ATTICUS GREENE HAYGOOD

Methodist Bishop, Editor, and Educator

ATTICUS GREENE HAYGOOD

HAROLD W. MANN

ATTICUS GREENE HAYGOOD
Methodist Bishop, Editor,
and Educator

UNIVERSITY OF GEORGIA PRESS • Athens

To My Wife
BETTY PARKS MANN

Paperback edition, 2010
© 1965 by the University of Georgia Press
Athens, Georgia 30602
www.ugapress.org
All rights reserved
Printed digitally in the United States of America

The Library of Congress has cataloged the hardcover edition
of this book as follows:
Library of Congress Cataloging-in-Publication Data
LCCN Permalink: http://lccn.loc.gov/65019380

Mann, Harold W. [from old catalog]
Atticus Greene Haygood,
p. cm.
1. Haygood, Atticus Greene, Bp., 1839–1896. [from old catalog]
BX8495.H269 M3
65-19380

Paperback ISBN-13: 978-0-8203-3543-8
ISBN-10: 0-8203-3543-6

Contents

	Preface	vii
I	Early Life	1
II	College and the Word	17
III	The War Years	34
IV	The Merging and Submerging of Southern Methodist Culture	51
V	Last Hope for Southern Sectarian Literacy—The Sunday School	67
VI	Emory College in the 1870's	88
VII	The Editorialist and the *Advocates*	110
VIII	Northern Philanthropy and Southern Profits	135
IX	The Church in the Wilderness	150
X	The Uncommon Schoolman	169
XI	Dr. Haygood and Negrophilia	182
XII	Act of Faith: The Abdication of Will	198
	Notes	212
	Bibliography	234
	Index	250

Preface

ATTICUS GREENE HAYGOOD was a man of national prominence in the late 1800's—as agent for the John F. Slater Fund, which aided Negro colleges in the South, and as lecturer, editor and writer, educator, and Methodist Bishop.

Representing the most progressive and humanitarian qualities of a Southern man, Haygood, like Henry Grady, was an exhorter of the "New South" doctrine. Although his efforts in the area of intersectional and racial harmony were often misunderstood, Haygood refused to compromise his desire for a reconstructed South based on religion, education, and economic revitalization.

Haygood believed in the possibility of social progress through intelligent human direction. He specifically urged acceptance of the Negro as a permanent voting and propertied resident and counseled devotion to teaching the former slaves skills, dignity, and morality. His dedication to capitalistic expansion of the South through cooperation with Northern industrialists and his enthusiasm for education through common schools brought Haygood national recognition.

This biography is an attempt to use the life of a single man, whose successes were often overshadowed by shortcomings, as a tool for a better understanding of the social history of the postwar Deep South.

I am indebted to many people, but I wish especially to thank those named below. Vice President Judson C. Ward of Emory University first suggested to me in 1953 the importance of a biography of Haygood and frequently in the intervening years has given me advice and encouragement. Dr. Robert H. Woody of Duke University has given me invaluable counsel and criticism and was the chief civilizer of an unruly historiographical temperament. Dr. Louis D. Rubin, Jr., of Hollins College, through his editing of the Haygood-Hayes letters (in *Teach the Freeman*, 2 vols., Baton Rouge, 1959), shortened my investigation of the Slater Fund activities.

My obligations to colleagues and librarians are extensive. I cite particularly the knowledgeable help of Thomas Crowder and Mary Davis of the Special Collections staff, Emory University Library; Isabel Howell, director of the library division of the Tennessee State Library and Archives in Nashville; and Elizabeth Hughey, librarian of the Methodist Publishing House in that city. E. D. Johnson, librarian at Radford College, gave suggestions about the Index. Wesley M. Stevens, a former colleague at Oxford College of Emory University, helped me to organize a tangled ecclesiastical story in Chapter IX.

HAROLD W. MANN

Department of History
Radford College
Radford, Virginia

ONE
◊ ◊ ◊
◊

Early Life

ATTICUS GREENE HAYGOOD was born November 19, 1839, in Watkinsville, in the Piedmont section of northern Georgia. Greene Haygood, his father, still in his twenties, was a native of Clarke County, of which Watkinsville was then the county seat. Greene had studied law there as well as in Augusta and for five years had practiced before the local Superior Court. Professionally prospering, he bought a house and 17½ acres of land just outside Watkinsville three months before Atticus was born.[1]

Greene's wife was Martha Ann Askew. Her father, a Methodist preacher, had come from Buncombe County in western North Carolina. In 1839 he was nearly seventy years old and was living in semi-retirement next to Mossy Creek camp ground, north of Gainesville, Georgia. His daughter came to Clarke County to teach school in Salem, a village eleven miles south of Watkinsville. In that day towns like Salem possessed a self-autonomous dignity later lost. Situated on the Appalachee River, which formed Clarke's western boundary, and reached easily over the stage route from Greensboro to Watkinsville, the town boasted of its own academy, or semi-private school. In a way, Salem's location, near the southern border of Clarke County, was directly on the threshold of the more plebeian way of life of the upper Piedmont and the mountain regions. Greensboro, and Greene County, to the south, lay fully within the cotton belt, and their society considered itself "cotton aristocracy." Martha Askew had only just moved from Salem to Athens, six miles north of Watkinsville in Clarke County, when Greene Haygood persuaded her to give up teaching and be his wife.[2] Although Athens had several thousand citizens and the county seat had only 250, life with a rising lawyer in the smaller town must have been greatly appealing. The elite of Watkinsville included another lawyer, a doctor, two proprietors of shoe shops, and skilled hands at the carpentering, tailoring, tanning, saddle-making, blacksmithing, and wagon-making trades. Besides the "good brick court-house" the town had two churches, Baptist and Methodist, two taverns, two schools, two stores, three groceries, one billiard room, and a jail.[3]

Clarke County, formed in 1801, had in 1840 a total of 10,000 people, a few hundred more whites than Negroes. Forty years of careless land cultivation had reduced the agricultural potential. Decreased production of cotton in the county and the general economic depression of the 1830's slowed down Clarke's growth rate considerably, and the census figure of 1840 represents a sort of demographic plateau. Propertied whites who had not moved on to the more promising lands of the Old Southwest (Alabama and the Delta) continued to work the fields during the critical seasons, growing cotton and corn. In the thus reduced tempo of farm life, a good reputation, not cotton wealth, was all that a man could expect out of life. A few wealthy families in Athens were absentee farmowners, but even they were not far removed from generations of humbler origin; social status therefore was not determined entirely by personal wealth. The regular farm labor of the county was provided almost entirely by Negro slaves, and between them and their masters there often existed a strained sort of family relationship. Out of a total county population of nearly 5,000 Negroes, there were only fifteen free ones.[4]

In the mid-1840's those with money to invest became interested in the continuing railroad boom and in small industry. The Georgia Railroad, one of two main lines in the state, stretched east from its western terminus in the relatively raw new town of Atlanta toward the more mannered city of Augusta, with its business and social ties with South Carolina, especially Charleston. The route traversed Greene County, south of Clarke, but a spur from a junction farther east at Camak brought the rails to a landing on the bank of the Oconee River opposite Athens.

Athens and Watkinsville could both be reached by the stage route running north from Greensboro. The arrival of the coach, with its mail and with occasionally an unfamiliar face, was announced in Watkinsville, as was the custom elsewhere, by a horn sounded when the travelers were a mile from the hotel-tavern.[5]

The Piedmont county's industrial enterprise may not have amounted to much, but it was the source of great pride. Several small textile mills were built in Clarke County in the 1840's. The largest was erected on Barber's Creek which separated Watkinsville and Athens. By 1850 there was a paper mill on the same stream and a combination leather factory and grist mill in Watkinsville. By then there was a total of nearly twenty grist mills, more than twenty saw mills, and perhaps a half dozen lawful distilleries. Clarke cloth and paper found consumers outside the county, but most of the liquor was consumed in three established saloons, one of them at Watkinsville in the Eagle Hotel, where Athens lawyers stayed during the court sessions. Liquor drinking by respectable gentlemen in the 1840's is not to be confused with the riotous backwoods life of Georgia, especially two and three decades earlier, as recorded by Augustus Baldwin Longstreet in his *Georgia Scenes*. Clarke County was in 1845—or at least its grand jury said it was—favored by "comparative exemption . . . from crimes and misdemeanors."[6]

The improvement of manners and an increased moral awareness were the natural fruits of the social stability of the older Georgia counties, wherein an increasingly austere family life often tended to inhibit the exuberance of those youth "with a good family name." The Southerners' growing consciousness of the disfavor held toward slavery by the rest of the civilized world may have affected the region's attention to morals. Certainly a real need was felt, particularly in the churched families, for a good example to be set at all times for at least the household slaves—who in turn would certainly be examples often enough to their owner's children. In the 1840's in Georgia membership in a church was not uncommon, but devout Christians were decidedly in a minority: perhaps twenty per cent were loyal members of the two leading sects, the Baptists and the Methodists. While the churches provided the backbone of the demand for disciplined manners and morality, they in no wise challenged the way of life. The dominance of the male in an authoritarian slave-holding household did not end in church, where seating was segregated more rigidly according to sex than to race, with wives and daughters separated by the center aisle from the masculine relatives. Negroes attended these churches but kept apart, as they also did at home on solemn occasions.[7]

The churches were developing a more central role in the life of Georgians. In the open-air months the campmeetings, initially characteristic of the Methodists, provided a center for social activity as well as for good preaching and singing. Not the least of their functions was allowing more informal concourse between young beaux and belles looking for mates. In many areas local churches had grown out of transient preaching in the unwalled arbors which served as sanctuaries in the camp grounds, and the most eloquent preachers—sometimes, too, the ones most at ease with county leaders—became accepted into plantation and village life on a par with the lawyers. The preachers were all the more looked up to because in the 1830's the Protestant denominations in Georgia had begun to build colleges, the merits of education being recognized in the more established sections of the state. The churches—Presbyterian, Methodist, and Baptist—may have created a source for private criticism of state legislation for a slave society, since they favored teaching the Negroes to read at least the Bible. State law forbade teaching slaves to read. The Methodists, because of their habit of reappointing ministers throughout the state conference, usually every two years, probably were more effective in standardizing social attitudes on such questions than the more tactful and more permanently stationed Baptist and Presbyterian elders.[8]

In communities as small as Watkinsville the most important events were church services and court sessions. Every other year, though, election campaigns overshadowed the Lord's Day and the drama of the courtroom. Athens, with half a dozen mansions graced by Corinthian columns on their porches and other evidences of "refinement and taste" within such as expensive chandeliers in the ballrooms and elegant mirrors, regularly had a more exciting and diverting calendar. The commencement week in August of Franklin College, the original name of the University of Georgia, marked the height of the social season. Then Athens swarmed with families and kinfolks and friends of the graduates and with others drawn from as near as Greensboro and as far as Charleston. Athens served as a refuge for some Charlestonians escaping the malarial lowlands.[9] Politicians returned to speak at the exercises—to the graduates and visitors, not to the natives. The city itself enjoyed its politics the year round, encouraged by the local conservative Democratic organ, the *Southern Banner,* to remain true to party. The county as a whole usually voted Whig majorities during the 1840's. Watkinsville was the center of Whig strength, although the *Southern Whig* was published in Athens. In 1850 this paper was renamed the *Southern Herald*—symbolically marking the decline of the business-minded nationalist party in Clarke County, Georgia, and indeed throughout the South.[10] As a successful lawyer in Watkinsville, Greene Haygood was an ardent Whig.

.. Early Life

Born on Barber's Creek, one of a large family of Baptist farmers, Haygood had shown little promise in his boyhood of any degree of success, being remarkable only for his large stature. In fact, a minister in the county said of him, "He was the most awkward, unpromising young man I ever knew. He came raw from a country school. He was laughed at, and every effort was made to discourage him."[11] He began his career in Watkinsville working in a store and later was befriended and given legal training by Judge Joseph Ligon, a local resident. When Greene was twenty-five, having practiced law two years, he joined Watkinsville's Methodist church and, two years later, married Martha Askew. The following year, 1839, he bought his first property from the estate of Judge Ligon. In the 1840's he was the busiest lawyer in court.[12]

Between 1839 and 1852 Greene and Martha became the parents of four surviving children. The first-born son was called Atticus, perhaps because of his schoolteacher mother's interest in the classics. Essays by Cicero, with which Martha was possibly familiar (it was remarked as a wonder that she could "read Virgil"), are addressed to Titus Pomponius Atticus. The second and third children died as babies, but the fourth, Laura Askew, born in 1845, survived and was a companion for her brother later in life. The other surviving children were Myra and Willie. By this time the household included two slaves, Aunt Esther, a nurse and cook, and Uncle Jim, general handyman. The Haygoods expected their children to keep busy. Laura learned all the arts of housekeeping and Atticus, or Attie, as he was called, was taught to plow. To support his enlarging family, Greene in 1844 bought four hundred acres of farmland adjoining the original Ligon property.[13]

Atticus Greene Haygood was a sickly child, subject from ages six to eleven to epileptic fits. In later years he recalled the seizures as terrifying choking sensations associated with an emotional state, brought on by impulsive self-assertion or, as he put it, "unaccountable courage." For him, as for most epileptics, consciousness became a treasure and self-control a primary aim, since the involuntary loss of muscular control and of consciousness caused a "sense of inadequacy and incompleteness."[14] To be sure that Atticus was constantly watched, his parents put him under the supervision of Uncle Jim outside the house. This was a healthy association for the boy, for his widowed Grandmother Askew, who came to live with the family when Attie was nearly six, hovered over him, singing hymns and praying much of the time.[15]

The muscular Uncle Jim was a hero for Attie. Since the burly Negro's marvelous talents were mostly physical, kinesthetic rather than esthetic, they were a contrast with the fanciful events of the little boy's dream world. Uncle Jim once "cleared a space" in a fight with another Negro in the presence of his charge, and was a symbol of strength and vitality thereafter. His pet name for Attie was "Horse Fly." He taught the boy to use his five senses in the woods and taught him to fish and hunt with the relaxed absorption of the accomplished outdoorsman. Uncle Jim had a fine bass voice and even played the flute. The lifelong effect of this friendship must be conjectured; perhaps it left the boy with doubts concerning the desirability of civilizing, christianizing, and thus inhibiting the Negro. Perhaps the vigor of expression of his written language as an adult and the musical quality of his speaking voice owe something to his idealization of Uncle Jim. (Neither of Attie's parents could sing a note. It need hardly be added that he never saw his father or any other grown white man use his fists.)[16]

Greene and Martha Haygood were kind parents but firm disciplinarians who "made us mind, taught us . . . to think it . . . cowardly to cry for small hurts and to be afraid of ghosts." The most vivid memory he had of his preacher grandfather happened at Mossy Creek while the Reverend Askew was dressing a lamb. He asked Attie to fetch a special knife to complete the severing of the hide, and later gave his grandson the blade. The curiously shaped weapon thereafter no doubt came to mind at the recounting of Abraham's willingness to sacrifice his son. When Grandfather Askew died his widow came to live in the Greene Haygood home. Attie felt her influence from the start. When he was only five years old, at a service at the camp ground just outside the town she took him to "kneel . . . down among the mourners" at the altar. The oppressive religiosity of his grandmother did more to frighten young Attie than to comfort him. Although he was afraid to pass the tombstones of his infant brother and sister in the back yard in order to fetch the mail, he preferred that route to one which required walking past the doctor's apothecary shop with its terrifying "skeleton in the corner—peering over the counter at the folks who came to buy 'snake root' and such things."[17]

The boy's awe for things spiritual, mingled with anxiety, was increased by the somberness of the daily devotionals in the family parlor, the reverence accorded the Bible and the Methodist Discipline with its restrictions on behavior, and the deference given preachers. Atticus once recorded: "Our father's house was a preacher's home. Many times we blacked their shoes, brought their saddle-bags into the house, watered their horses."[18] One traveling preacher never forgot the "old-time, two-story house, built for room and convenience" on "a beautiful level site, with twenty-six varieties of fruit and forest trees . . ., a well of good water and a dry well in which to keep milk cool."[19] Atticus gave all preachers the special obedience he had had for his Grandfather Askew. He remembered the time that Preacher Askew spoke from the pulpit in Watkinsville—an eminence ascended by circular steps and a God-filled enclosure decorated by red swinging doors which kept on swinging for fascinating moments after the sermon had begun. Visiting preachers liked to sit on the porch of the Haygood house, just as Attie's grandfather had, speaking in sonorous tones about religious matters.[20]

Attie learned early how to escape from a somber world of ghosts, spirits, Bible verses, sermons, and prayers into one that was sunny and bright. It could be done by the simple act of pulling a book from the shelf. His first book was a collection of sketches of wild life by John J. Audubon—bought at an auction, but he and his precocious sister Laura when quite young graduated to reading Macaulay and Carlyle. When Carlyle died decades later Haygood wrote: "Tens of thousands felt a sense of personal bereavement. . . . It cannot be questioned that he did much good; alas! it is equally certain that some minds were blighted under the fierce heats of his strange and imperious genius."[21] Scott and Byron stirred him deeply and he read his volumes of them over and over again. Greene Haygood saw to it that his children did not read "flashy papers and low novels," but his and Martha's predilections for the *Southern Christian Advocate* and the Methodist Discipline did not weaken their son's preference for imaginative literature and imaginatively recreated history. Laura was a better memorizer of the schoolbooks, in Latin and in mathematics, than her brother. She was able to go directly from her mother's tutoring to the junior class of Wesleyan Female College in Macon.[22]

In his twelfth year Attie's health improved greatly, and he began to prefer outdoor physical activity to reading books with Laura. Fishing or rabbit hunting on his own was an exhilarating advance over his first fishing trip, three years before, with his father, sister, and some school girls. He loved plowing, even with "a recalcitrant mouse-colored mule, named 'Beck,' who had truly a head of her own . . ., always coming to an immovable standstill when she heard the dinner horn...."[23] Heavy labor and strenuous hiking and the magic biochemistry of adolescence made of the frail child a strapping young man, particularly noticeable for his deep chest and short adroit hands. There were still traces of his childhood sickness, in a muscular jerkiness and the peculiar way in which he walked. And as he grew older, he was often unnaturally attentive to older people when they spoke, another habit of his childhood. If not his physical, certainly his emotional health was hampered because his father, fearful of a return of the choking spells, insisted that Attie sleep in his parents' bedroom. He was well into his teens before he had a room of his own.[24]

In his thirteenth year, Atticus moved with his family to Atlanta. Greene Haygood's motives for moving from Clarke County, where he was a successful lawyer in his prime, are not clear; political dissatisfaction with the ebbing of Whig fortunes in Clarke County (Atlanta was dominated by Whig leaders), the quest for greater economic security, and a desire to make his own way somewhere other than in his native county must have been factors. According to what Greene himself wrote in 1859, the most pressing reason was a desire to bring his children up where the gospel of manual work was still respected:

> Most of the inhabitants came here [Atlanta] for the purpose of bettering their fortunes by engaging actively in some kind of business ... our people show their democratic impulses by each allowing his neighbor to attend to their own business, and our ladies even are allowed to attend to their own domestic and household affairs without being ruled out of respectable society.[25]

In 1852 Atlanta was the fastest growing city in Georgia. It claimed four thousand citizens, almost double the census figure of 1850. In 1854 the population had jumped to six thousand, and by 1860 the official figure was nearly ten thousand, to the dismay of rivals Macon, Augusta, and Savannah. It was a city divided into two equal parts by the railroad tracks which justified its existence. The most important street was Whitehall, which crossed the tracks at a right angle, in an east-of-north direction. Alabama Street intersected Whitehall, in the southern half of the town, and the corner of Alabama and Whitehall was the business center. Greene's new law office was a half-block from this corner. Most of the residences of the Whig business leaders were south of the tracks, and Greene Haygood bought a large tract of property, with a house, on the southeastern edge of the city. (He sold much of his Clarke

.. *Early Life* 9

County property, but retained the house and ten acres he had bought in 1839.)²⁶

Atticus found life in the city exciting. The Haygoods lived in a two-story house near the end of Mitchell street, which paralleled Alabama. Although many of the streets were primitive, being "cut through new ground," there were also sidewalks of brick, stone, and planks, and there were many more stores than in Watkinsville—about sixty. Still, the city was not extraordinarily large in area, for

with his barefoot playmates, he could cross it at a run. A few hundred yards of badly laid brick pavement fronted the little stores. Ox-teams and such like struggled along Whitehall street in mud, axle deep, through the cotton season. First church—our first church—was a shackling affair, wood shingles, smoking stove, chicken coop belfry.... The car-shed [railroad terminal] was side-posts and shingle roof.... Then the fire department was "No. 1." How they yelled and ran like mad over roots and rocks and mud to fight the occasional shanty fires. How we worked ourselves (the boys of the day counted it glory to run with the machine almost into a dead faint)....²⁷

It was on frolics into the shanty section north of the tracks that Attie saw the saloons centering around Five Points and must surely have heard tales from the other boys about the painted women on Line Street.

When the Haygoods arrived in Atlanta in 1852 it was safe enough to walk north of the tracks in daylight, but no self-respecting gentleman would go out at night toward Five Points, where the "rowdy male crowd, drunkards and gamblers" made and kept their own folk law. There was as yet little respect for duly constituted authority. The first jail, built in 1851, was a flimsy structure, and Atlanta's Mayor Jonathan Norcross—a Maine preacher's son—had been physically threatened in 1851 while presiding over city court. Night order improved after 1853 with the hiring of three men as a police force. The victory of the law abiding was complete after 1854 for another reason: Atlanta became a new county seat as Fulton County was created out of DeKalb County. The influx of population included many lawyers, and the building of a new combination courthouse and city hall, south of the tracks and a block from the Haygood home, guaranteed greater respect for propriety—and for the Mayor. Fulton's first grand jury congratulated the county on the moral reforms accomplished since 1851, while asserting that there were still too many saloons, and unrestricted "desecration of the Sabbath."²⁸

Between 1854 and 1860 Atlanta was transformed from a fledgling railroad town to a city not much different from older Macon. Of its 6,000 inhabitants in 1854, 728 were registered "polls." The tax digest of that year listed forty-one professionals in town—over twenty lawyers, three dentists, and one daguerreotype artist among them. Six hundred shanty children received free education. One fourth of the population was Negro, counted in the digest as "1024½" slaves, an interesting way of registering parturition. There were sixteen free Negroes, plus one "slave on hire," because of skill at a trade.

Greene Haygood was one of the twenty lawyers in 1854, but a year later he and his partner, I. A. Whitaker, had to compete for business as counsel with twenty additional advocates. Whitaker prospered more than his more limited "country boy" partner, and by the end of the 1850's Haygood was in partnership instead with a man by the name of Bates. Nevertheless, partly because of his democratic manner which made him "a people's man," he was the city's first paid and official lawyer, after 1860.[29]

Greene Haygood was fortunate in being Democratic in mien while Whiggish in politics, since such a stance allowed him entrée into both the professional and "mechanic's" classes. Atlanta was thoroughly a Whig stronghold. The city fathers entertained Millard Fillmore in 1854, put a portrait of Zachary Taylor on the wall of the chamber in which the city council assembled, and in 1856 sponsored a political rally supporting the presidential candidacy of Fillmore on the third-party, Know-Nothing ticket. *The Daily Intelligencer* reported that 12,000 attended the rally.

Soon after his arrival in Atlanta, Greene Haygood, no doubt because of his political sympathies, was appointed by the council as a trustee for the poor-children's school. Shortly afterward he was appointed a member of the Board of Health. The latter responsibility required supervising well digging so that water would not be contaminated by the wastes from the tanyards and slaughter pens and persuading property owners to keep their pigs and cows off the streets. In the mid-1850's he was appointed to a delegation sent to the state capital in Milledgeville to lobby for the removal of the state offices to Atlanta. During the last half of 1856 Greene sat on the council, winning a vacant seat in a special election. His principal activity there was the recommendation, in good Whig fashion, that Atlanta subsidize the building of a projected Georgia Air Line Railroad to Charlotte—as a link in a future New York-to-New Orleans line. The council acted affirmatively on the recom-

.. Early Life

mendation. Greene's family, especially his relatively immature seventeen-year-old son Atticus, considered as phenomenal this peak of Greene's public career. Later Atticus grew to understand that his father was on the periphery of power and that "his great worth" was not "being recognized or appreciated."[30]

Greene left the council in January 1857. The next three years were turbulent ones in city politics, as they were in the South and the nation at large. The Whig leadership was successfully attacked by the mechanic class, and the Democrats captured city hall in January 1858. They condemned the buying of the stock in the prospective railroad as extravagance. They complained of the tax rates. They said the new jail, which cost the taxpayers $14,000, had walls which could be punctured by a "tenpenny nail." And they won many votes by objecting to the hiring of a free Negro as guard of the jail when, in the wake of the recession of 1857, there were many unemployed white men available. The final outrage upon which they capitalized, in the overheated national political climate, was the fining of a white mechanic in city court on the strength of a free Negro's swearing to the mechanic's guilt. When Greene Haygood was chosen city attorney in 1860, it was because his Democratic nature outweighed his Whiggish sentiments. (Greene voted for John Bell for President that year, to the applause of his newly politically conscious older son.)[31]

None of his father's public accomplishments thrilled Attie more than Greene's participation, after the city hall turn-over, in an effort to establish a state system of public education. Already in college himself, Attie learned that the movement was supported by the better educated ministers who were professors and presidents of the denominational colleges of the state and by the more cultivated citizens, especially those in Augusta, Savannah, and Macon. Greene was the enthusiastic host at a meeting held in Atlanta in the fall of 1858, in conjunction with the state fair, to organize lobbying for the proposal before the upcoming legislative session. The state had decades before established academies, but the diminution of financial support during the Jacksonian period and the resulting subsidizing by towns, cities, and the more urban counties had destroyed the public character of the academies. Where academies were not available, educated parents had to teach their own children. The only other elementary education available was in poor-schools, attendance upon which in effect served as public announcement of the parents' poverty—and disgrace. Greene Haygood was outraged by the existing stratification of facilities. In 1858, the new governor of Georgia, Joseph E. Brown, though in favor of more educational opportunity, was politician enough to realize his legislative support would be hurt by a direct backing of the proposal to consolidate all schools into a state system. Anything that would require an increase in taxes would be anathema. He did secure the voting for an additional $100,000, most of it from state railroad income, as a help to the counties to better their poor-schools. Atticus, aged nineteen, never forgot the near-victory of the idealists, and resolved that when he himself reached a position of influence he would make possible for all children in Georgia an elementary education in a classless state system, through the political support of enlightened statesman.[32] Throughout his life Atticus would remember his father's devotion to progressive causes, both commercial and cultural, and his championship of more railroads and better schools.[32]

Greene Haygood was an active Methodist layman in Atlanta. The spring after the family had moved to the city, 1853, Greene started a Sunday School in the front room in his house where his wife taught girls on weekdays. That summer a second Methodist church was chartered since the first church was somewhat inconvenient for residents of the southern half of the city to attend and since Atlanta was growing so rapidly. Greene included his two sons, Atticus and the baby boy Willie, as charter members. Other first members were Willis Peck, Joseph Winship, Edwin Payne, Dr. George Smith, and F. M. Richardson. Greene sparked the effort to buy a lot opposite the courthouse, on Mitchell Street, and a half-block from his home. In 1858 he paid the remaining debt on the sanctuary of what eventually would be called Trinity Methodist Church. Bishop James O. Andrew consecrated the new building in December 1854, during the first state annual Methodist Conference held in Atlanta. Greene also helped to organize a third and a fourth Methodist church, as missions of Trinity, and continued to act within the membership of Trinity as a "class-leader," or "exhorter" toward spiritual improvement for a group of about a dozen adult members in full standing. He seems, however, to have lost a portion of his interest in Methodist needs as his public activities increased after 1857. However, the Haygoods kept up family connections in the Trinity church even after Greene's death.[33]

Atticus when only thirteen became Sunday School librarian of Trinity. In July 1854, at fourteen, he was "Born of the Spirit" by grace and through the vessel of the preaching of the Rev. J. P.

Duncan, whose fervent oratory on the occasion of the visit of Millard Fillmore to Atlanta had brought tears to the eyes of the distinguished guest. Attie was baptized in September, and despite his complete loyalty had to remain a "probationer" for a year—this was the ante-bellum requirement of the sect. During this time he continued as Sunday School librarian and became church sexton. He even worked for awhile as a hod carrier to help pay off the debt incurred in building the new sanctuary. Because his unusual and strained religiosity pleased his increasingly frail and pietistic grandmother, Attie's loyalty for the church was a practiced one, and he knew it.[34] It would take years of honest self-examination, however, for him to admit that he was more excited by railroads, politics, romantic book heroes, and the noise of life in Atlanta than by prayer and piety. His parents' refusal to allow him to attend plays presented at the Athenaeum, north of the tracks, or to participate in a Christmas carnival called the "Fantastics" confirmed their strict Methodist discipline but nevertheless awoke the fun-loving core of Attie's Welsh nature. It is significant that during these years he openly admired the language of the impious Thomas Carlyle.[35]

Nevertheless, the thoughts and habits of Atticus Greene Haygood were conditioned primarily by the accident of his being in his teens during the 1850's when the Methodist Episcopal Church, South, was coming into its own as a distinctive pietistic sect within Southern society. The split of the church in 1844 indirectly over the question of the propriety of a bishop's owning a slave had, if anything, increased Southern idealism about personal conduct. There remained, too, a social conscience—with sharp boundaries—since the threefold mission of the Methodists embraced evangelizing among unchurched whites, Negro slaves, and the heathen overseas, China being the chosen sphere of foreign missions.[36] The primary source of strong loyal support for the established churches of the rural counties, towns and cities in the 1850's came from laymen who, as young men twenty or thirty years before, had had highly moving spiritual experiences at the camp meetings. The "love-feast," a custom borrowed from the Moravians of eating breads and water in the closed meeting of members in good standing only, was perhaps the most meaningful service of all; it was held before the quarterly conference of the society (or church). In a sense it was exclusive, but the spiritual climate was that of a democracy of the elect, as the Presbyterians might have called it.[37]

Much of the high morale of the Southern Methodists, though, was due to the willingness of laymen and preachers to accept an authoritarian review of their yearly, quarterly, and monthly behavior. Each full member was assigned to a class, whose leader, called an exhorter, minutely kept up with the private lives of his class members. A persistent aberration from Methodist conduct might lead to a return to the probationary status, on decision of the pastor of the society, whose duties also included supervision of the behavior of the exhorters as well. The preachers and their "presiding elders," established preachers who regularly held the quarterly conferences in each church within a district, had their behavior examined yearly at the annual conference of preachers, over which a bishop presided. The bishop was answerable to God but not, in any clearly defined way, to the quadrennial general conference of the whole church, by which he had been elected to lifetime office.[38] Self-examination was so universal among the Methodists that individuals took pride in disclosing their inmost life, and preachers in the 1850's were not embarrassed by a high proportion of probationers among their membership. What is most important here is that this attention to behavior was not thought of as antithetical to the Methodist tradition of emphasizing salvation by faith entirely, not works.[39]

The importance of a glowing inner experience of salvation and a conscious growing in grace and righteousness had always precluded for Methodists any profound intellectual understanding of the theological traditions which had fostered their version of the gospel. The university-trained John Wesley left a theological and psychological confusion that his American followers would never be able to resolve. On the one hand Wesley accepted the Calvinistic (and Augustinian) idea of the total depravity of man at birth and, without a saving experience, throughout life. Wesley, however, also adopted the teaching of Dutch Arminianism, which agreed with the psychological premises of Enlightenment thinkers such as John Locke, that each life "starts from scratch," and that everyone is in a position to *will* to be saved. This cardinal point put American Methodists sometimes at violent loggerheads with high Calvinism, with its doctrine of the absence of personal option about salvation or damnation.[40] In effect Methodists believed that unctuous preaching—and devout and earnest hearing—might "trigger" a moment in which saving grace would justify man in the sight of God, relieving him of his inborn depravity. This act of will was to be followed by a constant striving, through daily resolution, to become more and more holy.[41]

No Georgia Methodist preacher in the 1850's knew enough theology to realize that the de facto declaration that God *must* save whoever *wills* it stringently enough was a terrifyingly heretical departure from the central Augustinian strand of the Western Christian tradition. The Methodists were so certain of an "automatic salvation," which, for the backslider, might be necessary more than once, that church leaders put the greatest emphasis on delineating righteous behavior for those presumably "saved." Wesley's delineation was found in the General Rules in the Discipline, in the pages after the Articles of Religion, placed first but never read. Wesley forbade his followers to "drink . . . unless in cases of necessity," to wrangle in court against a "brother," to haggle over prices during purchases, to buy or sell smuggled goods, to borrow with no intention of repaying, or to sing songs or read literature which does not "tend to the knowledge or love of God." Wesley predictably included general European Christian taboos against self-indulgence, fighting, profaning the Sabbath, and "giving or taking things on usury." In addition, Georgia Methodist taboos heartily forbade attendance at "germans" or dances, circuses, and plays.[42] Some of the twenty-and-more commandments would not deprive any Westerner of full participation in civil society; thus, the Wesleyan follower was advised to obey authority, to swear in court, to make no criticism of private property rights, and to encourage his priesthood to marry.[43]

Here was the basis of a religion of works if ever behavior became coerced rather than really desirable to the individual. The Methodists promised that joy and ecstasy would follow upon the most rigorous striving after total purity, inward and outward. If depressions came, the Methodist had no theological or philosophical framework by which to explain the decline of the inner temperature he was constantly watching. Young Atticus Haygood tended to believe, when depressions replaced joy, that the same God who had made him an epileptic and given him only partial sovereignty over his consciousness was again reminding him of the futility of striving. When he became an adult he would reject completely the Wesleyan use of external behavior as a measure of inner righteousness. As a sixteen-year-old he merely recoiled when he read from the Discipline the condemnation of those who said that "'we are not to do good unless *our hearts be free to it.*'"[44] He knew that he would never be free not to do good—his grandmother's prayers forbade that—but the joys of his inner being would always be personal and secret.

TWO

College and the Word

ATTICUS GREENE HAYGOOD was enrolled in the sophomore class of Emory College in September 1856, when he was not quite seventeen. Any dream he had of attending a longer established Northern school with a large library and more complete educational facilities was not to be realized; Greene and Martha, being good Georgia Methodists, preferred for their son the twenty-year-old Emory, which had already produced prominent Methodist preachers and laymen. Similar monopolies were being established for the Baptists through their Mercer University at Penfield, and for the Presbyterians at Oglethorpe, in Milledgeville.[1] The earlier attractiveness of Franklin College in Athens was declining for church people, even though Georgia's Methodist bishop, George Foster Pierce, was a graduate of the school.

Franklin College in 1856 was not considered a fit place for a religiously trained boy in spite of the good reputation of its president, Alonzo Church, an ordained Calvinist preacher of New England origin. Baptist parents probably had fewer questions about the school than the Methodists, since the professor of literature in Athens was the Reverend William Brantley, a Baptist minister. The Baptists also would have felt more at home with the Calvinistic tone of the administration's voice. President Church had expected all of his young faculty members to enforce pious manners upon their students outside the classroom. In 1855 he had been sustained in his demand by the state Board of Trustees, over the protests of the younger faculty. As a result some of the college's best young teachers resigned, including notably the scientifically oriented LeConte brothers who went to South Carolina. The trustees apparently did not attribute the school's loss of teachers and patronage to Church's policies, but rather to limited state financial support and to the fact that "denominational institutions under vigorous sectarian patronage" were more and more being considered by responsible parents in Georgia as providing the best educational advantages for their children.[2]

Emory College in 1856 had an enviable reputation for faculty harmony—and a somewhat undeserved name for having a student body comparatively "holier" than the average. All but two of the teachers were either elders or local preachers in the Methodist Episcopal Church, South. Being a literate preacher was the first professional requirement of Emory's faculty; supervision of memorized recitation from textbooks required attentiveness and a clergyman's ability to keep order among young people. Thus the existence at Emory in 1856 of at least one intellectually alert professor was entirely an accident. Whether or not the bookish, thoughtful Attie Haygood realized the scholarly shortcomings of the Emory faculty in advance, he was visibly distressed by the countryman's cast of the professors and by the smallness of the campus and its buildings when he arrived at Oxford from the Georgia Railroad depot in nearby Covington. A senior that fall of 1856 read disappointment on the face of the boy from Atlanta:

The first thing I remember hearing about him was from one of the boys who joined the sophomore class with him. He said they met him in a professor's room when he was being examined for admission. He walked around and looked at the rooms, walking with a very firm step and stood very erect, casting his eyes about as if he felt rather let down in getting into such a place. This boy said that was the way he looked, and it was some time before he got that look off him. He was very full of histories, about all the great universities . . . (those little professors did look dingy) and the impression made upon young Haygood by the buildings they were then using . . . were [sic] evidently disappointing. . . .[3]

Emory College possessed five buildings, described by a delegation of visiting preachers as "one main building, of large and elegant proportions, besides several others, which are appropriated as dormitories for students, . . . [and] two commodious and elegant halls, used by the two Literary Societies. . . ."[4]

The two-story white main building housed a chapel and all the classrooms and was surmounted by a tower of squat Masonic proportions. The four square columns in the front of the building were somewhat constricted by jutting walls on either end. Inside, the classrooms were quite plain. The walls were lined with wooden benches which were disfigured by knife carving; a few bore sticky patches of tar in evidence of "an ancient joke."[5] The literary society buildings were more typically "Southern Greek." Their four columns were spaced evenly across high masonry porches. The interiors of both Phi Gamma and Few were indeed rather elegant, if not ostentatious. The debating rooms for both were on the upper floor and were dominated by wooden platforms reminiscent of the courtroom. On its lower floor each of the societies had a library full of stimulating volumes—unlike the library of the college proper.

The other two buildings on the campus were East Hall and West Hall, dormitories which housed ten students each. Most of the one hundred and fifty college students, and all of the college preparatory boys, lived and boarded in the homes of Oxford citizens. A significant proportion of the entire student body lived in the homes of four faculty members and of the resident active or retired Methodist preachers. It was not unusual for parents—like the mother of L. Q. C. Lamar—to move to Oxford in order to be near their sons during their academic training. Oxford was a pleasant town to Methodist preachers and laity. Physically, it was noted for its wide tree-lined avenues and its malaria-free climate. It was, moreover, designed as an active Utopian experiment in moral excellence; all lots were sold "with the express understanding that if ardent spirits could be sold upon them, they should be considered as forfeited."[6] Methodists liked the isolation from the worldly spirit of even nearby Covington, and they liked being able to hear great preaching throughout the year by resident and visiting ministers. Some students found the psychic climate confining; but once accustomed to it, they joined, often as alumni, with Oxfordites in thinking of the institution as the shrine of Southern Methodism. To all Georgia Methodists the pulpit at Oxford from which commencement sermons were preached was thought to be, verily, a holy place.[7]

Into this wonderful isolation came Attie Haygood, with the somberness only youth can affect. On registration day he and his father, who came with him, participated in the perpetually observed ritual of confusion observed by all students on that day. Atticus signed the Matriculation Book, thereby swearing to obey the "statutes and the Discipline" of Emory, including a new covenant not to join "with any of the secret societies [two fraternities] . . . that now . . . or . . . may hereafter exist under pain of forfeiting college membership."[8] Above his name he saw the signatures of John Heidt, son of a Savannah preacher; R. U. Hardeman, son of a lawyer in Macon; Isaac Hopkins of Augusta, ward of a Dr. Newton; and John C. Floyd, from a noted Covington family. Of all those who registered, Haygood was the only one to write down his exact age in months—"16 and 9 mos."—being very conscious that he was the youngest enrollee. One student who matriculated that day was twenty-eight. Registration was followed by brief oral examinations in mathematics and Latin; Attie's showing in these was such that he was placed in the sophomore class.[9]

In the wearing heat of the September afternoon, Greene took his son to find a place to board. Peter G. Bessent, a lay resident, was startled when the Atlanta lawyer who came to see him said that "he would have to take Atticus in his family room, that he had never slept out of the family room at home."[10] Bessent, rubbing his chin, said no young adult could sleep in his bedroom. Reluctantly Greene agreed to let Atticus risk the perils of a future epileptic relapse in the presence of two students, John Hammond and Edward Bates, who roomed together at the Bessent home. Atticus stayed with these upperclassmen (who ignored him) till Christmas. He initiated no acquaintances until November, and seems to have spent a large part of his time in his room keeping an account book, a record of how he was spending his father's money. He spent over $100 before Christmas, half of it before the end of September! Besides his books for Greek and Latin, and a book of lectures about oratory, he had to pay $20 for his tuition, $40 to Mr. Bessent for the room and food, and smaller amounts for winter clothing. In November he paid $3 to have all his clothes (sixty-four pieces) washed for the first time since his arrival, and he lost $15, which, he wrote on his account margin, "I have good reasons to believe . . . was stolen."[11] Although he continued the account for his three years at Emory, during which time he recorded spending $915.40, he generally lost interest in the arithmetical tracking of his affairs, and in his adult life refused to bother himself with what he considered such minor details. The resolution of his college days not to keep full accounts in the future was an unfortunate decision.[12]

In lieu of close friendships with students, Atticus paid special note to his teachers during the fall, transferring to them the extreme deference he had learned to exhibit toward preachers. He won the respect of everyone because he could recite well—he had been trained in speaking by his mother and a teacher in Atlanta. Before Christmas, though, he had found the round of recitation in classes, by an absolutely predictable alphabetical

.. *College and the Word* 21

order, dull and monotonous. He worked on his own to learn Greek, but soon turned for stimulation to the books he found in the Phi Gamma library.

The students accepted him at once as an immature boy, who did well in class without any particular involvement in the assignments. Although he had not so far engaged in any rough and tumble, he was let alone: the heavy build on the five-foot-six frame guaranteed that. In the casual conversations he had he was filled with "nervous energy," never kept still, and "did most of the talking." His dark brown eyes, already myopic, rarely focused on the persons with whom he talked, and he acted as though he would rather talk with somebody else—former epileptics "have difficulty in adjusting to . . . complexity."[13] Before Christmas, though, he struck up a conversational relationship with a junior, Young J. Allen. A friend, John Heidt, later said that Allen was "the only man I ever saw who impressed him [Atticus] enough to keep perfectly quiet when he was talking. He would sit close to him and listen, like a child talking with his father."[14]

Young Allen was a drudge, a quiet student, like Atticus, without much conviviality, and utterly serious. During his junior and senior years, from 1856 until graduation in 1858, Allen was to the faculty and Oxford preachers the outstanding student. He was a mature-looking nineteen-year-old with piercing eyes, a handsome aloofness of manner, and a fancy trimmed black beard. On Sundays he wore a costume marked by a silk vest—as though he fancied English gentry dressed that way. He was the ward of a wealthy family in western Georgia, and his clothes and the books he bought for his personal library were his main extravagances. The plain-clothed Atticus was awed to find such a man so serious. Young's disinterest in girls was a puzzle to the other students, who did not know that he was secretly engaged. Atticus, the timid and immature, found this lack of interest somehow reassuring.[15]

The dashing aristocrat while an adolescent had become "convicted of his sins" through the agency of the preaching at Salem campground in the western part of Newton County, wherein Oxford and Covington were centrally located. Two years earlier, in 1854, he knew that he wanted to be a preacher; but in 1856 he was emotionally overwrought because he could make no firm decision to be a missionary to China, a decision which he understood would be a major one in his life. (The Southern Methodists had sent five missionaries to China since 1848, but three had since retreated from the challenge of Christianizing the entire nation.)

Allen's secret half-resolved intention had been "nursed in silence ... till finally in 1857 ... he opened his mind to his dear friend, Atticus Haygood ... and later to a few other ... advisers, among them being Bishops Andrew and Pierce."[16] Beginning in November 1856 he held prayer meetings in his room and by late January had made a clear resolution to "press forward to entire consecration, entire sanctification, of body, mind, and spirit to the Lord" and to give to God his earthly career and ambition by being a missionary. Those closeted with him and Haygood were some of the best students at Oxford. Atticus found his new idol's decision an irresistible guidepost, and in the spring revivals of 1857 experienced a religious ecstasy. It is significant that in later years he recalled the sophomoric fervor with amusement: "I was greatly troubled with this question: 'Why is faith, and not something else, made the condition of salvation?' "[17] Five months of attempts to find in his own being a faith equal to Young Allen's had left him weary.

By the end of his first year Atticus had come to know other students besides the 'pray-ers'; he had begun a life-long friendship with three "H's," boys who sat beside him in the required twice-daily chapel, in Sunday church, and in some classes. They were Robert Hardeman, John Heidt, and Ike Hopkins. Heidt and Hopkins became preachers and Hardeman a "local preacher," or deacon; they were likable boys of easy temperament, untouched by the necessity to grope after greater holiness. Through these boys, but not directly, Attie learned to his surprise that Emory College had enrolled its quota of unruly students also, any of whom would have been notable delinquents—even at Franklin College in Athens. All Emory's rules against swearing, cock-fighting, attending horse races and circuses, and carrying firearms were broken. And the boys knew that there was drinking in the two unsupervised domitories. During Haygood's three years at Emory, known misdemeanors by the students included fishing on Sunday, wrestling in the recitation rooms, exceeding a leave to visit LaGrange Female Seminary, and assaulting an innocent person walking down the main road through Oxford.[18]

Indeed, during Haygood's senior year six students were seriously punished, four being expelled, for "riotous and grossly disorderly conduct" of an unspecified nature. Of the two who were suspended only until the end of the term, one was George Foster Pierce, Jr., son of Bishop Pierce (who had been the President of Emory College until 1854.)[19] Most of the students, Haygood learned gradually, were neither delinquents nor pray-ers. The chief amusement was fishing, other sports being wrestling, running and broad-jumping in the road on the way back from the post office, shooting marbles, playing musical instruments, and playing cards. Occasionally even the calmest boys indulged in stealing chickens or placing an ox or horse in a professor's classroom. As a sophomore, particularly, Haygood was something of a prig, never "going with us on anything like a frolic, or outdoor recreation."[20]

For the spring term of his sophomore year, in January 1857, Atticus moved to the house of John W. Yarbrough, across the street from the post office. Yarbrough was the assigned preacher for rural churches in Newton County and a man in his professional prime. He had several sons in various levels of the academy and the college, and several daughters. Atticus from the first was most impressed by the oldest of the daughters, a poised girl named Mary or Mollie, just a few days older than he, but grown mature with her responsibilities in the household. On the second night Atticus was put into the room with Mollie's brother, George, a senior, and his roommate William Patillo, where he stayed until the end of the term. These boys, who were planning to be preachers, introduced Attie to their practice of praying privately behind the bed nearest the door to their room, so that they would be concealed when the door opened. Besides the prayer sessions with George and William, those with Young Allen, and the twice-daily chapel devotions, there was the Yarbrough family service at supper time downstairs in which all the boarders joined. Atticus liked this best because the Yarbrough's had a piano, and there was good singing. He eventually learned to sing "very respectably" in this environment. For two calendar years Attie stayed at the Yarbroughs.[21]

Although Atticus joined wholeheartedly in the devotionals of his roommates, which at one time led to all-night shouting, he learned during the spring of 1857 to sit up far into the night, "with a green baise shade over his eyes," as a way to absent himself from the enforced religious rounds. After he had tired of private work on his Greek, he turned to narrative history in the grand manner—Prescott's *History of the Conquest of Mexico* and Motley's *Rise of the Dutch Republic*. In the Phi Gamma library he also found a book by Hugh Miller, *The Foot-Prints of the Creator*, published in Boston in 1857, and Miller's earlier book, *The Two Records: The Mosaic and the Geological*.[22] Miller was a popularizer of the findings of the geologists which challenged the literal

Biblical estimation of the age of the earth, especially the calculations of James Ussher. The idea of an organic evolution of the world was in no way as dangerous to pietistic thought as the contemporary cosmology of Herbert Spencer (seemingly not available in Oxford), but Miller was dangerous enough. A book added to Few Society's library a year after Haygood's graduation averred that what Miller "declares to be SCIENCE, is simply a matter of FAITH, . . . this FAITH . . . inferior to the BIBLICAL CHRISTIAN FAITH. . . ."[23] George Yarbrough remembered that his sophomore roommate was "much taken with Hugh Miller." That Haygood was aware at the age of eighteen of the implied epistemological challenges made by physical evidences upon revealed truth seems, in the light of his adult grappling with the threats of Darwinism, incontrovertible. The tragedy is that in the Southern Methodist milieu, Atticus Haygood, an intellect of profound—as opposed to brilliant—insight, never allowed himself conscious resolution of the problems of knowledge and truth which he knew by some sort of prophetic sense. Albeit he may have "increasingly suspected that man was an animal, that the universe was a self-governed machine, . . . that the peculiar human concern with ethics had no backing outside man, and that any kind of theism was supererogatory," he spent the force of his intellect in denying such an understanding.[24]

Atticus Haygood energetically engaged himself in preparing for the debates held weekly at Phi Gamma, the literary society of which he was a member. Sometimes the debates were on ponderous issues, like the legality of secession. With his facility for language Atticus excelled in debate, and "they were afraid to tackle him." The traditional climax to the debating activities was an inter-society debate during commencement week, and orations by the best speakers of the three upper classes. Part of the regular curriculum required sophomores and juniors to memorize orations found in books as well as original compositions. At commencement his sophomore year, in July 1857, Atticus Haygood declaimed on a Monday after his father had drilled him on the speech in the woods the day before. Greene was disappointed that his son failed to win the sophomore prize, but Atticus—oblivious to his standing in such competition—was more interested in Young's speech on Tuesday on the subject of "Man Born to Labor," a most interesting theme for a Southern aristocrat.[25]

Atticus Haygood had learned by the end of his first year at Emory of the learning limits in the memory-work of a college curriculum. Emory's regime was a close model of that of Yale, having been shaped by Augustus Longstreet, president during most of the 1840's. The president during the late 1850's was James R. Thomas, who accepted the dictum that education "is drill." He was in the process of formulating a formal statement of his educational philosophy during Haygood's sophomore year. Education, Thomas thought, was meant to "secure diligence in study" from "conscientious motives," to "regulate the general habits, refine the feelings, and polish the manners," and especially "to effect a proper adjustment and expansion of the intellectual and moral forces."[26]

Thomas, a tall, raw-boned country fellow who liked to pan for gold in mountain streams, was well liked. He was kind and a just disciplinarian, believing that in the role of punisher he should be "an angel of mercy" rather than "an avenging instrument."[27] Atticus loved him and admired his campaign to end the troublesome fraternities, a campaign at its climax his sophomore year. However, Atticus could not agree that the four or five hours a day spent in memorization of Greek or Latin texts and mathematical rules served to "refine the feelings." It was a rare day when the classics professor deserted this routine to give a lecture on Greek or Roman society or political history. Attie could not condemn those students who used the "pony" to reduce the time spent in preparation. In some classes, like that in rhetoric, memorization of slight text assignments was no bother: "we could go through the lessons like a deer in a walk and have plenty of time to write the names of our sweethearts on the margins," wrote a classmate.[28]

The traditional dryness of classroom hours was somewhat relieved because in such a small community the students were able to learn the real interests of the professors. Thus, George W. W. Stone, a timid and ineffective mathematics professor, further burdened by having to teach physical science because of the departure of Alexander Means, still endeared himself to all Emory students by his sterling character and obvious spiritual dignity. Some students—not Atticus— also liked William J. Sassnett, Oxford's "political economist," who left during the fall of Haygood's junior year. Sassnett was a doctrinaire Southern Democrat who liked to talk, and who represented biases of planters in Georgia's cotton belt. He justified slavery on the premise that men are born unequal, defended the strictest censorship of literature for church members, and was a violent enemy to public education, which he felt would lead to moral decay.[29]

The only course work Haygood enjoyed was his study of French. His favorite teacher, Gustavus J. Orr, taught the difficult subject of civil engineering. "By his power of illustration and his clearness of exposition he made subjects attractive which are often looked forward to with dread."[30] When Haygood was a senior, the class requested Orr to spend the last day talking about vocational choices available to them. Since Emory students were exhorted constantly into the ranks of the ministry—approximately one sixth of all Emory's graduates so far had become deacons or elders—Orr's upholding of the law, medicine, and teaching made a lasting impression on Atticus, although he chose to follow in Young Allen's steps and be a preacher, making his decision during a famous spring revival in 1858, his junior year. Amid the mass fervor of that genuine working of grace even among the delinquent students the conscientious Professor Orr was troubled because grace passed him by. His being, along with the French professor, not even a local preacher and a Presbyterian at a Methodist school had resulted in a demeaned status, and Orr did not stay long at Emory. Orr's importance in public education in the decades ahead would thrill his ante-bellum student. This intense admiration can be seen, possibly, in the latter-day Reverend Haygood's studious avoidance of clerical costume and his carefully conversational manner of speaking.[31]

If it had not been for his prospective marriage to Mollie Yarbrough, Haygood would have considered his senior year an irritation rather than a climax to a college career. With Allen gone, the mantle of religious leadership among the students rested on his shoulders—those of Allen's closest friend, everyone knew. He received his license to preach at Salem campground in the late summer of 1858,[32] before school started. It was true that he enjoyed preaching, much more so than "exhorting" his contemporaries. Preaching required a complicated self-control of consciousness. There was no denying, too, the pleasure of being in authority, as one grasped the lectern upon which the Holy Bible lay. Out there were the attentive faces of saints of the church, now listening to him. But the pleasure of hearing his own rich baritone voice rebound from the plain walls of a church frequently distracted him from attention to his congregation. He never as a young man experienced "unction" in the pulpit, but at times when he thought of how proud his parents and grandmother must be of his surviving his epilepsy to live to this day, there was a sweet tightening in his chest and even occasionaly a choking sob in his throat. Out of the pulpit, however, as the most prominent senior ministerial student, he felt awkward at Oxford. Sought out by younger students, he became tired of endless questions about the possibility of "pressing forward to full sanctification."

The revivals of 1858 were not duplicated in the spring of 1859. After Christmas Atticus moved out of the Yarbroughs' house, he and Mollie now being engaged. On a beautiful April day the seniors held their traditional picnic at the "Rock." The events—secondary in interest to the opportunity for strolling—were music by a band, a picnic dinner, and "an eloquent speech by A. G. Haygood on behalf of his class."[33] Mollie and Attie had planned to wait until after his graduation in July to marry, but Grandmother Askew's impending death made them move the date up to June so that "the sweet old soul" could "bless her young preacher's wife."[34] The honeymoon in the distraught and funereal Atlanta household was not unusual in being two parts wretchedness and one part bliss. The excitement of the new relationship reached its peak on the return to Oxford, so much so that graduation on July 20, even though he was one of a chosen dozen orators, was barely engaging. He was the only married senior. All of the other speakers that day received flowers from their girl friends, and one old man in the audience, admiring Haygood's Phi Gamma-trained oratorical style, asked loudly why the neglect of him.[35]

From July until Christmas Atticus served as junior preacher of the Oxford Circuit, shepherded in this apprenticeship by the Reverend J. W. Talley. Services at the many churches on the circuit required him to sleep away from Oxford every weekend, and also usually on Wednesday and Thursday nights. The one place in which the evenings were easy for him was the Burge plantation in the southeastern edge of the county, where "Aunt Dolly" presided in her womanly prime.[36] Mollie spent these nights in her father's house alone, outwardly serene, having been trained for such neglect. John Yarbrough no doubt had told her before her marriage what she should expect. Twenty-five years earlier Bishop Pierce, on the threshold of matrimony, had had his bride instructed by his father the Reverend Lovick Pierce, in these words:

> You will necessarily have many privations and sufferings not common to wives of mechants, planters, etc. And so also will you have many pleasures not common to them.
> My dear Ann, I have seen many of our young preachers make themselves contemptible, by what they allowed to be a *respectful com-*

pliance with the wishes of a fond wife, in neglecting their ministerial duties, and letting the idea get out that their wife could not bear their absence, and all such nonsense. I hope you and George will banish from you such *disgusting foolishness*. Always remember that *fondness misplaced . . . is weakness, ignorance, and folly. . . .* Be faithful, pray much, and live a life of daily *self-sacrifice*.[37]

Traveling out on the circuit that summer and fall with "Brother Talley" was good training. Crops were well watered that year, and fifty new members joined the various churches of the circuit in gratitude to the God of signs and seasons; by conference time the total of members "growing in Grace" was 800. The probationary class of about one hundred in all the churches was not diminished or added to that year. An unusual change in the circuit's statistics for 1859 shows a decline of Negro members from 195 to 91. This may have been Atticus's business. He was at ease with Negro slaves and found out that the fifty black probationers, plus fifty more allegedly converted members, were on the roll to please their masters, and for that reason alone. The increase of Sunday school membership was surely Haygood's achievement. White membership doubled, and five out of the fourteen congregations began to hold a school for the first time, most of them on Sunday afternoon. The junior preacher bought books for the Sunday school libraries. His accomplishments did not go unnoticed by the hierarchy, and he was assured of acceptance into the "First-Year Class." Haygood's class contained those who wanted to become fully ordained elders four years after admission in December 1859 to the Georgia Conference of the Methodist Episcopal Church, South. That fall, before conference, he gave his farewell to Young J. Allen, who was leaving for China. It would be eighteen and a half years before the Christian missionary and his disciple would meet again.[38]

The Annual Conference—the term referring to both the whole body of the preachers and to their yearly congress—assembled in Rome in December 1859, under the gavel of the Kentucky bishop, H. H. Kavanaugh. Business was conducted in a sequence of twenty-one questions asked by the itinerant bishop, the first being "Who are admitted on trial [as members of the First-Year Class]?" Haygood had been examined over a year before by his presiding elder as to the seriousness of his professional intention and was one of those named by the secretary as being admitted. The next five items dealt with those young preachers in the four years of examination. "Trial" for deacons, for "local preachers," required only two years; to become a traveling preacher and full elder required four. Atticus could look forward to becoming an elder in 1863, if he fulfilled the self-study requirements suggested by the conference for the several classes. Examinations took place immediately preceding the four conferences. One of the surprises at Rome was learning from those "on trial" that the examinations were a farce. A young man completing his Second Year told Atticus that "None of the Class but myself had paid any attention to this primary study."[39] Haygood resolved that he would be equally conscientious. The story came out of the examinations that fall that one boy was passed without comment after he said that the divisions of the Holy Land were "Europe, Asia and Africa." But then, the examiner had admitted beforehand that "I reckon you know as much about it as I do."[40] The examiners were established leaders of the conference, often college graduates.

Conferences varied in their degree of spirituality, but Atticus was amazed at the jocularity, contentiousness, and sometimes (off the floor) the vulgarity of Methodist preachers away from their flocks. A main part of the business was the statistical reporting of the accomplishments of the preachers, a competitive sport especially for preachers established in the cities and the prosperous towns in plantation counties. To the recipients of the conference subsidies—the old-lady widows of preachers, struggling new "mission churches," the American Bible Society agent, and the man in charge of buying religious tracts for the conference—these totals were of serious moment. It was the last two questions that interested all the members of the conference and brought full attendance on the business managed by the bishop (when he was not out of the chair conferring with the "presiding elders" and visiting laymen and their wives). Next to last was the decision about the locale for the conference a year later. Bids would have already been made by two or three towns, and the decision would be in Protestant Georgia a matter of considerable local prestige. Without a doubt the majority vote often reflected the preachers' consensus on the town with the nicest host homes and the best cooking.

The last question provoked the only silence ever allowed during conference business: the bishop announced where the preachers would reside for the next year. All those who had a two-year residence knew that they would move. Young preachers were often moved annually. Only the presiding elders, the itinerant bishop's "cabinet," knew beforehand what the assignments were—they having suggested most of them. J. R. Branham, the presiding elder who had examined Haygood and found him fit to preach, and John Yarbrough, his father-in-law, were prominent members of the conference and gave good words in Haygood's behalf to Bishop Kavanaugh, from faraway Kentucky. As a result, Atticus Haygood was honored by being assigned to be the "junior" to Lovick Pierce, the oldest active preacher, father of Georgia's resident bishop, and by far the most venerated man in Georgia Methodism.[41]

The conference of 1859 acted on a special matter. It approved the establishment of a "Book Depository" in Macon to sell at just above cost denominational tracts and books, for the most part religious, all published by the new Publishing House of Nashville. Its manager would be the Reverend John W. Burke, a friend of the Haygoods, having gone to school in Athens to Martha Askew. The conference of 1858 had appointed a committee of preachers and laymen to suggest a method for increasing the use of books and tracts; they recommended a bookstore. There were four laymen on the committee. One, James W. Chambers, was President of Emory College's Board of Trustees. He and a second member, Albon Chase of Athens, had stock in textile mills. Chase also had been the editor of *The Southern Banner* when the Haygoods lived in Watkinsville. Greene Haygood himself was the third member, the fourth being a man named T. M. Furlow.[42]

Atticus and Mollie, who was bearing their first child, moved to Lovick Pierce's home in Columbus after Christmas. Lovick refused to serve big churches and was working to build up a new church to be called Pierce Chapel. His "charge" included the congregation in Girard, Alabama, across the Chattahoochee River and southwest from Columbus. This responsibility was even more challenging than the Newton County circuit Atticus had served, since the first circuit had been in a prosperous agricultural district. Pierce's churches had all together only seventy-five members, with ten on probation. There were no slaves on the rolls. Atticus did preach to Negroes in Columbus in a mission on Sunday afternoons.

Lovick Pierce was called a "saint," but Haygood knew him as a widower of near eighty, and of a dynamic and inflexible nature. He was still 'a great man physically," a hard worker—and a crack shot. His mind was flexible. He was perhaps more interested in theology than any other Methodist preacher in Georgia. He worked hard thinking out his sermons, but would not write them down even in outline, insisting on spontaneity: "A man preaching without the Spirit is a mere lecturer on theology," he would say.

Almost alone among old preachers, he insisted that "God's grace does not work alone, or chiefly through the pulpit." His awareness of the mystery surrounding the workings of grace was his most important gift to Atticus Haygood.[43]

Lovick also taught Atticus his prejudice against lectures and literarily pretentious sermons. But the main influence was in teaching the necessity of a doctrinal orientation and an intellectual core. (Atticus found it best as a young preacher to make outlines of his thoughts and to refer to these; this became the method of a lifetime, although he also found that he could read fully written manuscripts without losing the valuable sound of spontaneous speech.) Lovick's interest in theology dated back to the first decade of the century when Wesleyan teaching had to be maintained in a backwoods intellectual battle with high Calvinist doctrine. The early Methodist preachers—Lovick being the sole survivor of those days before the War of 1812—had sharpened their wits in denying the Calvinist teaching of the "necessary indwelling of sin" in the earthly body until death, of "limited atonement" promised only to the elect, and of the "unconditioned perseverance" until death and beyond for any who experienced signs of election.[44] The democratic Methodists promised a possible working of grace for all, the eternal danger of "backsliding," and the desirability and possibility of total righteousness of this earth.

The Wesleyan quest for total "sanctification" always fascinated Lovick, but apparently more intellectually than as an experience. He never "doubted his conversion" but he recognized that he "had . . . seasons or moods of depression in which he 'mourned the loss of grace' " and he pointed these facts out to Atticus, who had sometimes lost patience with the sanctification-seekers in Oxford.[45] It is significant that Lovick's son, the bishop, never concerned himself with the necessity of constant inward growing toward a greater, a total purity.[46]

Haygood's determination to be a model probationer in the conference was well matched to Lovick Pierce's theological orientation. The junior would be examined on "the historical and biographical parts of the Bible," the first volume of Wesley's sermons, the denomination's hymnbook, Part III of Richard Watson's *Institutes,* and Watson's *Biblical and Theological Dictionary.* Watson, British Methodist, had organized Wesleyan theology in what may be called the scholastic manner in a work completed in the 1820's. Thomas O. Summers, himself a former Britisher, was the Methodist Publishing House's editor, and in 1857 brought out an edition of the *Institutes,* printed first in New York in 1823.[47] The title obviously was chosen to distinguish the formal statement of "Arminianism" from Calvin's far more famous and influential *Institutes* of three centuries earlier. Lovick Pierce applauded and sustained his junior preacher in his close study of Part III. During the year Haygood acquired the ability to restate in his own language all of the arguments of this portion of the ponderous volume.

Watson's main premise was appealing to the young preacher: the power of reason resided in all normal beings, thus all beings could be taught the reasonableness of the holy, compassionate life. Haygood read more into Watson than was there: the Southern Whig's enthusiasm for social improvement—from more railroads to wider literacy. Unfortunately, the Arminian assumption that all the burden of salvation depended on the energy of preachers was psychologically oppressive to Haygood. There was to be no relaxation in his life. *His* only hope for salvation was in remembering Lovick Pierce's words that grace worked its own way, in its own time (and, the Calvinists would have added, on whomever it chose). Watson put Haygood directly and tragically into the Enlightenment mainstream of belief about the sovereignty of the will; the former epileptic, proud of his self-control, found this belief irresistible until he was past forty. As Watson said: "It is decided by the word of GOD itself that men who perish might have 'chosen life.' It is confirmed, also by natural reason."[48]

It was on the mornings before and after the Sabbath that Lovick delivered his "monologues concerning Bible teaching, Methodist history and doctrine and religious experience."[49] Lovick also taught by faithful example the duties stated in the Discipline, which younger preachers were beginning to neglect: "To see that the General Rules be read . . . once a year . . . To see that a fast be held . . . on the Friday preceding every quarterly meeting. . . . To renew the tickets for the admission of members into lovefeasts quarterly."[50]

It was the fateful year of 1860. The Methodist Episcopal Church, South, had forged a happy compromise with plantation society. For the eighty-year-old patriarch and the twenty-year-old son of a determinedly middle-class Southerner, though, the forces destroying the sectarian spirit of the denomination were invisible. Services in Pierce Chapel and at Girard were as plain as camp meetings for pioneers had been. Only the Sunday morning service was formal. Much of the magic of worship was carried through the singing. There was no piano in churches such as these, and the two preachers had to "line out" the tunes either by verse or stanza, Lovick in his shaky old voice, or Atticus in his still uncertain pitch.

Lovick Pierce felt that Atticus Haygood was one of the best junior preachers ever sent him. He judged Mollie a quiet undemanding wife, as might be expected of the sister of George Yarbrough, his junior two years before. The word was passed to his son Bishop Pierce, who would that year preside over the Georgia Conference meeting in Augusta. The conference met in December 1860; the preachers were "simply panic stricken." They were not panicky over any impending war following the certain secession of nearby South Carolina, for war seemed unlikely. Their panic was over what Lincoln's election would do to those Southern states which did not follow South Carolina's example. Nevertheless, the early sensation of the conference was the trial of a young man (all the preachers were regularly examined as to probity of character). The preacher had not shown up for his own wedding. The conference acquitted him when he said he "had heard things" about his prospective bride's character. Another young preacher thought otherwise, that "while he was away from her another maid had won his heart."[51] By the last day of the conference, given the overriding political excitement, this incident was forgotten. The appointment watchers, the gaugers of careers on the make and careers forfeited, listened intently. Atticus Haygood was one of the names watched. The news was that young Haygood would be Bishop Pierce's own preacher in the town of Sparta. For Haygood additional excitement lay in Sparta's nearness to Georgia's state capital of Milledgeville, where the dramatic struggle over secession would take place after Christmas. In his heart he knew his star had risen—even if the Southland's firmament was so topsy-turvy that no star would be sure of the direction toward its zenith![52]

THREE

The War Years

ATTICUS AND MOLLIE, with their baby boy Paul, moved to Sparta, in Hancock County, in early January of the turbulent year 1861. Hancock County was a cotton county; and Sparta was one of several Georgia villages in such counties, "in which the planters resided." Sparta was thus a Methodist "station," giving to the pastor a regular congregation. This closer relationship—in the areas where planters predominated—ironically lessened the possibility that the Methodist system of behavior supervision would work in strict sectarian fashion. Certainly Bishop Pierce, who resided four miles outside Sparta, would never send to his neighbors' pulpit a young preacher offensive of manner. As a result, in Sparta, as throughout the plantation area in central Georgia, liberties were taken with the "General Rules":

> Women wore rings, ruffles and ribbons, without rebuke, and men neglected family prayer and did not go to class meeting, with no other penalty than a general rebuke from the pulpit. The old straight-breasted coat was still worn by many of the preachers; but the young men did not follow the example . . . , and sometimes one was found daring enough to let a part of his beard grow.[1]

Atticus—a young man with a beard (Young Allen had had one)—had been picked partly because the Bishop knew him to be bright, capable of engaging in conversation with older men, and docile. Neighbors of his like John L. Culver, David Dickson, Dr. E. M. Pendleton, Richard Malcolm Johnston (an author in the mold of Judge Longstreet), and Professor Sasnett, men in their prime and confirmed in their eccentricities, would be let alone, preached *to* but never *at*.[2] The Bishop treasured the good life of Hancock, where "The plantations were not too large to make the white population too sparse for social enjoyment, and yet they were large enough to make every man independent."[3] Indeed the

.. The War Years

Bishop's home at "Sunshine" was a social center, for whites and blacks. He preached the weddings and funerals of his white brothers (it was said that he saved his mightiest sermons for these occasions in "his own pulpit" in Sparta), and he married his slaves to the slaves of other Hancock planters. Nearly seven years of episcopal service had sapped some of his vigor, but he was still an extraordinarily magnetic figure on the platform. In a patriarchal society men were not ashamed to admire the physique and bearing of other men (or even their phrenological contours), and Bishop George Pierce was "the most beautiful of mankind." Men loved to "look upon, and listen to a man whom they knew to be as consistent as he was beautiful."[4]

Atticus felt acutely his unusual relationship with the Bishop, and with the Bishop's friends. Having been close to the Bishop's father, he could claim the friendly but deferential status of a younger brother; he was welcome at "Sunshine." In another sense, however, the Bishop's poise was unnerving; Atticus became again Attie the child tending the horses of the itinerant preachers in Watkinsville. A Southern Methodist Bishop, even without the *presence* of George Foster Pierce, was in 1861 a cornerstone of "Christian civilization," which, being built on slavery, was necessarily authoritarian, a civilization to be defended by secession from a North disrespectful of tradition and authority. Bishop Pierce had voted for the Unionist candidate John Bell in November (as did Greene Haygood), but the Bishop agreed with the planters' political psychology; he would write to his son away in the Army, in the fall of 1861: "I hope no one in whom flows any of my blood will ever be a Democrat. A sound, sensible, strong government can never be built upon democratic soil."[5] So close was Bishop Pierce to the Southern cause that he would in four years be identified with it in a manner analogous to that of the Yankee Methodist Bishop Matthew Simpson, untiring supporter of Lincoln.[6] So powerful, trusted, and respected was Pierce's voice that on a fasting Friday observed by the state legislature, March 27, 1863, he felt free to demand the repeal of the slave law which forbade preachers or anyone else to teach the Negroes to read even the Bible.[7] This was the man who during six months' association in 1861 fastened upon Atticus Haygood a domination that lasted until near his death two decades away. It is a tribute to the intellectual independence of Atticus Haygood that he never surrendered during this earlier time the democratic bias he had acquired from his father.

During the first months of the new pastorate in Sparta Greene Haygood was simultaneously engaged in a new part-time occupation, growing out of his educational interests. He was, after Christmas, editor of the second volume of a Southern Methodist periodical, *The Educational Repository and Family Monthly.* Since 1856 the concern of the Methodist parents in the South "for schools that shall advance their children beyond their own attainments in knowledge and culture" had initiated an Educational Institute, an annual gathering of teachers from the denomination's colleges and academies, Methodists who taught at state institutions, and interested laymen.[8] Most of the papers read at the Institute were discussions of the relative qualities of various textbooks in use.

In 1859 the members of the Institute voted to publish a monthly organ; this was favored by the contributors of papers, most of them professors, who had to "give over their summer leisure" in preparation for the Institute. The new publication began its issue in January 1860; Greene Haygood was "Junior Editor," and after the resignation of W. H. C. Price of Auburn, Alabama, in December, succeeded as editor.[9] Expressing with fervor the new Southern nationalist position his son would copy, Greene considered the *Repository* "an important step . . . towards the accomplishment of Southern Independence, and the elevation of Southern . . . education." He was glad that children of Southern Methodist parents would be hereafter protected, in securing textbooks, "from the infectious character of those plague-spots which are so often found in our school books of Northern Production."[10]

Atticus wrote two articles for the *Repository,* one each for the January and February issues. The first is entitled "Agur the Teacher" with an author's nom de plume, but all the marks of Haygood *fils* are there. "Agur" 's theme is that both wealth and poverty in their extremes are morally dangerous; it is from the middle class that the "greatest reformers" are furnished, and by it true Christian regard of others and Christian morality are furthered. The article was used by the twenty-one-year-old disciple of Young Allen to criticize the parents of his Emory colleagues who had encouraged their sons to "make a rise" professionally and who judged college years not spent in finding "some . . . profitable profession" as wasted time. Atticus concluded the article with a blast at materialistic Southerners (Whigs?) who equated potential marriage partners in terms of additional income: "We live in an age of steam and telegraph, and we have generally got rid of those simple old notions about *love*'s being a *sine qua non* to a proper marriage."[11]

The February article was signed by the editor's son and given the title of "Southern Independence and Southern Literature." It was an echo of his father's sentiments: "Our literary vassalage ... [is] galling and humiliating." Southern dependence on Northern papers, periodicals, and books was due to the fact that Southerners would not buy Southern papers. He cited the case of "a monthly magazine, published somewhere in the 'Empire State of the South,'" five years before. "It barely completed its first volume when it met the fate of so many kindred publications." The young man bitterly recognized that the Southern editors who survived were gifted only with managerial ability rather than with true journalistic talent. Without realizing it, Atticus was a prophet. The *Educational Repository* ceased publication after the May issue. But then, the beginning of the War for Southern Independence made even editorial ventures less of a necessity than they had seemed in February.[12]

The shooting at Fort Sumter, April 1861, unleashed demonic spirits that Southern whites had labored to closet up through decades of civilizing through the institutions of court, pulpit, and college. One Georgia Conference preacher, only slightly older than Atticus, was that spring "wild with the war fever. I made political speeches. I wrote fiery poems and articles. I talked war all the time. I never did better preaching as far as the subject matter of my sermons was concerned but I did but little and expected to do but little." Restless to go into the Army, Atticus ignored the wishes of his "poor little wife," and accepted a chaplaincy.[13]

Mobilization in Georgia reached a fever pitch in April and May, after the Commonwealth of Virginia asked for two or three companies of Georgia infantry to help protect the port of Norfolk. The next request came from the Confederate Secretary of War, asking Governor Brown for two regiments to defend Richmond. The "Hancock Confederate Guards," a company of boys all from that county, was immediately organized, hoping to be one of the ten companies to be included in a regiment going to Virginia. Seventeen thousand men were organized into Georgia regiments and legions, electing their colonels, before the Battle of Bull Run in late July. Although Governor Brown delayed until very late, to the agony of Secretary of War L. P. Walker, before transporting the two regiments, Georgians participated in that glorious victory against the Yankee invader, sixty Georgians dying in the action.[14]

By the end of August, the number of Georgians in Confederate service was duly proportional to the population of the state. In Virginia near Richmond was encamped Cobb's Legion, led by the young politician T. R. R. Cobb of Athens; and at Camp Walker not far from Manassas were the Fifteenth and Sixteenth Infantry Regiments. The Sixteenth's colonel was the nationally known Howell Cobb; its chaplain was George Yarbrough; its lieutenant colonel, who would succeed the elder Cobb in six months and become a popular brigade leader, was Goode Bryan. The colonel of the Fifteenth, for slightly over six months, was Thomas W. Thomas; lieutenant colonel was Linton Stephens (half-brother of the Confederacy's Vice President, having been captain of the Hancock County company when it was first organized); the chaplain was Bishop Pierce's young pastor, Atticus G. Haygood. The Fifteenth was made up of company units from northeastern Georgia counties—Elbert, Hart, Franklin, Wilkes, Lincoln, Taliaferro, Hancock—from areas settled by Virginians since the Revolution. (Another Hancock County unit was a company in the Sixth Regiment, one of the first two organized.) Bishop Pierce's own contribution, besides the sacrifice of his young preacher-client, was his son Lovick, Jr., who was a private in Company E of the Fifteenth.[15]

Haygood and his brother-in-law were but two of over a dozen members of the Georgia Conference who joined the Confederate Army as chaplains. Eight others deserted the cloth to fight in the ranks, and one of these, a captain, was killed at Bull Run. Atticus could not resist the excitement and certainly was subject to the blessing of Bishop Pierce. None of the chaplains likely joined for base motives, although being on the "staff" of the colonels made them officers in effect; after August 31, though, an Act of Congress made their official rations enough for only one daily meal, putting them in the same category as privates.[16] Hope of preferment probably had little to do with Haygood's willingness to go and leave his infant son. He was closest to Lovick Pierce and Henry Middlebrooks, Lovick's brother-in-law, both Emory graduates and both privates. Lovick was instructed by his father, in a letter written July 23, to accept Thomas's offer to be his personal secretary, and to "Tell Haygood to write to me." (By fall Bishop Pierce missed his son, writing to him, "If you cannot come home this winter, I must . . . come to see you," and warned of the "moral pestilence . . . in camp life.")[17]

Until late October Atticus was sanguine about his military career. He was so busy nursing the sick and burying those who died of illness, and in writing letters for illiterate soldiers, not to mention conducting the open-air services, that he managed to suppress his loneliness. In early September he felt honored to be in charge of escorting one hundred seriously ill Georgia soldiers chosen for hospitalization in Richmond. Upon arrival he had a few hours of distress. Georgia's hospital had not yet been organized in the Confederacy's capital, and the sick had to be temporarily housed in hotels and private dwellings, these arrangements not having been made beforehand. Once the responsibility was discharged, Chaplain Haygood savored vicariously the life of Richmond, which he found to be "a very fine, wealthy, aristocratic and wicked place."[18] Through the courtesy of Lieutenant Colonel Stephens, he spent some hours in the Vice President's office, writing Mollie about the Yankee prisoners kept in the tobacco factories along the James River and about hearing a piano playing next door to his hotel, reminding him of the Yarbrough home in Oxford—in which he had lived with her two years before, and to which she and the baby boy, Paul, had gone. A second letter, to Atlanta Methodists, criticized Georgia's failure to provide for hospitalization of the sick soldiers and averred that "our regiment has not forgotten the Christian teaching. . . ."[19] He was delighted to meet his brother-in-law in Richmond, not having had time to locate him at Camp Walker, and boasted of working over his sermons "as if he had been in a first-class charge at home."[20]

Chaplain Atticus Haygood returned to Camp Walker, to a regiment seething with dissension. There was, as Linton Stephens said, at base the ill-health of a high percentage of officers and men, and discontent with an unknown but stagnant future: "The brigadiers seem to be as much in the dark as . . . the rest of us."[21] But the resignation of three officers of the regiment, including the staff adjutant, was the result of Col. Thomas's overbearing personality in the midst of doubt.[22] In August, Thomas had had to defend his ousting of one of the officers, William F. Price, who had "walked about Atlanta with his brave read [sic] cap on," using his office and the unusual situation to sell the men socks and cigars. A few weeks in Virginia had made Price unhappy:

. . . when he got here, the socks and segars were all sold, the weather was uncomfortable, and our arrangements for feeding were not completed. In addition to this, cannonading was occasionally heard on the Potomac. Price began to think the prospect not inviting. . . . The plan he adopted was to get as many as he could to back out with him . . .

so he coined stories about the hardship we were to endure, and the manner we would be treated when mustered in. . . .[23]

Mustering in would transfer the men to Confederate authority, and "About sixty men" in addition to thirty-eight of Price's fellow Hart Countians refused to be mustered in until Thomas convinced them of Price's cowardice. Thomas had to endure a situation in which "all are not with me," but he seems to have made no effort to make his officers happy.[24]

Dissension in a Confederate regiment was no remarkable thing, especially during the period of seasoning: "The esprit de corps of Confederate officers was surprisingly low."[25] With the advent of cool weather in October, the improvement in supply, and the rumor of combat before winter, morale rapidly improved, and Thomas took the occasion of a snappy drill to tell his Georgians how to act in combat—not to trust their rifles to hit beyond a hundred yards, not to be afraid of using their bayonets, and to ignore the harmless whistling of shells overhead before the fighting started. The chaplain was somewhat dismayed with the matter-of-fact manner in which Thomas talked about the bloody business of war, although he concurred in the colonel's fear that the South could not "afford to be defeated." The fate of Southerners would be to become "hewers of wood and drawers [of] water to an enemy we abhor."[26]

The rumor of combat, as Col. Thomas also suggested, was baseless, and officers and men felt that the Fifteenth's fate was to wither away from inertia. Before Christmas, half a dozen officers resigned, not least of these being Linton Stephens. Chaplain Haygood resigned on November 13, in time to be back in Georgia and see Mollie before conference met in Atlanta later that month. He had at first admired Col. Thomas, sympathizing with him in his problem with Price, and was thrilled at the regimental orders that the men would attend his services on Sunday. But the talking of the other officers, and the homesickness of the privates, had unnerved his resolve. He was already depressed to learn that Greene had failed in his bid to become state senator from Fulton County when word was sent him that his first-born son Paul had died in July, while he was on his way to Virginia. He consoled himself "on picket" by writing a sentimental poem about his "angel child," "Too pure for earth," who had joined Grandmother Askew where "we all meet . . . above."[27]

The meeting with Mollie took place in Atlanta. The young wife's restraint vanished even in front of her in-laws, and she purged her grief with tears and the joy of her husband's nearness. The general air of the Greene Haygood home was one of excitement. Brother Willie, now nine, was eager to hear stories of the war. Preachers were congregating in Atlanta for conference, and the family was happy over Haygood's prospect of being ordained a deacon. At the conference George Yarbrough by special vote was "called and elected" an elder even though he was still in Virginia, although he would have to be ordained when he returned. A reporter for an Atlanta paper was amazed at the "fine body of dignified, business and intellectual men" who made up the Georgia Conference.[28] Experienced men knew that the show of fine clothes and dignity was an election year gambit: this conference elected its most prominent preachers to be delegates to the quadrennial General Conference of Southern Methodism (a conference which never met). The spirit of patriotism pervaded the gathering in Atlanta, a Confederacy supply center. A resolution passed unanimously which affirmed that "there is no such thing as a Union party among us."[29] Haygood spent far less time on the floor than at his two preceding conferences.

Bishop Pierce sought out his former preacher to inquire after Lovick and showed no dissatisfaction with Haygood's resignation from the chaplaincy. He had heard talk of general denominational unhappiness with the situation. As proof of this, the new appointment could not have been more to Atticus's liking. He was to be the senior preacher of the Watkinsville circuit; he and Mollie could live in the old family place in Watkinsville; and now *he* would have a junior—Anderson J. Jarrell, an able recent Emory graduate.[30] Before the year of 1862 was out they were joined by a portly eighteen-year-old country fellow, Asbury Dodge, just licensed to preach. Watkinsville circuit embraced two counties, Clarke and Jackson, and contained some fifteen hundred Methodists in twenty-one country and crossroads chapels. "It was hardly allowable for a young preacher to go on wheels,"[31] but Haygood and Jarrell were so enamored of their horsemanship that they would not have considered using a buggy even were it proper. Atticus boasted of his own horse's capabilities:

'Jack Morgan,' a blood bay and a mover for true, from Jefferson to Watkinsville one October day in three hours . . . . Dodge drove a one-eyed flea-bitten mare with a short tail . . . . Jarrell had a dignified, reliable white horse—'Selim' by name. He had a vexing habit of jerking up his right hind leg when starting out in the morning.[32]

This was a happy year for Atticus Haygood. The experiences in Virginia, and his grief, had matured him; he had shed the doleful affectation of religious seriousness that he had brought with him to Oxford in 1856. He was a man of nearly twenty-three, enjoying the most romantic year of his married life. Being master of the Watkinsville house was inexpressibly exhilarating. Both Jarrell and Dodge ventured comments on Haygood's unpreacherly high spirits. Even the presiding elder, R. W. Bigham, who relived his own youth in observing such gladness, gave Atticus a mild reproof at a camp meeting in Jackson County when he saw Atticus in "a bob-tail brown jeans sack coat," admitting that he "was somewhat inclined to be a rowdy himself." It was at this same camp meeting that after preaching himself hoarse Atticus took a "big swig of 'Number Six' " as cough medicine, and "For a time I had fire in me."[33]

The Watkinsville house became a center for the young people who "used to spend our evenings at the parsonage playing innocent games, playing on the piano, and singing." Brother Haygood became the father of a baby girl in midsummer, who was named Pauline. Attie Haygood was erasing the memory of a panicky, sickly childhood and uncertain adolescence, reliving his previous life in the gaiety of others. He was "so full of life and fun and loved young people" that on "moonlight nights we used to get out in the streets . . . and drill. He was always our captain. . . ."[34]

The Reverend Haygood became, during this year of 1862, thoroughly at home with the professional expectations of a Methodist preacher. He conscientiously continued to work on "developing a text"—evolving a sermon from the well of meaning in perhaps a single Bible verse—he being one of the few preachers in the conference with enough knowledge of history, theology, and nineteenth-century homiletics to do this. As the senior preacher of the circuit he even dared to reprove the planters. At least once he spoke about the "vast problem of the colored people among us, and the great responsibility under which the white people of the South were thereby placed."[35] He tactfully applauded those planters who allowed "their negroes the privileges of the sanctuary. The result was that a number of their servants were soundly converted."[36] Such references from the pulpit were certainly rare during the Civil War. In 1859, however, Josiah Lewis, a Georgia Methodist preacher, father of a classmate of Haygood's, had created a "sensation" in using an entire sermon to criticize church-

.. The War Years

going planters for physical neglect of their slaves.[37] Before the end of the Watkinsville appointment Haygood had become somewhat estranged from Jarrell, and especially from Dodge, both of whom within fifteen years would become leaders of a narrow "social gospel" limited to the behavior requirements of the "Holiness movement," a supradenominational development in the post-war South. Haygood seems to have retained greater loyalty to the Pierce version of the Wesleyan gospel, with its realistic acceptance of the continuing perversity of man (even after conversion).

Haygood's developing interest in improving society in spite of the recognized difficulties was relatively secular and relatively Whiggish, but not weakened because of any failure to understand the stubborn resistance to change, especially of religious men and women. His efforts along with those of the local Watkinsville preacher—Deacon John Calvin Johnson, with whom he worked better than with Dodge—in bringing the Arminian gospel to eastern Clarke County (a haven for "hard-shell" high Calvinists) indicates a comprehension of the orthodox Augustinian distrust of "total sanctification" while in the flesh. Dodge and Jarrell, on the other hand, felt that the Methodist gospel was designed to preach hope in earthly purity—a purity which would make the blessed one free of responsibility for the depravities of the society of the unsaved.[38]

The intellectual divergences between the assigned preachers of the Watkinsville circuit, during 1862, concerned their parishioners not at all. The most important event to the "planters" (large and small) was a covenant in the spring to grow more wheat and less cotton.[39] John Calvin Johnson, who helped his good friend Greene Haygood's son in gospeling among the Primitive Baptists, marked the year by exhorting Clarke County boys into the company of "Johnson Guards."[40] Johnson was still Clerk of the Superior Court, as he had been in the 1840's when Greene Haygood was the leading lawyer before the court; in July 1862, he issued Atticus a pass identifying him as "attached to the Government," and so gave him freer movement throughout the two counties.[41] The war intruded into the church itself. There were periodically rumors of cavalry raids by the Yankees from the Union base in Tennessee. One Sunday night when Atticus was on his knees somewhat exceeding the Discipline's limit of ten minutes in impromptu prayer, an incoming worshipper whispered that Watkinsville was to be raided that night. When the Reverend Haygood stood up, he was astonished to find that his congregation had vanished.[42]

The fall and winter of 1862-1863 cruelly mocked the joy and freedom of the previous spring and summer. Atticus was aware of a despondence at the conference, held in Macon in November. Decision by the bishops not to hold the General Conference scheduled for the spring of 1862 caused demoralization among the leading preachers and apathy among the less notable. At the conference a perfunctorily patriotic resolution was passed, but a Macon lady's request was needed to prod the conference into setting aside an hour to "pray for peace."[43] Haygood managed to stay buoyed up by the knowledge that 1863 would be his last year "on trial," and he looked forward to Christmas with gleeful anticipation—it would be his first as a parent since the death of his son Paul.

But Christmas Day in Atlanta, 1862, brought another personal sorrow to Atticus: Greene died that day of smallpox. The "pious widow and four children," in the words of the *Southern Christian Advocate* (a recent literary refugee in Augusta, having moved from Charleston), turned toward Atticus, now the head of the family. That he was, at twenty-three, not yet ready for this responsibility is indicated by the obituary in the *Advocate*, which singled out Willie as a "promising boy of nine or ten summers" without mentioning Atticus at all.[44] The conference had appointed Haygood, junior, to the charge of Palmetto, a village twenty miles southwest of Atlanta, and Newnan, ten miles farther in the same direction. In an ordinary year this would have been a fine appointment, for Newnan and Palmetto both were planters' villages, with the former boasting a wartime hospital and a school for girls.[45] But the tribulations of the family rendered impossible any regular attention to his charge, and after the death of Greene's widow, Pauline, in the spring, Atticus decided to go back into the chaplaincy (his resignation having put him into a sort of inactive status.)[46]

By 1863 a new sort of chaplaincy organization had emerged in the Confederacy. The Southern Baptists had the previous year decided to send only "missionary chaplains" to the Army, men under their pay and control. Both Presbyterians and Methodists agreed that denominational interests would be better served by preachers who were not on regimental staffs. In April 1863, Bishop Pierce met in Macon with other Southern Methodist bishops, counseling especially with John B. McFerrin, the denomination's secretary for the Board of Missions, who had fled to Georgia from Nashville, a city occupied by Federal troops. The Methodist plan, possibly suggested by McFerrin, was the creation of a superintendent of missions for each Army Department, or area of troop deployment. McFerrin was named superintendent of the Confederate troops stationed south of the Tennessee River—in Alabama, Georgia, and Tennessee. In May he "appointed" the first missionary to the troops at Shelbyville, Tennessee. Actually the new plan encouraged interdenominational worship, since the chaplains were freer to roam in their ministry to the sick, wounded, bereft, and despondent—Catholic priests and Protestant preachers joining in the field in instinctive association of priestly function. The interdenominational worship experienced by officers and men during the Civil War had an important effect: there is no doubt that it destroyed the sectarian characteristics of Southern Methodism.[47]

Atticus Haygood was appointed by McFerrin to Confederate troops in northwestern Georgia, sometime before the Battle of Chickamauga, which began September 18. The casualties in this struggle amounted to over 25,000, and for days McFerrin and other distressed chaplains, Atticus Haygood included, wandered among the untended wounded and the unconsecrated dead. An Atlanta man, his leg blown off, woke from a coma to see

> before me . . . two civilians, as their . . . genteel appearance clearly indicated . . . , upon each one of their arms . . . a large basket well filled, and under the other . . . a large feather pillow . . . [;] each one immediately recognized me, and . . . Haygood exclaimed, "Why, Frank, it seems as if God has directed our footsteps." . . . the two . . . were the Rev. Atticus Haygood . . . and the Rev. Father O'Neal, the . . . priest. . . .[48]

After the battle the surviving Confederates went into winter quarters in a withdrawn battle "line" centered on Dalton, closer to Atlanta and its supplies. The missionary chaplains here were given their greatest preaching opportunity of the war. Revival services were held in jerry-built log churches, as many as seven hundred troops crowding into some of the congregations. From December 1863 until early May the preachers converted hundreds of soldiers. An attempt was made to preserve denominational lines in the revivals; newly baptized soldiers were given a certificate to take back to the Christian church of their choice as a sort of petition for home membership.[49]

By appointment of the Georgia Conference, Atticus Haygood was given charge of the denomination's church at Rome and continued service as missionary chaplain to these soldiers. These were months of mounting distress; it would seem that his own helplessness to hold back the furious momentums of Confederate military history, to deny the auguries of defeat in 1863, was experienced as a doctrinal problem. His most important sermon, repeated before soldiers and civilians at Rome, was an argument against the fatalism about the end of the Southern fight for independence which he had heard discussed, primarily he judged, by Presbyterian and Hardshell soldiers. On the other hand he deplored the unrealistic statements of the still sanguine who talked as though history had no "law"—in theological terms, as he stated it, that history was entirely free of a "governor." Calvinistic doctrine, as he heard it in the revivals, limiting man's place in the City of God and (by implication) in his chances of earthly happiness, he found "unscriptural and unphilosophical." But the optimists possessed an equally disturbing "proud but superficial philosophy." Haygood clung to a deterministic faith that demanded a voluntaristic accompaniment: "Your PRESENT PREACHER REVERENTLY ACKNOWLEDGES THAT HIS LIFE, AS FAR AS WE CAN SEE, WAS RESCUED FROM THE DOMINION OF EPILEPSY IN ANSWER TO PRAYER."[50]

The Georgia Conference which sent Haygood to Rome met in Columbus in late November 1863. In a strenuous effort to maintain the "connectional ties" throughout the section Bishop Pierce held the conferences in Virginia and South Carolina while Bishop John Early traveled from Lynchburg to preside in Georgia. The bishops had no income from the church but enough from their private estate to live on. They were far better off than the preachers, who "were pressed beyond measure to get means of substinence." Even had there been freedom from economic concern the pulpit "had little to say" since there was nothing to say about the war. Formerly devoted members were given to "heartless gaiety and shameless rapacity," and, most crucially, to ignoring their preachers.[51]

More frightening even than the declining influence of the pulpit was the prospect for the *Southern* church if the South lost the war. In Columbus, E. H. Myers, editor of the *Southern Christian Advocate,* read a "Report on the State of the Church and Country" at a time when the news was of Bragg's retreat into Georgia from Lookout Mountain and Missionary Ridge. Myers drew his prophetic inspiration from Jeremiah:

> We need no prophet to foretell, that if we succeed not, every religious establishment of our land will pass under the power of our

enemies [the northern Methodist Episcopal Church]. They come with the sword in one hand, and a new gospel in the other, and woe to the minister or church of Christ who will not receive that gospel.[52]

Myers referred to the displacement already made in some areas, notably Louisiana, of preachers appointed by Southern Methodist bishops. It was not an auspicious time to be ordained an elder in the Southern establishment; but the four years were ordained to end on November 29, 1863, and Bishop Early anointed Atticus Haygood an elder, a "traveling preacher" in the Georgia Conference of the Methodist Episcopal Church, South.[53]

Haygood preached Sunday afternoon at the little church in Girard, Alabama, which he had served until three years before, and on Monday all the preachers left, the conference having been shortened from its customary week. Resolutions of the preachers included a memorial to the Confederate Congress for some financial aid in supporting the missionary chaplains, a specification that there should be one chaplain for each brigade, and permission to use mission money to pay the chaplains. The Eagle Factory of Columbus let it be known that each preacher could buy "a bolt of homespun . . . and eight yards of jeans apiece at reduced prices," and a few of the preachers were in a position to benefit.[54]

Atticus Haygood served in Rome and at Dalton only till February 1864, when he went to join Bryan's Brigade in eastern Tennessee. He left Mollie in Oxford with their third child, a boy named Wilbur Fletcher Haygood, born January 15. Atticus was one of only eight Methodist chaplains in Johnston's army, and had to reach Tennessee in a roundabout ten-day trip via Greensboro, North Carolina. He wrote the *Advocate* about his trip; from Greensboro

the traveller may enter the luxury of a primitive stage ride of twenty-four miles. I greatly enjoyed the ride, especially the eating and the hot genuine 'Rio' at the dinner house. Just think of it, ye half-starved denizens of cities, pure coffee, away up there near the Virginia line! From Greensboro to the Southside and Richmond and Danville Rail Roads, we had no crowd, while we made the trip as quick as those unfortunates who took the squeeze by way of Wilmington and Petersburg.[55]

The Sunday after his arrival he left the brigade to "three Baptist co-laborers, and a visiting Presbyterian" and assisted George Yarbrough in a morning communion service which utilized a red-oak stump as an altar. Hundreds joined in, "many Christians wept, and sinners looked seriously and wonderingly by."[56]

Chaplain Haygood remained with the right flank of Johnston's army only briefly. In May, Sherman opened his campaign to capture Atlanta, the important railroad center of the Southeast and a supply depot. By July the Confederates had been forced back to Atlanta's perimeter, the line of defense being the Chattahoochee River. The siege of the city, as the Federals crossed the river and formed a semicircle around its northern and eastern boundaries, began in late July. Atticus Haygood arrived at his family's home in Atlanta sometime that summer, sickness having forced him out of the field. Bishop Pierce gave him an interim appointment to Trinity Church, the church his father had organized in 1853, and Atticus preached there until Atlanta surrendered. These services, Catholic mass, and the newspaper were the last comforts of "Southern civilization" before the fall. The hardy citizens, those who had remained through the siege, began to leave the first day of September, when an advance party of Sherman's army arrived on Peachtree Street.

Atticus left about midnight on September 2, the warehouse and car shed fires lighting "the road to Decatur," the explosions shaking windows in Conyers, thirty miles away.[57] Martha and Laura Haygood driving a wagon with "sixty packages" were evacuated September 4; Willie and sister Myra were already in Watkinsville.[58] It is not known whether Mollie was in Oxford or in Watkinsville.

The fall of Atlanta was almost a relief. For nearly six months yet there would be extreme privation, but no worse experiences than were happening could be anticipated. Atticus Haygood thrived in this period, in which the established order was disestablished and every day demanded its own routine. Although there was little food on the Watkinsville farm, a family friend allowed Atticus to cut up the paper from the inventory of Clarke County's paper mill, and sale of envelopes fashioned from the paper brought him in a small amount of currency.

Haygood heard through Athens that the Georgia Conference, already changed as to location, would not be held in November in Milledgeville, the second location chosen by Bishop Pierce (since Sherman's soldiers were headed in that direction). He consequently decided, in early December, to go back to Atlanta by way of Oxford, which had been undisturbed, and stood "waiting' the good times coming.'" Such was not the situation as he approached Atlanta, forty miles to the west. The armies had trampled the fields of unharvested wheat and had mangled the rails of the Georgia Railroad. In Decatur he witnessed the burned Presbyterian manse, but he found the southeastern section of Atlanta, six miles farther on, generally untouched by the fires. Sherman had spared the churches around the city-hall square on the petition of the Catholic priests. Everywhere, however, there were ugly emplacements, one "on a vacant lot of my mother's . . . near Trinity Church." The most disturbing vandalism he found in Oakland Cemetery, where his father, grandmother, and two children were buried: the Yankees had stolen a marble shaft from "Mr. Oatman's Marble Yard" to honor their own dead.[59]

Conference met in Athens in January. Haygood, occupying Dr. Myers's place, opened the first session with the doleful report that "hindrance of the gospel" had reached unmanageable proportions. It was evident enough to the preachers that spiritual degradation had reached their own ranks. One preacher was dispelled for "disgraceful conduct," and another received a public reprimand for "brutal treatment to a negro boy." The conference voted to memorialize the Georgia legislature to consider the "better securing of matrimonial relations among the slaves."[60] Bishop Pierce appointed Haygood as pastor of Trinity in Atlanta, where he held services the first Sunday in February. By then the sanctuary had been cleared of the furniture which had been stored in the church to save it from destruction. On the second Sunday in February, F. M. Richardson reopened the Sunday school. With some rail service restored, Atlantans acted as though Sherman had been driven out of their city and as if they were certain that the boom of the 1850's and the chaotic 1860's would continue.[61]

March, April, and early May were nevertheless dangerous months, and Atticus would not let the Haygoods leave Watkinsville. In all of northwest Georgia there were reported to be thousands of deserting Confederate soldiers, and one report listed only "two legitimate" men in the area wearing the Confederate uniform. A single officer in Atlanta in charge of dispensing the commissary stores to the civilians had a heartbreaking task of apportionment. Every morning his office was crowded with women and children literally begging for crusts. Some women walked as far as sixteen miles, through the mud and ice of March roads, to secure a sack of meal which they had to carry home on their shoulders. The surrenders of the Confederate generals in April temporarily heightened the dangers: there was now not even Confederate authority in force "to defend either private or public property from the marauding parties." The new order arrived on

May 4 in the person of B. B. Eggleston, colonel, Ohio Cavalry. Atlanta was relieved and after a gasp or two began immediately to plan its postwar prosperity based on rebuilt railroads and the mercantile needs of northwest Georgia.[62]

Atticus Haygood, now twenty-five and a half, could not so easily forget the dreams of a Southern civilization in which great writers and editors would become world renowned. The Providence in which his faith had lain had proven not an infallible stay. Ahead now for a Southern Methodist preacher stretched a destiny in a defeated, impoverished section on the periphery of the civilized Western world, so far removed from the highest circle of wit and learning that a Haygood's talents would never be known.[63] May 1865 in Atlanta was warm, anxiety for the safety of the family dissipated, and memory abandoned recall of the stench of death. But the relaxation of emotional controls served in Haygood only to stimulate him to an irrational, unbridled bitterness against the Confederacy. He knew that his life would be without any professional options, that he could hope for nothing but an increasingly routine round of church services and conferences. His bitterness came out in sermons disguised as a wrath toward sinners "at a country campmeeting . . . at the close of the war." As he had never done before, there he exhibited "a power of invective . . . never equaled."[64]

FOUR
◊ ◊ ◊
◊

The Merging and Submerging of Southern Methodist Culture

PASTOR HAYGOOD preached at Trinity Church in Atlanta during 1865 and 1866, the two years of Johnsonian reconstruction of the old Union. Atlanta did not become the official capital of Georgia until 1867-1868, but it was the headquarters for the Union Army, and that was what mattered now. Federal troops were everywhere—in the streets, in the rebuilt saloon-and-solicit area, and occasionally in the churches. For old Atlanta families like the Haygoods and Richardsons the most disturbing element in the swollen population of nearly 20,000 was a swarm of skinny, sallow transplanted upcountry Southern whites, some from mountain areas which had hardly recognized the Confederate cause as existing, much less as worthy of sacrifice. The Methodist pastors of Trinity and "First Church," formerly called Wesley Chapel, Haygood and Alexander Thigpen, had as chaplains encountered such types who, even when they were loyal to the cause, were bewilderingly unlettered and unmoved by the Protestant ethic. Of course, the white ladies were most afraid of the idle Negro population, ex-slaves, to the number of 10,000. After June 1865 the Freedmen's Bureau in Atlanta began to issue rations to them; the rest of the day they indulged their new "liberty of movement" in contented idleness, dozens lolling about near the railroad tracks.[1]

It seems that Southern Methodism was not in a position to reinterpret its "mission" in circumstances so vastly altered from the ante-bellum status quo. The General Conference had not met; the bishops had not yet given any direction; and individual preachers had to improvise more than ever. A few pastors taught individual Negroes to read and write, but in the large towns— where the Negroes were no longer subject to their former masters' orders about attendance on worship—the black population in Georgia was neglected. Since Trinity Church had not had any

Negro communicants, a decision in this area was not of immediate concern. Soldiers did occasionally visit Trinity Church, as did Yankee huckster types, but they were free to do no more than wander in one Sunday and never be seen again. They even felt free to be quietly amused by such sermons as the one Atticus preached during the summer of 1865, on "Endless Punishment."[2]

The Haygoods and the Richardsons were concerned most consistently with the physical and spiritual welfare of the Southern whites, many of whom lived in freight cars, tents, and flimsy tin-roofed shacks. The State of Georgia fed them that summer with corn bought in Missouri and some given by Kentucky; an environment of squalor could, however, mark shanty children for life with visible and invisible signs of early disease and distress. When a smallpox epidemic struck, Richardson organized Atlanta's Southern Protestants to help at least through donations.[3] It was perfectly clear to Thigpen and Haygood, however, that their congregations were not really happy with the prospect of shanty children in their Sunday schools—and that the more responsible shanty parents sensed the prejudice against their children. Atticus, his bitterness dissipated, realized during his two years in Atlanta that his main work was among those who had been Southern Methodists before the war. Among them values had shifted to embrace more unashamedly the pleasures of the world. The male population, moreover, had for four years not recognized pulpit authority—those who had exhorted their spirits had been able battle commandants capable of appropriate improvisations of behavior. The preachers in the main had stayed home with the women and children and old men, and the chaplains' work had been a minor consideration during wartime.

After the war in Atlanta, on Sunday, the older prewar business leadership once again showed respect for the pulpit's authority. Haygood easily learned that younger Southern men were of a different breed. Atlanta appeared to be a permanent military cantonment and, as a railroad center, was a good stopping place for enterprisers from the North. Despite the severe limitation of inventories, by July 1865 the volume of sales began to increase noticeably every week. The result was three hundred new licensed businesses in the burned-out city, most of them operating in lean-to stores. By late summer there was a vegetable market, and those who sold produce could buy cloth and medicine. The stores created large demands on lumber planing mills. By the spring of 1866 Atlanta's business prospects had passed the primitive level.

Eight large concerns were incorporated during 1866, most of them "building and loan associations." Joseph E. Brown was one among many ex-Confederates to open a law office and to do business with former enemies and lukewarm supporters of the war—for Brown, of course, a not unnatural relationship.[4] Southern Methodist laymen who identified with the new regime then being born through hard competition were more inclined to celebrate "the sacrament" on Saturday in the elevation of Yankee coin than on Sunday in the elevation of the host or reception of the Word.

Since a large segment of Atlanta's new economic elite remained in, or joined the Southern churches, the values of the marketplace invaded the sanctuaries in a manner never allowed when the preacher was more closely associated with the elite, as in antebellum Hancock County. Not only in Atlanta but also in town stations, no impecunious Methodist pastor could afford to antagonize the very men who were beginning to be able to support the church with their new money, especially if they attended services fairly regularly. And their wives would be less likely the targets for sermons or reproof on the score of the vanity of display. Proof of this change lies in the unaltered lists of "probationers" in conference statistics; new numbers were not added. Another symptom of the shift of values and authority even within the churches was the radical tampering with the worship service and with the traditionally plain Southern Methodist architecture. Copying Northern and "high-church" models, both Trinity and Wesley acquired organs and acceded to requests to pretty up the services with organ preludes and offertories during the worship hour and an anthem sung by the choir. From Haygood's point of view these demands, incorporated into Trinity's church life more harmoniously than at Wesley, grew out of a desire to display the wealth and "culture" of the congregation and a hedonistic wish to make the worship-hour "enjoyable." He was quite certain that formerly a capella hymn-singing suffered from loud organ accompaniments and that the sermon had to compete for central attention with musical divertissements.

Wesley Chapel's evolution as a "fashionable church" was accelerated after 1866 when Thigpen was succeeded by W. P. Harrison. A courtly Savannahian, Harrison encouraged his parishioners in their desire to dignify attendance on worship. His sermons were full of literary allusions, some in foreign languages. He referred to himself as their "minister"—a new term—and he furnished the inspiration for building a new, larger sanctuary farther out on Peachtree Street (the direction in which new mansions were beginning to be built). The new church would be, not Wesley Chapel, but "the First Methodist Church of Atlanta." Harrison stayed only a short while in Atlanta because the Bishop disapproved of the encouragement of urban airs, and of overlong appointments to town churches. Harrison's career of prominence ahead, however, in a Southern Methodist church in Washington, D. C., and as chaplain of the House of Representatives, was more in tune with the life of Southern cities after the war than was the planter Bishop's. For that matter, neither Atticus Haygood at Trinity, nor his assistant pastor, the elderly Dr. Alexander Means, could be criticized by ante-bellum standards for any un-Methodist vanity in personal dress or affectation of manners.[5]

Atlanta was typical of cities of the deep South, last bastions of the Confederacy, where despite or because of civilities toward carpetbaggers, to the extent of full acceptance, the congregations of the Presbyterians, the Baptists, and the Methodists became social meeting places for the new business elite. Elsewhere the Southern churches were not so fortunate. In border areas like Louisiana, Tennessee, and Missouri the Federal army had supported the Northern Methodists in their ousting of pastors with Confederate loyalties. The Northerners reasoned that since the split of Methodism in 1844 had resulted—from their point of view—because a Southern bishop owned a slave, now that slavery was destroyed by the Thirteenth Amendment a schismatic slavery-defending Methodist sect had no reason for existing. Just as the Union was being restored in the errant area, so the church of Asbury would be re-established.[6] Bishop Pierce, who was the most vigorous of the ante-bellum "general superintendents" of the Southern church, resented bitterly such claims. He was alarmed most that several preachers in Georgia, one of them Haygood's father-in-law, John W. Yarbrough, accepted the Yankees' rationale. Indeed, Yarbrough in 1866 began to preach to the Negroes in Oxford as an appointee of the Northern church. Bishop Pierce was less disturbed that the Negroes were being lost, some to the Northern white denominations. (The Negroes, it was soon evident, would swarm permanently into all-black churches, from the democratic Baptist congregations to more hierarchical organizations like the African Methodist Episcopal Church.)[7]

Bishop Pierce, the "Jefferson Davis" of the planter sect, which was now being remolded without design, felt threatened most by "democracy." He did not approve of the kind of laymen in Atlanta to whom Harrison catered. He did not approve of Harrison, or of E. H. Myers, or of Holland N. McTyeire, all of whom were opposed to the authoritarian genius of the prewar sect.[8] Certainly he felt that the move of the state capital from Milledgeville to Atlanta was a portent of the decline of "Sunshine" and Sparta as the center of conference power. It is likely that Atticus Haygood had only infrequent communication with Bishop Pierce during 1865-1866, but the removal of Harrison according to the old rule after a two-year pastorate in Atlanta was a vivid example of the Bishop's preference for rural, camp-meeting religion, an orientation which Atticus tended to share. On the other hand, Mollie's father was one of those who had dared to transfer to the Northern church, evidently admiring its more limited episcopal authority. But Atticus at twenty-seven felt at ease in a denomination where bishops had authority even to be unreasonable if they felt like it, and he was grateful to Bishop Pierce.

The uncompromising nature of Bishop Pierce, and of the Georgia Conference which he continued to dominate, had in fact determined the course of John Yarbrough, who resigned in 1866. During June 1865, the Reverend John W. Caldwell, pastor at the Southern Methodist church in Newnan (Haygood's assigned pulpit two years before) preached a sermon scathingly denouncing slavery and by implication condemning the rottenness of the planter society which tolerated such institutionalized moral evil. His congregation sat in shocked silence at first. Before he had finished, however, a third of his hearers had left and the remainder were trying to interrupt his abuse. During the next week "The commotion . . . surpassed anything that had ever been witnessed in the town. The people were . . . enraged, and some even made threats of personal violence." Caldwell said that "some even atempted to excite the soldiers against me, alleging that I had charged them with stealing more property within the last four years than all the negroes put together . . . in all their lives!"[9] One ex-slaveholder agreed that slavery had "occasioned . . . more sin . . . than any other single thing," and the next Sunday Caldwell openly blamed the major spiritual weaknesses in the planters' sect on slaveholding and its results.

His congregation refused to hear another sermon, and the presiding elder of the district removed Caldwell from his charge. Appealing to a Federal army officer for protection for his house, he was told that the pulpit was his in spite of the presiding elder's action. In November 1865, Caldwell was tried before the Georgia

Conference, and was accused of calling on the army for help in order to further his professional advance to a higher pulpit. He was censured for warning the preachers that "the eyes of the president . . ., the military authorities, . . . of the world are fixed upon your action here."[10] The presiding elder's removal of Caldwell was declared just. Caldwell was not expelled, but "allowed to resign." It was after this incident that John Yarbrough left the conference. Bishop Pierce of course approved the conference's handling of the matter.

It was at the same conference, in mid-November 1865, that Atticus learned of the statewide loss of city Negroes by the Southern church. Petitions were received by the conference from Negroes in Atlanta, Augusta, and Savannah asking that former mission chapels be given to them. The Macon Negro "charge . . . passed away from us," said one pastor. Thigpen spoke in favor of transfer of Negroes to their own churches, and for resigned acceptance of their loss from the rolls.[11] The ex-slaves in the cities were joining African Methodist Episcopal congregations, the first organization in Savannah by James Lynch in 1865. An A. M. E. conference in Charleston in May 1866 was the springboard for intensive proselyting; in the summer of 1866 William Gaines helped establish Negro congregations in Macon, Columbus, and Atlanta. From Savannah, Macon, Columbus, and Atlanta the Negro church moved to smaller cities. For instance, Andrew Brown, "a poor bare-footed, bareheaded man," was licensed to preach in the most informal manner after a conversation with the A. M. E. preacher in Atlanta, who "appointed" him to Dalton.[12] Bishop Pierce genuinely felt that "In the change from slaves to freedmen . . . our obligations to promote their spiritual welfare have not ceased," but he believed the Negroes would return to the churches of their former masters (and apparently from temporary residence in the cities back to the rural counties). That the Bishop was a realist was demonstrated nevertheless by his appointing a white preacher to the "colored mission" in Dalton.[13]

The Methodist Episcopal Church, South, held its first General Conference since 1858 in New Orleans in April and May 1866—at the same time that the A. M. E. conference was taking place in Charleston. In New Orleans the statistical loss of former members made the decline in Negro membership from 200,000 to 80,000 look more serious than it had seemed at the annual conferences in the fall. Besides, the news was now widespread that the Negro A. M. E. leader, Bishop A. W. Wayman, had made a triumphant tour of the city congregations during the winter, including Georgia.[14] The Southern white Methodists voted in New Orleans to enact a plan which would keep the A. M. E. from further successes among Methodist Negroes. Negro congregations throughout the South would be henceforth under the supervision of J. E. Evans, a Georgia preacher known as the "weeping prophet"; when there were enough Negro congregations in an area, with enough able Negro preachers who had served four years on trial, the preachers would be named presiding elders of Negro districts. It was hoped that by 1870 a general conference of loyal Negro preachers from all the Southern states could be held to create a rival for the A. M. E connection with its own black bishops.

The plan worked rather well. In 1870 the Colored Methodist Episcopal Church in America was organized—obviously "separate and unequal." Its intended client relationship to its parent denomination is clearly shown in the consecration of one of the early bishops, Lucius H. Holsey. Holsey had grown up as a slave in Hancock County, had been married in Bishop Pierce's home in 1862, and had been ordained a deacon by Bishop Pierce in 1871. In 1873, he was chosen a bishop of the C. M. E. Church.[15]

Atticus Haygood was a silent witness of a far more crucial political battle within Southern Methodism. His chief sources of information were the anti-episcopal conversations of his father-in-law and, during the winter of 1866, of W. P. Harrison. To a regular reader of E. H. Myers' *Southern Christian Advocate,* moreover, the accounts from the New Orleans conference were as sanguine of constitutional victories as Confederate news from the war had been in 1862. Myers, and Holland McTyeire, "had hinted [even] before the war at changes which was to be great improvements . . . more practical, less emotional religion, more culture in the pulpit . . ., fewer changes in appointments . . ., more bishops, more lay power, no probation, no class-meetings, less rigidity in general rules."[16]

In 1864 the Northern Methodists had pointed the way to such changes by extending the time limit of pastoral appointments from two to three years. The Southern desire for more bishops came partly from a belief that the more there were the more diluted the power of each would become and partly because city pastors could more easily become bishops. The Southern progressives did not, however, agree with the Northerners' insistence that the bishop was the creature of the General Conference since he was elected by it. Episcopal ordination had greater meaning to

Southerners and those who knew their history likened the Northern confusion of *episkopos* with *presbyteros* to the unfortunate tamperings with the episcopal polity that occurred in England during the 1640's.[17] The proposals for greater lay influence, for the end of probation and of class-meetings, and for a de-emphasis of the love feasts and strict adherence to the behavior rules prescribed by Wesley were derived from a hostility to the authoritarian, supervisional character of the prewar sect. The old practices were believed unsuited to the more democratic economic and political order certain to emerge even without a military defeat for the South. The psychology of the progressives, moreover, was clearly anti-rural. As E. H. Myers worded the progressives' position, "This is the age of clubs" and the church needed to have an egalitarian association as in clubs so that men could "act and react directly upon each other."[18] Moderates like Haygood might applaud the democratic direction pointed out by the progressives, but he valued more highly than they the emotional and introspective values of the class-meeting and the love feast. Moreover, he regretted the new emphasis on superficialities—organs, "high steeples," literariness for its own sake.

The progressives won control of the New Orleans conference because of Bishop Pierce's intransigence. Pierce threatened to resign if the conference voted against his wishes to remove the limit in years that a pastor might stay in one (city) pulpit. Forced to compromise with a four-year limit, the progressives, supported by outraged moderates, found it easier to have their way in other matters. The most touted victory was in the election of four new bishops (though the progressives had wanted six). Three of the four—the forty-two-year-old Holland McTyeire, David W. Doggett, and William Wightman—were progressively inclined. McTyeire was the real leader of the progressives. Both Doggett and Wightman respected high literacy and urban proprieties. The fourth new bishop, however, was Enoch Marvin, a rough Missourian unbalanced in his hatred of Northern Methodists and Roman Catholics. Pierce would still predominate in the council (the two other older bishops, Kavanaugh and Robert Paine, siding with him).[19]

The conference legislated changes that were more radical than the diminution of Pierce's episcopal influence. It modified the probation system so that new members would not have to undergo a probationary status for six months, "provided they are converted," decision on this matter being left up to the individual pastor. The class-meeting was relegated to the minor status of the voluntary prayer-meeting. Love feasts were to be observed only at a new annual meeting of representatives from each church in a district. Since lay representation at quarterly, district, annual, and general conference was also approved, this meant that rival businessmen from competing towns and villages in a district conference would be expected to unbare their private difficulties at the love feast—something they would certainly never do![20]

The progressives made no headway in gaining support for the establishment of a theological school to educate a learned ministry, although a resolution was passed recommending the inauguration of "a Biblical chair . . . with each of our Colleges."[21] The greatest enthusiasm for literacy expressed in 1866 concerned the Sunday school population. Although conservatives preferred the teaching of the catechism, while the progressives favored making the classes attractive with songs, story-telling, and the use of illustrated papers, there was general agreement that the Sunday school must replace "probationary status" as an avenue to informed church membership.[22]

No legislation was needed to encourage town and even village churches to effect a remodeling of the church building and also of the worship service after the new habits of Atlanta and other cities. No one really objected to the beautification of the sanctuary with finer pulpit furniture and choir lofts; most learned to tolerate badly performed operatic solos and anthems; but Bishop Pierce drew the line on the renting of pews (an Episcopalian tradition with definite social implication). His disapproval stopped the burgeoning practice, already manifest in Columbus, Macon, Savannah, and LaGrange. Though many churches responded to the new model, a large majority of the churches of the Methodist South in 1866 and later had the most primitive of arrangements. Many of them were plain boxlike affairs without comfort or beauty, some nothing but cabins. In the country very few had any method of being heated.[23]

Among the important legislation for the church in 1866 was the attempt to strengthen lay support. The progressives hoped that if laymen had the vote in the conferences, this representative feature would make the church more attractive. A war within the nation had accomplished the destruction of an authoritarian social regime in the South. If the progressives had intended, by making Southern Methodism more "republican," to keep Negroes within the client C. M. E. church, their hopes were mostly disappointing. Since

Congress, the Northern churches, and the occupying army of the Radical Reconstruction years following 1867 taught the Negroes to distrust their former masters, it is not surprising that the ex-slaves continued to leave both white parishes and tentative places in Colored Methodist congregations. The progressives were equally misled in anticipating a new spiritual morale among white laymen because of their anti-authoritarian measure.

The chief result, totally unexpected, was to make the denomination more Erastian, more closely identified with the power structure of the world than it had been when dominated by planter-type bishops. Laymen's values did become more prominent, but unfortunately town laymen too often used church and Sunday school offices as a sign of status. It is clear that most laymen were not interested enough in church politics to make any substantial difference in conference voting, much to the disappointment of the progressive preachers.

A convincing demonstration of the use of the church by laymen for their own reasons may be found in the spectacular career of H. I. Kimball. Kimball came from Chicago to Atlanta as a real carpetbagger and was the power behind Rufus Bullock's gubernatorial chair during Georgia's Radical Reconstruction. Despite his background and the widespread belief that he enriched himself at the public trough, Kimball became a devoted member of Harrison's First Methodist Church and through the respectability gained here was by 1880 one of the city's two or three leading citizens.[24]

The Northern Methodists during the years of reconstruction, being unaware that men like Kimball would add to the town strength of the Southern church (a denomination they thought of as the refuge for diehard Conferedates), undertook to establish their churches, districts, and conferences throughout the defeated South, thereby duplicating territorially the divisions of the Southern organization. Efforts in Georgia were directed from the earlier occupied Tennessee. In the spring of 1866 Wesley Prettyman began to preach in the courthouse of Fulton County, across the street from Trinity Church, where his rival Atticus Haygood held forth. In the fall of 1867, about the time of the Reconstruction-enforced elections for a constitutional convention, the Northern Methodists organized and held a Georgia Conference of their own. Yarbrough, Caldwell, and John Murphy, formerly Southern elders, were half of the conference cadre on this occasion.[25]

A year later the Northern Methodists claimed 15,000 members in Georgia, including some Negroes. The denomination hoped that Southern ex-slaves would be attracted because of its close association with the Republican party and because it provided schools to teach the Negroes to read. Despite the fact that the Northern Methodists' Freedmen's Aid Society might have sometimes been confused with the Army's Freedman's Bureau, the Negroes learned rather quickly that Northern Methodists were often transient rather than permanent friends. In 1869 nine Negro preachers in the Northern church's Georgia organization requested and received a separate district of their own. With the growing disrepute of Radical governments, and the return of states to normal relationships, the Northern Methodists, after 1870, used most of their educational money on institutions of higher learning, almost abandoning elementary education in the South except as special training at the colleges—and abandoning completely their political efforts.[26] Northern Methodist conferences continued to minister to Southerners, but primarily in proletarian areas in which the Southern church with its new urban orientation had less appeal. People in specifically mountain areas and the lower middle class cities like Atlanta were catered to. John Yarbrough, Haygood's father-in-law, returned to the Southern church between 1872 and 1874. Caldwell, the unpopular Newnan pastor, eventually became pastor of the Methodist Protestant Church in Atlanta, yet another anti-episcopal variety of Wesleyanism.[27]

During the period of Radical Reconstruction in Georgia, 1867-1871, Atticus Haygood was a presiding elder of the North Georgia Conference of the Southern church. The state conference was split into halves in late 1866, at which time the Trinity pastor was named presiding elder of the Rome District, which would be his responsibility until the end of 1868. The Rome District corresponded to "Cherokee Georgia" of thirty years before. Here also was the scene of General Sherman's maneuvering in his approach to Atlanta during the spring of 1864, using as his supply route the Western and Atlantic Railroad. This state-owned road was the main link between the "Gate City" and Chattanooga and was familiar to Brother Haygood because of his activities in the Rome and Dalton area during 1863 and 1864. Approximately half of the charges of the preachers whom Haygood would supervise were close to depots on the railroad: Ringgold, Dalton, Calhoun,

Manassas, and Kingston. There was another line of churches, not so easily reached, stretching from Cedartown in western Georgia, west of Atlanta, north through Rome to Summerville and LaFayette. This ravaged country promised only a minimal subsistence for the dependent preachers. Even before the war, the district was not promising for Southern Methodists, since the region had not supported many plantations. As an added difficulty, both Rome and Dalton were faced with rival Northern Methodist chapels.

Haygood of course was flattered at being named, at twenty-seven, a presiding elder for even such a poor district, and he seems to have been optimistic about the prospect for financial support of the church, its foreign missions, and its publications. He held a district conference in Rome that first year—when the district conference was still optional—and persuaded the progressive Bishop Holland McTyeire to preach at it.[28]

As for Atticus, moments of depression and some bitterness came to him on his quarterly rounds of the churches. His memory as an old man may have shown him as more bitter than he really was. At any rate, the description he gave of the district he served during this early appointment gives good reason for discouragement.

A Bishop from Americus . . . sent me to a district embracing nine counties. . . . There was one railroad and a piece of one. . . In 1866 the crops failed . . ., nothing was organized. Some never returned; those who got back found desolation. Fences burned, and many houses and homes. Horses and mules were scarce; broken down army stock were counted a treasure. Cows were as scarce as horses and of hogs there were very few. There was . . . hardly enough poultry to make a new start with. . . . The scarcity of money can hardly be exaggerated.

Many Churches had been burned or torn down. . . . Some preachers were afoot, others rode sorrier horses than ever carried itinerants before. . . . Through the entire district, men called "missionaries" of the "Mother Church" were going to and fro, prophesying the "disintegration and absorption" of the rebel Church. They were well paid. . . . Their confidence dismayed some of our people.

Many of us were young men and all poor. . . . There was not a decent parsonage in the district nor moderate support for any preacher.[29]

The diet of the preachers was mainly "sorghum, cornbread, and an occasional rabbit, with a mess of fish now and then."[30] There being no house provided in the district for a presiding elder, the parsonage had to be in Atlanta.

For Dalton and Rome, the trading centers of northwest Georgia (north of Marietta), Haygood could rely on two stalwarts. At

Rome was "Sandy" Thigpen, the young ex-chaplain who had been in Atlanta two years before. In Rome was John Norris, first honor graduate from Emory College in 1857, and a sincere "searcher" in Young Allen's prayer group. Norris reported to the *Advocate* that "If we except Atlanta, no place . . . suffered so much by the war. . . . In the midst of their poverty," nevertheless, the "old citizens . . . have undertaken the erection of a new house of worship." Most of the enlarged population of Dalton "have no controlling church affinities." As a result, Dalton was "a break-water against the aggressive tide of Northern proselytism," the Northern church offering $2,000 to construct a church building if the congregation would secede from the Southern denomination. Norris's group therefore built its sanctuary at *"real sacrifice."*[31] Dalton became an important town pulpit for the North Georgia Conference in the 1870's, and ironically became almost a perfect example of a "status church." One later pastor said: "I never . . . had charge of any Church so lacking in vital piety as this Church was."[32]

Thigpen was immediately successful in Rome, during 1867, in making a "Methodist Episcopal Church, South" an institution of postwar Confederate respectability. The outstanding layman in this congregation was J. I. Wright, a lawyer, who in April 1868 was the chief spirit behind a meeting organized to protest the section of Georgia's new constitution which gave Negroes the right to vote. All the Negro members of the Rome congregation— who had not yet made a decision to join the A. M. E., C. M. E., or Northern church—left Wright's church that year.[33] A third example of the urban orientation of even this impoverished section is the success of Clement A. Evans at Cartersville. Evans, a Confederate general, became a leading town pastor in North Georgia during the 1870's and 1880's, preaching eventually at the First Church in Atlanta.[34]

By the new canons of judgment, then, Haygood's presiding over the Rome District was successful. Dalton, Rome, Cartersville, and Cedartown were guided in the direction of development of the Southern churches in Atlanta, Augusta, Athens, Gainesville, Elberton, Griffin, and LaGrange. Giving to the Chinese missions doubled during 1868—Colonel Wright, the Rome lawyer, had a taste for saving the Chinese heathen almost equal to his distaste for Negro citizenship in Georgia. Since arrangements were being made for a separate organization of the Negroes, the drastic loss by the white churches in the Rome District during two years (from 463 down to 169) offended no one except the presiding elder, who remembered his rapport with the Negroes in 1859 in Newton County, in 1860 in Columbus, and in 1862 on the Watkinsville circuit. The statistics given to the annual conference registered the more important retention and enlargement of both urban and rural white support of the Southern church.[35]

The proceedings of the district conference held at Rome in May 1867 illustrate further the revival of what must be called Whiggish progressivism in a section of Georgia not dominated by the planters. Of the five lay delegates, W. H. Felton, a local preacher from Cartersville, within a decade would be an Independent U. S. Congressman; and Dr. H. V. M. Miller, delegate from Rome, that very fall would serve in the "scalawag and Negro dominated" constitutional convention for the state, would be elected U. S. Senator by the Reconstruction legislature in 1868, and would serve briefly in the Senate after February 1871.[36]

The resolutions of the conference, therefore, may reflect not only the views of Atticus Haygood and Bishop McTyeire, but an atypical progressive spirit among some of the laymen in those very town churches which were becoming stale and stilted. The conference delegates resolved:

[that] the pastor . . . urge upon . . . the membership . . . the great importance of giving . . . their children a good, substantial . . . English education, and . . . wherever . . . practicable . . . a finished and liberal education. . . .
That . . . the churches . . . inquire . . . whether . . . all the children . . . are attending school, and to . . . keep alive, by any available means, a lively . . . interest in this subject.
That . . . ministers and official members . . . feel charged with the duty of giving personal attention to securing competent teachers and sustaining . . . academies in their respective cities. . . .
That we regard it . . . important . . . in all cases, other things being equal, *to discriminate in favor of . . . Methodist schools and colleges.*[37]

(The state constitution which Dr. Miller later helped to write provided organic legal backing for a state system of common schools. There were no public schools in 1867. During that year Bishop Pierce was raising money to reopen Emory College.)[38]

Other resolutions of the conference encouraged whites to give aid to the education of Negro children " (in their own schools)" and to assist them to "secure . . . capable teachers who will not poison their minds against their former masters." Likewise, Sunday schools were exhorted to use the denomination's publications in order to avoid the teaching of "a faith antagonistic to . . . our Church."[39]

The two years on the district, 1867-1868, confirmed Bishop Pierce's high opinion of Haygood's abilities. The Rome district conference extended acknowledgement to Nashville, Bishop McTyeire's residence, and also the re-established administrative center of the Southern church. The older preachers, moreover, like John Glenn, who died in 1868 in Cedartown, spread the word throughout the North Georgia Conference that Greene Haygood's boy was motivated by the highest kind of idealism. He was deferential to his elders; he disliked polish for the sake of it—he was not one of those young men unhappy outside a town pulpit, seeming to have absorbed some of Lovick Pierce's unconcern with professional advancement. No one knew, no one read into his utterances his unfulfilled hidden ambition—to be a writer and editor.

There was not much time for meditation during 1867. When Atticus was not in Atlanta he was struggling to meet his appointments. At one preacher's cabin Haygood wrote, "I stayed four days—rain by day and by night. . . . His wife did all the work. There was only a little 'middling meat' and corn bread, meal after meal. But we were happy and healthy." Haygood's son Wilbur was three when he left on his first round in 1867; that year a baby boy named Lipscomb died and was buried in Oakland Cemetery. During 1868 Atticus decided not to return to Atlanta between rounds; he stayed at a little place called Oostanaula, on the river of the same name, not far from Calhoun, the county seat on the railroad. Mollie bore him that year a daughter named Mamie, the fifth child, and the second to survive past infancy.

Between March and May Haygood wrote, under the pseudonym of John Tryon, five long letters to the *Southern Christian Advocate*—published in Macon since the end of the war, by the progressive E. H. Myers.[40] The letters were all concerned with his church's loss of loyalty and of financial strength. Also, they were exercises in developing a style:

> We are making much ado about poverty. Many of us think more of the pelf we have lost than of the heaven we hope to gain. . . .
> Were these negroes, these cotton-fields, this gold and luxury . . . our only treasure, our god, that we cry out so bitterly?
> . . . Your correspondent is acquainted with congregations which can, in their poverty, sport brocades and velvets and laces, that before the war would have been thought extravagant; that can parade costly furs

now, when ten years ago it was not cold enough to need them; and if you talk about China and Allen and the conversion of the world, they begin to bleed afresh. . . .

As connected with this question . . ., let me ask what can Dan Castello's show or Robinson's circus do? . . . Yonder is another where people come twenty miles, and camp in the woods at night, to spend their money next day upon a vagabond troupe that demoralizes the country.[41]

He was relieved that the Atlanta and Augusta churches "have not yet reached the semi-heathenism of nearly all the great cities of the North and West." Yet they had already lost contact and concern with "the mass of our city populations." But the country people were little better:

I heard a prayer for Young Allen . . . the other day, that seemed actually to startle a congregation . . ., the people in some places actually browbeat the preachers out of their plain disciplinary duty of . . . taking up missionary collections. . . . I myself have heard a preacher apologize . . . as a preface to his collection.[42]

Haygood did not record the fact that his town churches, with all their religious superficiality and their money, had become the backbone of mission financing.

FIVE

Last Hope for Southern Sectarian Literacy— The Sunday School

THE PRESIDING ELDER of the Rome District, 1867-1868, was promoted by the North Georgia Conference of the Methodist Episcopal Church, South, to be the presiding elder of the district embracing Atlanta, Decatur, Covington, and Oxford, for the years 1869-1870. The appointment came about a month after Haygood's twenty-ninth birthday in 1868: there was obviously no one in his age bracket in the conference with his record of advancement after a mere nine years of membership. Moreover, in becoming an accepted part of the Bishop's cabinet the Reverend Haygood had reached a professional pinnacle; any higher office must be the gift of the next General Conference, scheduled to meet in Memphis in 1870. To other preachers the new Atlanta district superintendent gave clear evidence of ambition for South-wide recognition; his continuing letters to the *Advocate* looked like a bid for notice, even though written by "John Tryon."

Atticus himself felt the pressure from outside (although he actually "internalized" it); he must justify the confidence of the Pierces. These months in Atlanta were miserable; he chafed in spirit at the limits which the pulpit assigned to a preacher's voice, to a minister's involvements. In January 1869, when he commenced his rounds of supervision, the "Georgia case" was being investigated in the national capital by the Committee on Reconstruction. In September 1868 Negro members had been expelled from the Georgia house of representatives—one of these, a deponent in Washington, was a Negro preacher, H. M. Turner, who soon afterwards became a Methodist bishop. Because of the obvious unreadiness of Georgia to fulfill the Radical Republicans' prescription for suitability in the Union, the new Congressmen and the Senators elected by the 1868 legislature were not seated in the new Congress in March. And in December 1869, the Radicals passed a special bill which subjected Georgia once again to military government.[1] These political activities, reported by a competitive press in Georgia's capital, were far more meaningful than the increasingly unrewarding ritual of quarterly conferences.

The home life in Atlanta, to which he had looked forward after the isolation from his family in Cherokee Georgia over the past two years, proved almost unbearable. There was no privacy for Attie, Mollie, their five-year-old boy Wilbur, and baby Mamie, his special joy. Martha Askew Haygood was almost sixty, just young enough to cause her son inner anguish both in creating "harmony" with the daughter-in-law and in making financial decisions for the household. Specifically, his mother's acquiescence in the sale of some of their property was gained between her moods of tearful rebellion and resignation. A sale was completed right after his appointment, in December 1868, and in February he advertised "My mother's Residence, corner McDonough and Fair Streets, within two hundred yards of the City Hall, . . . CHEAP."[2] Martha, Laura, Willie (after his graduation from Emory in July), and Atticus's family lived together for almost a year in a house on Crew Street on their remaining property. Lots in Oxford were disposed of in 1867 and the home-place in Watkinsville was given to the church as a parsonage. About $4,000 came in through the sales. Sister Laura, twenty-four, used part of it to build a schoolhouse in which to teach young ladies the classic and modern languages, music, drawing, English, and mathematics. Her investment was a wise one; she prospered and soon had two assistants. Willie, upon graduation, entered the hurly-burly of Atlanta's marketplace, biding his time until he could become a lawyer and himself deal in real estate. Attie displayed little interest, or competence, in keeping accounts for the whole family—partly because his own income was not yet substantial, much to his embarrassment.[3]

There is no evidence, negative or positive, that Atticus Haygood experienced any kind of psychic crisis at twenty-nine or thirty. There is circumstantial indication, though, of some sort of dramatic breakthrough to completer maturity and poise when he was forty-one. The biographer must speculate about what was happening to the invisible man within, the guess of environmental and medical factors effecting changes. The documentable facts are simple enough: Haygood had not had a serious seizure of epilepsy since 1857 and, having been free of threats since his marriage in 1859, is reported to have learned how to relax, to enjoy life, to give the impression of appreciating people, a capacity noted primarily by those who knew him in his late thirties and early forties. He had a literally fruitful marriage, Mollie bearing him eight children during their first sixteen years together. He was, by any criterion, conscientious in his duties as pastor or presiding elder, as the Discipline outlined these tasks.

But nevertheless, there are implications that he disliked his profession. He hated being governed by "will." His nature, newly discovered in his late twenties, was that of a wildly romantic, creative "Celtic." Like many another proper man in the Victorian era, he was at a loss to explain his erotic sense of need, not altogether fulfilled in his marriage. Being at home more of the time made this part of his nature seem incompatible with his life. But his chafing "in the cloth" of the ministry was more than the restlessness of a young man's pride. He had always wanted to write, and for him preaching was a poor substitute. Between 1867 and about 1880, therefore, Atticus Haygood lived the life of what might be called a cultural schizophrenic; he was going through the motions required of him within the confined and confining crib of Southern Methodism. But he yearned meanwhile after salvation through the agency of some yet to be discovered source.

His inner conflict, a war between the instinctual and the professional halves of his personality, resulted frequently in a hostility directed outside, toward a changing and less familiar Atlanta, and even toward the congregations of the town and city churches in his district. Atlanta was already known as an important center of Southern Methodist strength. Enthusiasm for foreign missions in Georgia in 1869 was limited almost exclusively to the cities. It was an irritation to the Reverend Haygood that in the "best churches," from a statistical point of view, there was little piety or any real literacy, or concern with literacy, whether religious or literary.

In August 1869, as if to escape the oppressive artificiality of church life in Atlanta and to cultivate a close-knit family relationship, Atticus took Mollie and the children by buggy into the mountain districts. It was a strangely succoring moment when he pointed out to his son Wilbur the grave of Grandfather Askew at Mossy Creek, the man of God who had wielded the knife in severing the hide of the lamb. (He never gave the knife to Wilbur.) Circling westward in an arc back toward Atlanta, they stopped a few days at a camp meeting in Dawson County. He learned that a group of delinquent mountain boys known as "Taylor's Clan" had disturbed all the night meetings with their catcalls and irreverence, and had scared the "tenters" by their noisy pranks during the sleeping hours. The night Haygood preached, undeterred by the boys gathered in the rear, the regular pastor felt emboldened to get up, walk back toward them, and stand on a board-bench; he preached the boys into awe, repentance, and good behavior.[4] Nothing so dramatic and so earthy could be conceived of in Atlanta.

The raw side of life in Georgia's capital was less appealing. The continued presence of Federal troops required establishments catering to their pleasure while off duty. Most offensive to the presiding elder, and others of the old families, was a German saloon downtown which used barmaids as waitresses. The objection was not so much to the existence of another saloon; it was to the strange character and behavior of the Germans. One of them felt free to promenade in public in a costume dominated by a red turban with blue tassels, his gloved left hand thrusting forward a sword-hilt and his right arm arrogantly protecting his dark-hued mistress, whom he called his "vrow." Haygood, untypically of his Trinity folk, was less aroused by the flaunted miscegenation than by the open German consumption of liquor, which encouraged adverse effects on Methodist discipline. On a Sunday in the spring of 1869 he was outraged to see advertisements "presented . . . along with religious notices" in two of Atlanta's papers, *"extravagant laudations of a certain 'ale house' . . . that . . . had won editorial favor by the munificent present of a whole 'DEMI-JOHN OF WHISKEY.'"*[5] He wrote a protest article for the *Advocate,* joyously reprinted by the *Atlanta Constitution,* whose publisher, W. A. Hemphill, was a prominent member of Trinity. Hemphill used the article to undermine patronage of his competitors, the *New Era* and the *Intelligencer,* by the respectable. The *Intelligencer* countered with the information that Hemphill, Sunday school superintendent at Trinity Church, brazenly accepted advertisements for Clicquot's champagne.[6] The liveliness of the Atlanta journalistic exchange led papers in Rome, Columbus, Griffin, and Macon to reprint Haygood's article under the title of "Purity of the Press" during the early summer of 1869, thereby broadcasting among Georgia Baptists and Presbyterians the moral reputation of the Methodist presiding elder in Atlanta.[7]

This triumph helped reawaken in Atticus a hidden dream, to be the best kind of exhorter, the brave and eloquent editorialist. Such a man, given a literate public which would respond, could fashion a career fulfilling the highest ideals of service, in a professional calling he had long believed superior to that of minister, lawyer, hackneyed journalist, or teacher. Since editorial leadership required a literate following, it was providential that in July 1869 a meeting was held in Atlanta to further the establishment of a state public school system. As in 1858, when Greene Haygood had supported a similar effort, the leadership came from the denominational colleges and from those cities like Augusta and Savannah whose citizens supported public academies. Haygood was one of many Atlanta citizens (John B. Gordon, a Presbyterian layman and former Confederate general another) who attended the sessions, to be electrified by the speaking of Gustavus J. Orr, his teacher at Emory ten years before. Orr's future was to be organically related to the cause of education in Georgia. In 1870 he moved to Atlanta to be a professor at the Presbyterians' new Oglethorpe "University," and in the early 1870's was chosen superintendent of public instruction in a school system he organized almost by himself. In 1869 he was President of the Southern Masonic Female College, in Covington; Haygood in June spoke to the ladies' literary societies during commencement and was called by his former teacher one "among the rising men of our State" who "in promise and usefulness" had "few equals."[8]

Orr's efforts in Atlanta on the public platform had results, as Haygood ecstatically observed, as immediate and effective as editorial exhortation. The charter membership of the association thus formed (the presiding elder included) in November formally launched the Georgia Teachers' Association, an effective lobby with the state legislature.[9] In December 1869, moreover, the city council of Atlanta voted a bond issue of $1,000,000 to create its own public school system, to be activated in full by 1871. In Haygood's mind the simultaneous inauguration in Atlanta in the fall of 1869 of Atlanta University (a Negro institution teaching elementary as well as college students) was in some mysterious providential way more than a coincidence. This venture, though financed primarily by the gifts of Northern Protestants, evoked a state subsidy during Governor Bullock's administration. The proliferation of educational enterprise to the romantic Atticus was all a flowering and fruiting under Orr's garden husbandry.[10]

The interests in education and in larger matters commented upon by the editorialists of the secular press made Haygood's supervision of the Atlanta district during 1869 and 1870 a peripheral matter in his life. He was pleased at the progress of the city missions among Atlanta's shanty dwellers, nevertheless, a charge firmly handled by Asbury Dodge, his fellow circuit rider of 1862. Money and books for the mission enterprise came regularly from Trinity, notably from the Hemphills and Judge D. F. Hammond. Both Mr. and Mrs. Hemphill and his sister Laura, furthermore, visited the missions regularly on Sunday afternoons, to give additional moral encouragement to the poor.[11]

In view of his father-in-law's pastorate among the Negroes of Oxford, moreover, Atticus was concerned by the continued loss of Negro communicants from the white churches in the district—but since the loss furthered the establishment of the separate client denomination there was no great point in halting it. Until 1870, though, there were many Negroes still on the rolls of the churches at Stone Mountain, Lawrenceville, and Decatur—and in Atlanta a single Negro (presumably an aged body servant of the previous era), a member at First Methodist.[12]

Haygood's lack of sympathy with the prosperous churches in Atlanta and Covington, with what he felt was a superficial religiosity, grew rather than slackened, and he felt no real direct influence over what he knew was an unhealthy development. At least he could express his irritation when invited to preach in these pulpits: he would chide the generous parishioners for their "humiliating" unconcern "towards the heathen world," and he loved to point out that "Brigham Young has at least as many agents in Georgia as the whole half million of us sustain in China."[13] His own impotence in a city district led him to agree with Editor Myers of the *Advocate* that the Southern Methodists might benefit by the abolition of the office of presiding elder. Myers continued to feel that it would be better either to have a much larger number of bishops or to give the pastors of large city churches a supervisory control over the lesser pastors in the city's trade area. Either reform would reduce the influence within the denomination of the old-time bishop and presiding elder, with their distaste for the manners of city churches.[14]

The one church activity in his district which was unerringly meaningful to the Reverend Haygood was the Sunday school, that "nursery of patriotism and piety," as he termed it. He remembered his own happy hours with the books and periodicals he found in his older boyhood in Trinity's Sunday school library. Southern Methodism's autonomy after 1844 had led to the necessity of printing its own literature, a literature more warmly received since it fitted regional tastes for teaching children both moralistic and social attitudes. Dr. Thomas O. Summers edited the catechisms and produced the *Sunday-school Visitor,* a weekly paper with a guide for teachers, published after 1855 in Nashville.[15] After the war, as Haygood knew, the Northern Protestant churches provided the model for the improvement of the Sunday school, which was to loom large in the educational life of the nation for decades. The leading enthusiast was the Northern Methodist John H. Vincent. Vincent in 1867 organized an interdenominational Sunday School Union, later established a separate magazine for teachers, and in 1872 held the first "normal institute" for Sunday school teachers, at Chautauqua, in the western New York lake country. Since 1865 Northern Methodism had, besides, printed "lesson leaves," individual sheets for Sunday school children.[16]

The Reverend Haygood, already a regular reader of the periodical publications of the Northern churches, was keenly aware of the improved methods of teaching and of the more attractive literature. In 1869 he wrote the *Advocate* about the inferior nature of the literature used in the Southern churches—including some bought from the denomination's Publishing House in Nashville:

The amount of mere rubbish—the quantity of dreary platitudes and of shallow twaddlings—neatly boxed up and labeled 'Sunday school Library'—by enterprising publishers who pay small prices for cheap brains—is absolutely appalling. Mere stories of impossible little boys and girls who were too good to live and so died and went to heaven are not quite the things children need. . . . If we could compass the question of expense, and bring a child's weekly into all our Sunday-schools, it would be a . . . great advance.[17]

In October 1869 he held a Sunday school convention for his district in Covington for the twofold purpose of emphasizing that teachers be well trained and of exhorting the use of the best printed materials. The Sunday schools of the Atlanta district were flourishing, but the main emphasis seemed to be on the "Celebrations" and the annual spring excursions. Covington's Sunday school usually rode en masse, by train, for a day at Stone Mountain, and in May 1869 six hundred children and parents filled nine railroad cars for Trinity Sunday school's excursion the forty miles to Oxford.[18] At his convention the presiding elder talked most about the need for Sunday school lessons to utilize Bible teachings and for the songs used to have some relevance to the doctrines of the church.

Six months later the Georgian, just past the thirty-year mark, was given control of the production of Sunday-school literature and books for his denomination, by appointment to the newly created office of Sunday school Secretary, with headquarters in Nashville, the site of the Methodist Publishing House. Haygood was in the delegation from his North Georgia Conference to the General Conference in Memphis, and there served on the Sunday School Committee, where his recommendations were turned into resolutions. There was some previous knowledge of his intellectual energy because of his writing to the *Advocate,* and it was clear to the influential that he was Bishop Pierce's candidate for the new office—which the Sunday School Committee had recommended. On the third ballot he was elected, receiving 110 out of 150 votes.[19]

This was an auspicious general conference in which to gain Southwide attention: it was the first to which lay delegates were sent. The decided "Confederate" cast of the lay delegates gave assurance that Southern Methodism had survived the threats to it since 1865 and would henceforth be the mold of an important style of Southern respectability. From Georgia there had been elected James Jackson (a judge advocate in the Confederate Army) and a future state supreme court justice, and Alfred H. Colquitt of Atlanta, a future governor. Trusten Polk, a former governor, had been the pro-Confederacy Senator from Missouri during the secession crisis, and Roger Q. Mills, a colonel in the Texas cavalry during the war, would be known in the United States Congress for decades as one of the "Confederate Brigadiers." There were also junior members of other famous families, a Foote from Mississippi and a Vance from North Carolina. Perhaps the leading personalities, besides the bishops, were the secularist preachers, college men like James H. Carlisle of Wofford and Landon C. Garland of the University of Mississippi, and the manager of the Publishing House, the convivial Alfred H. Redford, a Kentuckian.[20]

The pace of Haygood's life immediately quickened with his elevation. Three days after his election he was back in Georgia—in late May, 1870—to make arrangements for his family and for his district. He was in Nashville after June 23, but returned to Georgia in July to attend several district conferences in north Georgia. During the month he was gone, June-July, two major events occurred in Georgia: Mollie bore him a son, whom he called Atticus Greene Haygood, Junior—a sure evidence of the high spirits he felt—and Emory College (Bishop George F. Pierce presiding over the Board of Trustees) honored him with the degree of Doctor of Divinity. He had returned, the triumphant native son, to Nashville by August 6. His family came later.[21]

As a sort of administrative capital for the Southern Methodists, Nashville was the emanating point for its major paper, the *Christian Advocate*. Being a railroad center, it also served the Cumberland Presbyterians and the Christian Church as an apt site for their publications. After 1872 the *Watchman* of the Primitive Baptists issued from the Tennessee capital.[22] Nashville was captured by the Federal army in 1862, and the city's reconstruction had begun early; with its railroad connection with Louisville it was, more than Atlanta, a "gate city" for the mid-South states. Along with Baltimore, which served commercially the older Southern states, Nashville was a dispenser of the "New South" spirit—long before the South self-consciously proclaimed its existence.[23] In 1870 Nashville, with 26,000 people, was considerably larger than Atlanta. Its major railroad, the Louisville and Nashville, dramatically entered the hilltopped city over the Cumberland River, the bridge having been rebuilt in 1867. Atticus came to Nashville over the Nashville and Chattanooga, a road dominated by E. W. Cole (a Methodist layman in Nashville) who was also one of the lessees of Georgia's Western and Atlantic, the state line from Chattanooga to Atlanta.[24]

The Tennessee city had access to the Midwest by sixteen steamers which traveled the Cumberland into the Ohio, docking at Cairo, Illinois. Given this wealth of connections, Nashville in 1870 was a major depot for cotton produced in Tennessee, northern Alabama, and even Georgia.[25] Since it had been a Federal army headquarters since early in the war, it was a mecca for freedmen. It was the site of several Negro institutions of higher learning— the Congregationalists' Fisk, the Northern Baptists' Roger Williams University, and the Northern Methodists' Walden (later Central Tennessee).[26] Both Negroes and whites attended the public schools in a flourishing system, but the whites' University of Nashville, in 1870 the object of the efforts of Confederate Generals Kirby Smith and A. P. Stewart, seemed unlikely to be revived. Nashville was not a city for Confederate romantics.[27]

The Methodists had been publishing in Nashville since 1834. The *Advocate* for Tennessee and Kentucky Methodists dated from 1848, and after 1854 this journal became one of three major organs of the denomination, the other two being the *New Orleans* and the *Southern*, the latter published in Charleston until the war. The Nashville weekly benefited from the editorial hand of McTyeire and, after 1866, of Dr. Summers, the omnipresent Nashville litteratist of the church. Within eight years it would be the "official" denominational paper.[28] Southern Methodists had become accustomed, since the late 1850's, to seeing the Nashville imprint on the bottom of the title page of hymnals, catechisms, theological works—and those rhetorically turgid children's books which Haygood deplored. Summers also edited the *Sunday-school Visitor*, printed on the Nashville press, which Haygood inherited in August 1870.[29] The manager, or book agent, was A. H. Redford. It was Redford who moved the presses back to the main floor of the House in 1866, after years of occupation of the property by the Federal army. He described his machines in 1870 as "seven book, one-cylinder, three hydraulic, and one screw press." Redford supervised the printing of the more than 15,000 *Advocates* and decided which books would be printed, the copyrights being in his name. Since his salary was ultimately dependent on the volume of trade, he was happy to encourage Haygood in his project for a magazine for Sunday school teachers, to launch a new serious quarterly review for the scholarly preachers, and to enlarge his "eclectic catalogue." Optimistic over the prospects of the book trade he had increased the number of employees of the House from six to almost eighty in just four years.[30]

The third member of the House (which was located at the northeast corner of Nashville's Public Square) was Haygood's supervisor when he was a missionary chaplain, John B. McFerrin, Secretary to the Board of Missions. McFerrin's son was Redford's assistant. Theoretically the Nashville publishing activity was supervised by a Book Committee, elected by the quadrennial General Conference. Apparently, however, the Nashville members of the Committee were satisfied with Redford and let him alone to make any decisions he wanted to, and most of the members of the Book Committee saw the plant briefly only during the few days of their annual May meeting. The exception was the Reverend A. L. P. Green of west Tennessee, who shared with Haygood a passion for increasing the literacy level of adult Southern Methodists.[31]

Upon taking charge in the summer of 1870, the young Dr. Haygood established rapport easily with McFerrin, Redford, and Summers, and was cordial toward W. P. Harrison, who came to edit the new quarterly review. He was happy at Redford's announcement that "no pains or expense shall be spared to meet the wants of our Sunday schools." Dr. Summers responded to the Georgian's accustomed deferential attitude to elders, and found the young man "a gentleman of high literary attainments." Haygood made no effort to take over the *Visitor* at once, and carefully asked the former editor's opinions about ordering new plates for illustrations. The transition could not have been smoother, especially considering that Dr. Summers was openly known for his "loud voice, . . . over-bearing manner," and "superabundant self-assertion."[32] Subscriptions for the *Visitor* increased by over 10,000 even before the summer was over (most of them no doubt from Georgia), and in the fall Summers agreed that it was wise, as before the war, to publish the magazine in a weekly version.[33]

The yearly salary of the Sunday school secretary was set at $3,000 by the conference resolution creating the office. For a little less than six months of apprenticeship during 1870 Haygood received more than a half year's salary, $1,625. This generous act resulted in Haygood's increased admiration of Redford, the Publishing House administrator. The editorial work was only part of his responsibilities. Haygood believed he had earned the salary easily by appearing in behalf of all the Nashville activities (including the Board of Missions) at annual conferences in Missouri, Virginia, and Georgia that fall. Bishop McTyeire took him to Missouri in September and reported back to the *Nashville Advocate* that

The Doctor is doing a fine work for his cause in Missouri. He likes the country and people . . . , and they reciprocate. . . . I am glad he has gone abroad; a new interest in our Sunday-school literature is sustained by his presence. . . . He is obliged to admit that this country, even on the hill-tops, can beat Georgia—for raising corn.[34]

But the corn-stalked hilltops did not amaze the Georgian as much as the sweep of the grassy prairies. He amused the Missourians by thinking that the flat expanses were "old fields turned out on the commons."[35]

Beginning, a little ruefully, to see Georgia in a new perspective, Haygood boasted in Nashville that Georgians by far outdid the Tennesseans in buying Methodist publications. His appearance later in the fall in Lynchburg at the Virginia Conference at first undermined his self-confidence. He was somewhat conscious that his baggy clothes were out of place in a city of considerable gentility; and he was more than a little aware that his black beard was being stared at—in the eastern South older preachers always were clean shaven despite the fashion of the war. However, he impressed the Virginians with an "address of great power" delivered at the conference's missionary meeting. The last conference appearance was in Augusta, where he was received with a hero's welcome, and the minor changes in the *Visitor's* format—new and "modern" typography for the title and reduced rates for volume buying—were acclaimed as major accomplishments.[36]

After January 1871 Georgia and the whole stretch of Southern Methodism—from Baltimore to Los Angeles—were on notice that the Sunday school literature was undergoing major improvements. The *Visitor,* now a weekly, but available also in monthly and semi-monthly editions, was henceforth a "take-home" four-page sheet of moralistic stories, rather than the starting point for Sunday school lessons. A few of the stories were original; most were borrowed—from the Northern Methodists' *Ladies' Repository* and *New York Advocate,* the *Presbyterian,* and the *New York Observer*—in a day of widespread freebooting among publishers. Old and new readers were pleased with the appearance of the new illustrations. Ironically, by 1874 repetition had become necessary so that the criticisms leveled against Dr. Summer's editions were once again valid. There was also, from 1871 on, considerable disappointment at the inferior quality of the paper used.[37]

Three new periodicals dedicated entirely to co-ordination of the lesson texts, from the nursery department to the adults' class, were *Our Little People*; for older children who could read fairly well, *Lesson Leaves;* and for adults, highly literate adolescents, and the teachers, the *Sunday-school Magazine*. The plan was for the Sabbath lesson for all groups to be drawn from a single scriptural text; and Dr. Haygood had already outlined two years of orderly study of the Gospels. The idea of a uniform lesson series he borrowed from the Northern churches. Both Vincent and Orange Judd had made similar outlines for the Northern Methodists, and the Presbyterians were beholden to Henry C. McCook. There was in existence already a series for the Sunday School Union.[38]

Haygood's unbounded confidence in his own abilities to plan and publish lesson-text material grew out of his personal success at exegesis in sermons and from the historical circumstance that Bible scholarship was still slight in the United States in the 1870's. The Doctor felt free to give a *standard* explanatory comment for his entire denomination, using as aids the Commentaries of Adam Clarke and Richard Watson, but primarily his own judgment.[39] The Nashville House's publications may thus, since the Secretary was restricted in his educational opportunities, be considered of little consequence intellectually, although they were certainly unusual because of the irrepressible vernacularisms of

.. *The Sunday School* 79

Haygood's style. On the other hand, Haygood improved on Vincent's *Picture Lesson Paper*: the type was larger—hence easier for little children to read—and *Our Little People* had its words hyphenated into syllables.[40]

Initial delight with Haygood's system, general at first, was replaced fairly soon by criticism, some well placed, some mere carping, all irritating to the new editor. The conservatives soon recognized that Bishop Pierce's boy was using his own questions for lessons in the *Magazine,* rather than part of the prewar catechism. To meet this objection, Haygood included in the questions for each lesson a single article from the catechism, along with his own questions, but in what he considered the order of pertinence to *his* outline. A major source of disagreement with the Sunday school secretary's aims of standardized study came from states like Kentucky, where union Sunday schools were rife, and pastors were untroubled by the demands that only Southern Methodist literature be used.[41]

Haygood's unyielding prejudice against denominational laxness was a major cause behind his decision, during 1872 and 1873, not to participate in the organization of the International Series of Lessons—even though he had met Vincent (in Nashville) and had the greatest respect for him. His denomination gave him a mild vote of confidence in this decision, at the General Conference of 1874, but the resolution suggested that later reconsideration would not offend the church. Dr. Haygood did not reconsider, and until he resigned in the fall of 1875 continued his own system. During 1873 and 1874 he used the Epistles as a starting point for his commentaries, and in January 1875 began again with the Gospels. He was deceiving himself when he claimed that he was accomplishing a major rewriting of the 1871 lessons.

Haygood's successor, W. G. E. Cunnyngham, pleased the progressives by at once utilizing the International Series, beginning with the year 1876.[42] Although the Georgian's stubbornness may be labeled primitivistic arrogance, nevertheless the new literature, standardized in effect for all American Protestants and suitable to the informal study habits of teachers in the town Sunday schools, made even more remote the prospects of *doctrinal* literacy—and of a rational morality based on an understanding of *each denomination's* intellectual heritage. Haygood's defeat was in effect a final blow against the sectarian discipline of enlightened Wesleyanism. It should not be concluded, however, that had Haygood survived in his office he could have stemmed the momentum by which the haphazard quality of religious life in the burgeoning city churches dominated Southern Methodism increasingly in an increasingly Erastian church.

The progressives were glad when Pierce's protégé returned to Georgia, but the Doctor's re-election in 1874 indicates that his popularity extended through the "connection." A few of the educated preachers, moreover, sensed the critical importance of the secretary's aims. Haygood wanted the Sunday schools to be used to prepare adults for total involvement in the life of the church—through a genuine, rather than a rote-learned, familiarity with the Bible. He agreed with the necessity of keeping the children's attention with many pictures and interesting stories, but he felt that there should be a *denominational* slant behind each lesson. This required that the eclectic use of literature be ended. At first he made phenomenal progress; by the end of 1871 it was estimated that half of the 300,000 children (most of them in the city churches) were using the new literature exclusively.[43] The expense of the attempt, coincident with the depression after 1873, cost the Publishing House about $30,000, but other enterprises somewhat underwrote the subsidy. Neither the Book Committee nor Redford nor, it goes without the recording, Dr. Haygood was disturbed by the debt. The effort was worth more than it cost, and, as Redford insisted, the book trade would be flourishing again in a couple of years.[44]

The major source of profit for the Publishing House, between 1871 and 1875, came from the sale of songbooks, the issuance of which was Haygood's responsibility by the resolution creating the secretary's office. Although there were many evidences of the impoverishment of the region by the losses of the war (marginal subsistence salaries for preachers being one), the South by 1870 had devoted itself to the new industrial desideratum of a consuming public, "conspicuously consumptive." No better evidence for this is there than the widespread buying of pianos and harmoniums for the home parlor. Often a loud, out-of-tune piano was donated to a Sunday school class when a new upright grand or more lavishly ornamented pump-organ replaced it in the home. The taste for livelier music, accompanied by a percussive instrumental emphasis of the major beats, was ultimately derived perhaps from the banjo and guitar music of the minstrels heard by Confederates during their war service. (Good Methodists, like

.. *The Sunday School* 81

Haygood, for instance, had never attended any form of theatrical during the 1850's, but avoiding minstrel songs in the camps was no doubt an impossibility.) It was inevitable, with the breakdown of sectarian discipline generally, that there should be a demand for livelier, accompanied music in the church.

As for the problem of the Sunday school lesson plans, Secretary Haygood had to mediate between postwar and antiquated preferences in hymn tunes. The first widely used Methodist songbook was *The Methodist Harmonist,* compiled in the East with awareness of the taste of Virginians, in 1821. This book assumed a high proficiency of unaccompanied part singing: intricate bass, tenor, and counter-tenor (rather than alto) lines paralleled the melody.[45] There is no evidence in the lower South, certainly not in the plantation counties, that such a civilized singing-school tradition was transmitted and preserved. The Southern Methodists' first hymnbook, printed in Nashville in 1847, *A Collection of Hymns,* was an anthology of hymn poems, chiefly by Isaac Watts and the Wesleys, safely metered and rhymed in the predictable style of Alexander Pope; their chief virtue was their theological pertinence and "soundness." Singing these hymns depended on the skill of the preacher; as a result, the number of known hymn tunes must have decreased, and the intricate patterns of harmony and rhythmic device of the 1821 book became unknown.[46] The first tune book for the Southern church appeared as late as 1859. Edited by L. C. Everett, a Virginian, it contained a simple piano accompaniment printed at the top of a page on which four or more poems were separately available for meter-matching. There were a few new tunes in this volume, called a *Wesleyan Hymn and Tune Book,* one by the young Tennessean, R. M. McIntosh.[47]

Fortunately for Atticus Haygood, who had learned to sing with difficulty when he was seventeen, Rigdon McCoy McIntosh was in 1870 a "singing-school teacher" in Nashville. Three years older than Atticus, he had been a roving youth as the son of an Indian agent. He had taught school in Alabama and had known Everett in Virginia, where he had gone to study and teach music. His war experience fitted his extravert personality: he had escaped after being captured by the Federals. In 1866 he edited a songbook of his own, *Tabor,* published in Nashville and Columbia, South Carolina, the sales of which warranted a second and third edition. McIntosh's experience in Virginia is signified by the inclusion of anthems and chants, and by his manner of separating the four parts in parallel scores—the alto replacing the counter-tenor line of the *Harmonist,* but the melody printed as the third rather than the first vocal line.⁴⁸

McIntosh's own tunes were uninfluenced by the banjo music with its de-emphasis of any vocal phrase beneath the melody. McIntosh thus was the heir of the older Methodist singing style and the stately harmonies of Lowell Mason, which Georgians particularly favored in unaccompanied singing. McIntosh's rhythms were livelier and some of the verses he used approach the ridiculous, the mere sound of the words seeming to please the composer; but his songs, even later, are musically superior to the "gospel music" which emerged triumphant in the 1870's and 1880's, songs with monotonous harmony, "foot-patting" rhythms, and doctrinally illiterate verses. The circumstances by which Haygood secured McIntosh's services are unknown, but during 1871 they were working together on a new Sunday school songbook, McIntosh donating his labor.⁴⁹

Haygood's book was not to be designed for use in formal worship; it was not a replacement for Dr. Summers' hymnbook. *The Amaranth,* which appeared in April 1871, reflected joint decisions. Haygood, influenced by Summers, excluded all mere "ditties" and songs "about 'the [Union] flag' "; furthermore there were more of the "glorious hymns" of Watts and Wesley than usual in "popular songbooks." Of the 180 tunes, twelve were by McIntosh, eight of them new, four reprinted from *Tabor* and his other collection, *Glad Tidings.* To avoid the dissatisfaction of a lively contemporary controversy, *Amaranth* was available both in round and shaped notes. In the preface, the Sunday school secretary candidly announced that the conference committee appointed to supervise the edition had "In the nature of the case not been consulted."⁵⁰ Dr. Summers approved of the exclusion of "namby-pamby, doggerel" songs. However, he must have become jealous of the immediate popularity of the book, for in the summer of 1871, he brought out a songbook of his own, printed by a friend in St. Louis, and later induced Redford to collaborate with him in the editing of another competing hymnbook.⁵¹ The *Amaranth* was nevertheless the star of 1871, selling 50,000 copies, and was succeeded by *The Emerald,* 1872, and *The Gem.* Both *The Gem* and *Amaranth* were reissued in several editions after editor Haygood returned to Georgia in 1874.⁵² All three of the books were suitable for worship in the smaller churches, all containing both simple chants and performable anthems.

Dr. Haygood necessarily depended heavily on McIntosh's musical judgments, but as in all other areas, he had a considered opinion about the developments in his church. Personally untouched by " 'operatic' music," anthems bowdlerized from French opera after the manner of Gounod, and disturbed by the unwillingness of organists to subordinate their voluntaries and offertories to the preacher's sermon, he nevertheless now had no quarrel with the musical additions, which so pleased city churches, provided congregational singing continued. As for his fellows in the Publishing House, the pageantry of the Episcopal liturgy in Nashville, with its "surpliced choristers, *processioning*, chanting, bowing," was the effort of a religiously effete denomination to win attention by attractive externals. The year he left Nashville, 1874, he made several important comments on the musical developments since the war:

... if there is no singing the public worship is imperfect.... I claim to be free from prejudice.... I am not organ or choir-made ... being able to enjoy either, provided the people sing.... The choir has no more right to sing what the people cannot sing (when they try) than the preacher ... to pray in a language they do not understand. Operatic singing ... is as much out of place as prayers ... in Greek.... Let us have solos and quartets ... in the parlor.... It is a *performance* in either case.

Our Methodist Church in Griffin, Ga., Rev. John W. Heidt, pastor, has an organ and a choir, and yet has congregational singing—and give[s] out the words two lines at a time. And there was no trouble or confusion about it. So well do they understand how to manage it that when the pastor had to give the colored organ-blower a slight pinch to wake him up (the choir being at the right of the pulpit), it did not throw anybody off his balance....[53]

The music Haygood liked best was the kind he heard in 1874, in August, at an African Methodist church in Columbus. The unoperatic Negroes, he said, " 'knew the lick it was done with.' "[54]

After 1871, the routine of the secretary's job left him time to edit books for Sunday school libraries. (His first church responsibility had been as librarian for Trinity in Atlanta.) Redford encouraged him in this activity as in the others. He hoped Haygood's new books would sell because of endorsement by the more widely used Sunday school literature; furthermore, an increase of buying by Sunday schools might help the House dispose of the stacks of books published by Dr. Summers after 1866, and other volumes bought from Northern presses. Thus, Haygood, in September 1871, announced a "new" boxed selection of five volumes for children under twelve, entitled "Our Little People's Library"—these were all old books. The first new editions appeared in 1872, even though a fire in April of that year destroyed nearly everything on the main floor of the plant, notably Dr. Summers' library, and unpublished manuscripts.[55]

While the Publishing House waited for new quarters, Mollie was pleased that her husband worked at their home, in the suburb called Edgefield, continuing to read children's books, especially imports from England. (Attie had gotten Mollie's brother Walter a job as mailing clerk at the House, so that someone could stay with her and the children while he was away, particularly during his fall visits to the conferences.)[56]

By late 1872 Redford was given the first of ten works intended for children between the ages of approximately nine or ten and thirteen or fourteen. Typical of the titles were *Papers for Thoughtful Girls* and *Junior Clerk*. A second series, selected by 1874, was for older children. The favorite author was the Englishman Samuel Smiles, but Haygood honored a north Georgia preacher, R. W. Bigham, by publishing his *Vinny Leal's Trip to the Golden Shore*. Haygood's minimal labor, and purposes, may be seen in his introduction to a book by Smiles:

> Thousands of our young people are well-endowed and only need to learn how to help themselves. . . . Those who do their best may expect the help of God; to encourage such effort and faith, we have reprinted this book. It is from the last English edition. . . . It has gone through several editions, and has been translated. . . . The present editor has done little, except to leave out a few paragraphs that would not be useful among our people. . . .[57]

The books were helpful in increasing the House's sales, especially after 1874 when "the trade" improved; but city Methodists knew that they were in paper, printing, and quality of illustrations inferior to Northern books of the same kind. The loyal Sunday schools, like Trinity in Atlanta, bought exclusively the Nashville products. As F. M. Richardson said: "We want no more essays on the depravity of Southern society. We are bad enough . . . , but if we seek books which tell us of our wickedness, let those books come from those who understand our malady."[58] Certainly, though, these little moralistic volumes were almost as ineffective in transforming the critical self-judgment of Southern Methodist children as they were in enhancing literary taste.

On the other hand, Dr. Haygood had a far more sensitive concern with style than the authors whose books he "edited." The main outlet for him, from 1870 to 1874, was the two pages of editorial comment in *The Sunday-School Magazine*, pungent observations on the deficiencies of schools which closed up for the winter, pastors who did not supervise the teaching activity of their "faculty," and teachers and superintendents lacking zeal and spiritual intent. His style, the most striking characteristic of which is its impromptu quality (his pieces often were unrevised), emerged in all its bold, exhortatory "Anglo-Saxon" during these years of his early thirties. During 1873 he wrote his first book, another exhortatory effort in support of financial strength for the foreign missions. He had served on the Board of Missions since he arrived in Nashville, and voted at the May 1873 meeting that a prize be offered for the best original missionary tract, as a gimmick for increasing denominational concern. He submitted his own manuscript under the nom de plume of "X. Y. Z." and won first place, even though he had exceeded the prescribed page length. It was published as a book in 1874 under the title of *Go or Send* and frequently reprinted. Second place went to the liberal and literate pastor of the leading church in Nashville, D. C. Kelley, who had briefly served as a missionary in China during the 1850's.[59]

Haygood's essay was an able argument directed at laymen. The author realistically started with the standard arguments against extensive giving to foreign missions, and rebutted them. He denied that the church was so poor that it ought to spend its money substantially at home (that is, in the defeated and devastated South). He argued against the proposition, seldom openly voiced, that the Southern whites had no obligation toward the yellow and brown peoples of the world—especially since their wardship of the Negroes had been severely curtailed by the victory of the North. Haygood answered all objections by an appeal to the Southern male's strong sense of honor and lively awareness of "duty." He said that Arminians had to accept the possibility that all men could be saved through missionary effort, and asserted the spiritual unity of the human race. Since it was not possible for each Southern Methodist personally to evangelize abroad, those who could not go must send their money instead. Otherwise the un-Christianized world would be deprived of Christian civilization in this life and of heaven in the next.[60]

The second half of the book was an appeal to history, citing advances in the behavior of primitive peoples made since European Protestants began seriously during the eighteenth century to send missionaries. He contrasted modern life in Hawaii, Madagascar, Tonga, the Fiji Islands, and India with life there in the pre-mission days. He cited the extirpation of suttee, infanticide, idolatry. A most important "proof of the pudding" was the elimination of cannibalism (as flesh-eating was replaced by hymn-singing). Even in the Fijis, a native would be punished for killing his wife, with "no pretense of emotional insanity made." In his argument Haygood shrewdly cited the commercial progress coincident to the extension of missionary influence. To the son of a Whig, such a merging of spiritual and material values was natural. Men of property, Greene Haygood's son said, might appreciate "a word upon the commercial value of missions . . . though no religious man will need such an argument to induce him to do his duty." The process of "civilization of the heathen creates new wants, which must be largely supplied by Christian countries." Those who abandoned nakedness would be a market for new consumer goods, "the profit on which . . . Christian nations—get the largest share."[61] The book appeared shortly before the 1874 General Conference; that body of preachers and laymen made Dr. Haygood assistant secretary of the Board of Missions so that he might continue his effective exhortation.

In July there appeared a new periodical, called *The Missionary*, the forerunner of a proposed voluminous publication by the House in behalf of missions, which because of Haygood's leaving Nashville in the fall never developed. During the 1870's, the decade of reawakened imperialism on the part of the European powers, the Southern Methodists did become more substantially committed to foreign missions, beginning in that decade the penetration of Mexico. However, it was the ladies, in their Woman's Missionary Society, organized between 1873 and 1878, who provided the major zeal and interest.[62] (Haygood's tract had been pointed toward the men.)

The effectiveness of Haygood's rhetoric owed much to his visits to the conferences as a salesman for the Nashville enterprises, for support of missions, for the Sunday school publications, for the books, for the *Advocate,* and at first for Harrison's *Quarterly Review*. Gifted with a natural exuberance, endowed with a Georgian's friendly charm of manner, disarmingly unusual in his unpreacherly conversational tone and his avoidance of preachers' clothes, he developed a great fondness for the leading laymen in the states he visited, and for those preachers who were like himself engaged outside the sanctuary—in writing or in school work. He met the builder of Trinity College in North Carolina, Braxton

Craven, during the commencement of 1871. There he rejoiced at Trinity's advancement at the expense of the University of North Carolina, which "has fallen into the hands of the Philistines," the Reconstructionists.[63]

In the fall of 1871 he ventured to the edge of the Southerners' universe, taking a slow steamboat up the Ohio River on his way to meet Bishop Pierce in Charleston, West Virginia. A night in Cincinnati on the return confirmed Haygood's opinion that Christian civilization had been endangered in America by the Germans. On the boat trip he experienced the discomfort of combined admiration and revulsion for the crew. He saw Negroes "with a full stock of sensation papers," and men "forty years old" (he was thirty-two) "gloating over these indecencies."[64] In Kentucky he saw a borderland where Southern Methodism petered out, as Bishop Pierce pointed out—a state, he said, where "the preachers were timid . . . and quietly gave the . . . country to Campbellism."

This analysis was not merely the reaction of the Erastian bishop from Georgia. A collection of Kentucky Methodist sermons in 1874 included such statements as these: "The Methodist Church does not claim to be '*The* Church of Christ' "—safe enough—but also, "It is not essential to a religious development that a man should believe in Calvinism or its opposite; . . . the whole question . . . is relegated to the individual."[65] Kentucky would be the nursery of heterodoxy, spreading doctrinal uncertainty into the lower South during the late 1870's and early 1880's.

A much more pleasant visit for Bishop Pierce and Dr. Haygood was to the two conferences in 1873 in Arkansas, a state behind Georgia in population and the development of town-centered life. Perhaps it reminded the Bishop of the Georgia of the 1830's, when he was a young man. The happy association with the buoyant Atticus convinced Pierce that this man's future must be in Georgia. The first conference was held in Forrest City, a railroad town on a line running from Memphis to Little Rock. In order to get to the other conference, at Camden in the southern part of the state, days of rain storms having made impassable the carriage road, they traveled through sparsely settled country down the Ouachita River, via a large yawl. Both bishop and Sunday school secretary robustly helped with the rowing, which in the swollen waters was necessary to keep straight in the channel downstream, the Georgian hierarch lustily timing his strokes to the metric grandness of his favorite hymn, "How Firm a Foundation."[66]

SIX

Emory College in the 1870's

ON JULY 21, 1874, Dr. Atticus G. Haygood, distinguished alumnus of Emory College, gave the annual Address to the Alumni, one of the highlights of the college's commencement week. The subject chosen was "The Christian Church and the Education of the People." To the undergraduates listening, and certainly to the young ladies who attended commencement (some for reasons unrelated to the events on the platform), there was nothing remarkable in the address, other than the fact that the speaker was a preacher rather than a lay alumnus. (The usual occasion for the appearance of older, well-known laymen during the commencement was the Address to the Societies.) Perhaps some of the seniors—and the alert junior Warren A. Candler—knew that Dr. Haygood was a favorite of Bishop Pierce, who was Chairman of the Board of Trustees of Emory College.

Emory's president in 1874, the Reverend O. L. Smith, was aging, and unhappy in his office. The small enrollment of 1873-74 at Emory reflected the severity of the depression from which the South was suffering. The faculty was being paid only token salaries. Young Dr. Haygood looked like a possible successor as President. It is unlikely, however, that the most knowledgeable who listened to Haygood's address knew the magnitude of Bishop Pierce's plans for the use of the Sunday school secretary's talents. Such awareness was limited to the presiding-elder types who had come to the annual commencement meeting of the Board of Trustees. On July 20, the day before his address, Dr. Haygood was easily elected to the seat of "Uncle Billy" Parks, well-loved North Georgia preacher, and resident of Oxford, who had died in October 1873.[1] Even some of the lay Trustees probably thought of Haygood's election as merely a sign of the dying-out of ante bellum leadership—a final seal of the Confederacy's defeat.

.. *Emory College* 89

But the election and speech had a threefold significance. It was a sign of Bishop Pierce's determination to destroy a proposal (by a Georgia Methodist preacher, formerly a professor at Emory) for the creation of a joint church-state educational system in Georgia, at the college level. This proposal had won adherents among the Emory faculty and the lay Trustees because of the apparent hopelessness, during the depression, of keeping the denominational colleges alive. The Emory speech was furthermore a challenge to Bishop H. N. McTyeire, and his sponsorship of Vanderbilt University in Nashville—the cornerstone of which had been laid in May—in defiance of the interests of the established Southern Methodist men's colleges in the older Southern states. Vanderbilt would have a divinity school, disguised as a Biblical Department, a progressive innovation which Bishop Pierce had violently opposed as hostile to the "genius" of the Methodist denomination. Dr. Haygood's new position on the Board, which gave added prestige to his speech, meant, moreover, that Bishop Pierce intended to remove him from the Nashville offices earlier than he had planned because of a yet hidden financial scandal in the management of the Publishing House, an affair which would surely ruin A. H. Redford and might hurt the promising career of the young Georgian.

Dr. Haygood's address understandably is rather strange. He seems to have been conscious that he must restate the Bishop's educational philosophy in a form palatable to his own generation; the pragmatic result hoped for would be an emergence of Emory College, in contradistinction to the University of Georgia and Commodore Vanderbilt's institution in Nashville, as a model for denominational ventures in higher education. Alliance with secular education, he said, was alliance with the "strange and unholy," the Romanists, the Jews, French infidels, and American Darwinists. Although "real discoveries" had been made about scientific truth by "even pantheists and atheists," nevertheless "We can give no rational account of a single atom in the universe if we leave God out," and a curriculum that did not include the Bible as its guide could not inculcate "a rational history of our world or a sound philosophy of morals." Furthermore, the Christian college should not be contaminated by the new universities which, bribed by patronage, would teach "trades, agriculture, mechanical arts, or book-keeping." If higher education surrendered to the demands of "those who want the name and the benefits of education without the labor of securing it," and began to teach "men their trades instead of educating them—its occupation is gone."

The primary slap against Vanderbilt was given in a censure of those "foolish people" who decried the denominational slant of denominational colleges as "bigotry." The core of Pierce's, and his own, educational philosophy was found in the statement that although "man's moral nature is more susceptible of educational influence than the . . . intellectual . . . and . . . requires education," nevertheless "If human history teaches anything, it teaches that depravity and not ignorance is the source of crime." (Haygood was in the process of rejecting this last, pre-Enlightenment sentiment, and would within five years drop his hostility to teaching trades at a Christian college.) His own most bigoted statement was that the godless French had been defeated in 1870-1871 because of the "decay of national virtue . . . not the lack of . . . schools."[2]

Bishop Pierce's conception of the role of the college had been stated in 1872 when he was forced by circumstances to an open "controversy between Bishop McTyeire and myself in the Churchpaper," which he knew would be neither "comely or profitable." MyTyeire had bypassed the majority feeling of the 1870 General Conference by engineering the collaboration of several annual conferences of the Mid-South in the projected "Central University," with a professional school for ministerial training, the institution which he later persuaded Vanderbilt to endow.[3] Miffed that he had been defeated, Bishop Pierce complained both of the "unconstitutional" bypassing of the resolutions of the church's central body and of the educational principle of a ministry with specialized academic training.

The following statements appeared in the *Nashville Advocate* in what must have been an embarrassing situation to many, between January and May 1872. Bishop McTyeire had the better of the exchange since he never lost his editorial temper.

University education [Pierce declared] is not *a*, certainly not *the*, *desideratum* in Southern Methodism. Church-schools in every city and every circuit—at least in every District—would be far better in my judgment. The mission of Methodism is to the masses . . . not to the select few. . . . University education is . . . not adapted to boys, the young, the immature. . . .

Methodist Colleges will furnish to the Conferences educated men. . ., without any of the delays and risks of a stereotyped training in a professional school. . . . Bishop M. himself is a specimen, . . . he would have been utterly spoiled by three years' arbitrary training in a professional school. He would have been stiff, cold, dry, powderless [McTyeire was widely held to be a man without warmth]. But graduating young, thrust out on a circuit, brought into contact . . . with the people, he is every inch a man. . . .

I do not want a man shut up in a seminary, lectured and molded by a given pattern, till all individuality be destroyed. . . .

The Presbyterians claim an educated ministry. . . . But they have not all the learning. . . . I know the Methodists and the Baptists are regarded by 'certain' as a plebeian set, but to these common people the whole country is largely indebted for the gospel. The Episcopal sect is too *delicate* for country fare. It must dwell in town. The Presbyterian training is too slow and stiff to meet the urgent and diversified calls of a promiscuous population. The Methodists and Baptists have a ministry right out from the people. . . . Let God call, the Church indorse, the Conference receive, and *the Bishop* send forth. . . .[4] [Italics not his, in the final phrase.]

Vanderbilt's rapid development in Nashville with professional schools in theology, law, and medicine could be countered only by the re-invigoration of the male colleges: Randolph-Macon in Virginia; Wofford in South Carolina, and especially Emory in Georgia. It was therefore severely painful to Bishop Pierce when the Rev. J. O. A. Clark (e) proposed in 1874 that a joint Board of Trustees representing the denominational colleges and the University of Georgia be created, to make possible the establishment of a graduate school in Athens and some possibility of solvency for the Baptists' Mercer, the Presbyterians' newly re-established Oglethorpe, and the Methodists' Emory. After all, this kind of cooperation had created the economic security and intellectual distinction of Harvard in Massachusetts, Brown in Rhode Island, and Yale in Connecticut—in the latter cases particularly without any harm to the Christian orientation of what had been founded as denominational schools designed to train ministers.

Clark, it may be assumed, had sounded out the Emory faculty, on which he had sat, his arguments being especially appealing in that depression year. Bishop Pierce, despite continued solicitation of paper pledges by Methodists to increase the college's income, had given up on the possibility of collection until the depression lifted. Clark's proposal was warmly endorsed by the Presbyterian John B. Gordon and the Baptist layman Joseph E. Brown, the latter also an alumnus and Trustee of the University of Georgia. The Trustees of Oglethorpe had already given their approval when Emory's Trustees met in July 1874. Following instructions perfectly, the first act of the newly seated Dr. Haygood was to resolve that Emory reject the proposition in any form. This the Emory Trustees refused to do.[5]

More indirect ways had to be found to defeat Clark's plan. Emory's commencement meeting ended with a condition attached to the proposal: any joint Board must give half its seats to the denominational colleges. Much to Bishop Pierce's chagrin, the August meeting of the Georgia Trustees accepted the condition. The chancellor, a Baptist minister, and Brown had wrought this miracle. With leading Baptist preachers, including part of the Mercer faculty, supporting the idea (probably out of a belief that the Baptists would dominate the joint Board as they did the present University), the only hope was the encouragement of Baptist suspicions. The editor of the *Christian Index*, in the fall, indicated his opposition. Bishop Pierce had shrewdly left Georgia by this time for an episcopal tour of the Pacific conferences.

After Christmas, during the winter of 1875, Dr. Haygood wrote a series of articles in the *Southern Christian Advocate*—in the style of Haygood but with the authority of a Methodist bishop. The unhappy Reverend Clark publicly accused Haygood of being Pierce's voice, and of pretending to be able to speak for the popular sentiment of Georgia Methodists. The Baptists, of course, knew that with the Methodist Bishop's utter opposition, even if stated so indirectly, Emory College would never be joined in collaboration: the Trustees would repudiate the proposal even if the Baptist convention accepted it. Haygood's articles, published between January and March 1875, thus dealt the *coup de grâce* to the possibility for a pooling of financial resources in Georgia for immediate improvement of higher education.[6] This demonstration of the power of a Bishop and his agent, and of the power of denominational prejudice in Georgia, was not lost on a precocious and ambitious young preacher, a senior in Emory College, who was living with the Haygoods when the articles appeared in the *Advocate*. The teen-aged preacher, Warren A. Candler, would as President of Emory College continue the denigration of the state's University in order to increase patronage of Emory.

During 1874-1875, as Clark, Emory's faculty, and some of the Trustees feared, patronage of Emory College sank to a new low. Enrollment of college students fell below the one-hundred mark. Income from the endowment, most of it railroad stock, dropped to about $3,500. An endowment of $50,000 and a larger enrollment were needed to guarantee full payment of the official salaries. The Trustees, as a last prospect of increasing income, raised the year's tuition to $60, a futile gesture, since it only furthered the irregular attendance of students—one term in Oxford, two at work—in a poverty-stricken era. President Smith was anxious to resign. The sole source of satisfaction was the erection of four new buildings, even though Bishop Pierce's brave decision to do this was taken without certainty that he could ever collect all the pledges given. The faculty certainly must have experienced anger and despair with the pride they felt in the visible improvements. One of the new buildings was a chapel for the twice-daily services, a special project of Bishop Pierce. The putting of brick and mortar ahead of the welfare of the faculty families in a decision taken entirely on his own was, they felt, typical of the bishop's priority in values.[7]

The bishop was withal sanguine about Emory's future. The Sunday school secretary's family moved back to Oxford from Nashville in the fall of 1874, after Christmas sharing the old Few home with "Aunt Dolly" Burge-Parks, who according to her husband's will would have to sell it. Both the bishop and Mollie were elated at the retreat from Nashville. Mollie's seventh child, appropriately named George Pierce Haygood, had died in an epidemic in the fall of 1873, and she was determined that her infant baby daughter, Laura, to be called Lollie, born in the spring of 1874, would survive. The Nashville doctor agreed that Mollie's "delicate health" would be improved by residence within hailing distance of her father's house in Oxford.[8]

The bishop was glad to get Atticus out of the developing Publishing House scandal. Dr. McFerrin and Haygood had learned to their amazement, in May or June of 1874, that Redford's salary was $5,000 a year; he had taken this amount on the basis of a single resolution, for one year alone, by vote of a subcommittee of the Book Committee. This irregularity suggested that Redford's accounts would disclose other improprieties, in the yearly statement of assets and liabilities. Haygood was not as yet disturbed by any harm to his own reputation that any disclosure would show. His only questionable benefit from Redford's administration had been making the stereotype plates of the *Sunday-school Magazine*, with Redford's sanction, his own property. (The questions at the end of each weekly lesson were republished, in Macon and St. Louis, in 1877-1878.)[9] Redford, however, had refused to give him a commission on the subscriptions secured by his eloquent appeals to the annual conferences—income additional to his $3,000 salary which the Doctor felt he was owed because his travel expenses were his own burden.[10]

Dr. Haygood was not disturbed by the prospect of scandal in the Publishing House; he was, however, pleased with the evidence that Bishop Pierce wanted him to succeed Smith as President of Emory. The sounding-out probably occurred on the return of the bishop from the West Coast, in the spring of 1875, if not before he left. Atticus was full of self-confidence because of his part in the Clark affair. He was glad, furthermore, of a graceful way to avoid enlarged objections to his decision not to use the International Series of Lessons.

At a special meeting of the Book Committee in Nashville on August 30, 1875, a resolution was passed that Dr. Haygood ought to resign if he refused to live in the Tennessee capital. It is unknown whether this demand was made with Dr. Haygood's collusion, but he cheerfully complied and resigned, averring that Mrs. Haygood could not survive another Tennessee winter. (In May he had already resigned his position as assistant secretary to the Board of Missions.) On November 1, he bought for $3,000 the "President's Home" in Oxford from the estate of Uncle Billy; Aunt Dolly had let the Haygoods live there since January. After the sale she moved back to the Burge plantation in the county.[11]

On December 2, the Emory Board, meeting in Griffin, voted to appoint Dr. Haygood President of Emory College, and Financial Agent. This arrangement meant that, since O. L. Smith remained as a professor of Latin, the faculty would have its half-salaries diluted only by an official half-salary for the additional faculty members. Haygood was to receive an additional $1,000 of the money he collected on pledges Pierce had garnered, and from pledges he solicited as Agent.[12] That the faculty nevertheless was unhappy with the change of regime may be inferred from the resignation (not accepted) of the vice-president, treasurer, and professor of mathematics, Haygood's old teacher, G. W. W. Stone. Smith, though, was delighted that he could now teach Latin, and Morgan Callaway was pleased that he could teach his first love, "philology," that is, the study of language through the vivisection of literature.[13]

Dr. Haygood had the burdensome task of being a collections agent for Emory College, as well as Professor of Mental and Moral Philosophy, until July 1878. His sacrificial willingness to live on a reduced salary rapidly ended the faculty's unhappiness, especially since the enrollment showed an immediate increase, from ninety-four college students in the spring term of 1876, Haygood's first as President, to almost 140 two years later. Some remembered that the enrollment had been 186 during 1870-1871 and realized that part of the increase was the result of bettering economic conditions; but Dr. Haygood was a decided success with faculty and students. They began to share his self-confidence and to believe that Emory would overtake Mercer, the University, and the new state college for men in Dahlonega, where tuition was free and the enrollment in 1876 surpassed that in Athens.[14] Since the teachers were receiving, during 1876-1877, only $700, or much less than half their official salary of $2,000, any ground for hope saved them from absolute despair. Blindly believing that Providence would solve his and the school's financial problems, Haygood himself received only $400 from the regular income, eking out an existence from his collections on the pledges.[15]

An adjustment was made by the Board in July 1878, after Dr. Haygood forced the issue by offering his resignation. He was thereafter relieved of the responsibility as Agent, allowed to keep the $1,100 he had collected, permitted to become editor of a new church periodical, the *Wesleyan Christian Advocate,* in Macon (with a salary of $3,000, part of which he had to pay an assistant), and relieved of regular class responsibilities.[16] Because income from the increased numbers of students and from the endowment was rising, he received *half* of his half-salary, or $500, for the *first* time during 1879-1880. Most of the endowment of Emory was in securities of the Central of Georgia, the Georgia, and the Memphis and Charleston railroads. The last-named was the least valuable investment, and the bonds might have been surrendered upon their maturation in 1880 without the intervention, through the Atlanta Trustees of Emory, by E. W. Cole, Methodist layman of Nashville. These trustees, E. E. and W. A. Rawson, and Alfred H. Colquitt, Governor of Georgia since the election of 1876, were influential in giving Dr. Haygood an awareness of the path to financial security for Emory College—the securing of major gifts from a few capable of such gifts—the finding of "A Vanderbilt" for Emory, perhaps. He was convinced after 1878 that Bishop Pierce's naive belief that individual gifts of $5 or $10 could endow Emory properly was an antiquated hope.[17]

Although his financial responsibilities from January 1876 until July 1878 made the presidency of Emory College onerous, the experience of being looked upon as a pillar of strength and keystone of hope was exhilarating to a man of thirty-six and -seven.

The sickly epileptic had become the embodiment of vigor. The professors, moreover, deeply warmed by his friendly manner and his total absence of arrogance—so annoying to them in the self-contained young men whom they taught—quickly forgot the circumstances of his coming. Smith gloried in freedom from the job of chief disciplinarian; he had failed in this office by his alternation from imperious threats to weak resignation and acceptance. He had begun to teach Latin at Wesleyan Female College in Macon, thirty years before, and he was content to fill out his years from the prestigious classical chair. He died in January 1878, having headed for home after hearing a recitation. His passing was memorialized by a student thus:

I was the last man that he called upon to recite, and having studiously prepared the lesson by the aid of an Interlinear . . ., I gave a most beautiful translation, but failed to parse a single line correctly. He dropped dead as he went . . . home . . . and the boys always insisted that my . . . recitation was too much for him.[18]

Professor Stone, the vice-president and treasurer, taught mathematics—as he said in the first class of each term: "Mathematics is an exact science, young gentlemen." A man of exalted character and the single active professor left from ante-bellum days, he was honored by the students. In class, though, his high-pitched, faltering voice made him less than a completely effective teacher. Haygood learned the inner strength of the man after they became regular fishing companions "in chosen retreats . . . upon the Yellow River." Stone, he learned, was well versed in Wesleyan theology, something increasingly rare in local preachers. The Stones' virtues were evidenced in these years, moreover, by the professor's two sons. Harry, who became a teacher at Emory College after graduation, was an able student in the Class of 1880. His brother George, a blind boy, made all Oxford proud by earning his own living by making and selling brooms.[19]

The star of the faculty, especially from the students' point of view, was Morgan Callaway, who taught English literature but was chiefly interested in etymology and what would today be called linguistics. The students adored him: he was a scion of "Southern aristocracy," coming from a plantation family. He had been wounded during the Civil War, was "the perfect gentleman" —and never gave any student a grade lower than 97. Haygood, the conscious democrat, was somewhat awed by a book-reading type of aristocrat, already the object of general Southern romanticization. Actually, Callaway's teaching meant little to the students, but they never admitted it. They were required to memorize and recite the expository sections of Hippolyte Taine's history of English literature; the pages containing excerpts from literary gems were ignored in the concentration on the development of the language, on "philology." Since President Haygood shared Callaway's fascination with words and his glorification of Anglo-Saxon directness, he altered the curriculum during his first term, the spring of 1876, so that Callaway could teach both sophomores and seniors what was billed as the "science of language." (Haygood had worn out several unabridged dictionaries in the quest for vigorous expression, during the twenty years since he became an Emory sophomore.)[20]

Despite his own interest in Greek as a student, Haygood shared, in typical honesty, the growing prejudice in America against giving Latin and Greek a central place in the curriculum. At Emory in the 1870's the effect of this prejudice was not yet apparent. When Smith died, "Ike" Hopkins returned to Oxford from the presidency of a college in Alabama to teach Latin. Hopkins, Haygood's friend from years of sitting next to each other in chapel and church while students, was a vigorous extravert, not at all the pedant. Haygood was therefore inclined to admire him in his love of Horace. Hopkins would read from the Odes in class, exclaiming to the daydreaming students, "See how fine this sounds!" They quickly learned that with slight agreement from them Professor Hopkins would complete the class hour in professorial recitation.[21]

Despite the financial limitations, President Haygood was determined to reintroduce to Emory College the study of contemporary languages; he had loved French and still called Mollie "amie" sometimes. To replace Professor Doggett, who retired after the spring term of 1876 to travel in Europe, he persuaded Henry A. Scomp to come to Oxford from the presidency of a small college in Kentucky. Scomp accepted on the promise that he could teach Hebrew and German as well as Greek (French was not in demand because of the nation's "weakness" in losing the war of five years before). Scomp was a bearded, eccentric pedant who talked Greek in class and made reference to his experiences as a student in German universities. His eyesight was so bad that it was soon learned that translations need not be prepared even with the use of the "Interlinear," or pony: good students could sit in for bad on the recitation bench, and Scomp would not know even from the difference of voice that the exchange had been made. An Emory graduate later mused: "Why we studied Greek at all I have not been able to discover, for there is not a man . . . who at the present day can repeat or even name the Greek alphabet."[22] President Haygood quickly decided that Scomp was not the man for the modern languages. The teaching of German and French did not start until the 1880's.

The special friendships with Hopkins, Callaway, and Stone, and the rationing of his time because he was financial agent and afterward the editor of a church paper, meant that President Haygood had little contact with the remainder of the faculty. They were John F. Bonnell; the emeritus professor Dr. Alexander Means; and the teacher of the college preparatory students resident in Oxford, young Rufus Smith. When Smith left to become a professor in a Methodist school in Dalton, in 1879, Haygood initiated a "Sub-Freshman Department," henceforth to be considered part of the college, hiring Lundy H. Harris, a recent graduate who had been for a year his assistant in editing the *Wesleyan Christian Advocate* in Macon.[23] Dr. Means was something of a bother. He considered himself the guardian of the "scientific apparatus" and the mineralogical collection (the latter still boxed up from 1861-1862 and hence unused); Dr. Means had purchased most of the college's property in this area, some of it during the 1840's. John F. Bonnell was the science professor. At the time he was an inexperienced teacher but his background included study at Harvard. Usually he heard recitations from the textbooks, whether the subject was geology, chemistry, or physics.

There was as yet no formal study of biology at Emory, a matter of some security to Dr. Haygood in 1878, when the zoology professor at Vanderbilt, Alexander Winchell, outraged the Methodist preachers on the faculty and Board by refusing to resign after writing an article which accepted the evolutionary hypothesis of human development. Haygood approved of the action of Vanderbilt in abolishing the chair of zoology since Winchell would not resign. He wrote: "The relation . . . was first of all a business relation. . . . Circumstances occurred to lessen his worth, . . . that our Northern critics are quite competent to appreciate."[24] Science and religion were to be happily mated in Oxford for at least thirty more years. The feeble Dr. Means once preached at chapel on the theme of "Electricity, the Vice-gerent of the Almighty."[25]

The only extraordinary aspects of the curriculum of a thoroughly denominational college was a Chair of Vocal Music, created by vote of the Trustees on the recommendation of Haygood in July 1876, especially for his friend of five years, R. M. McIntosh. McIntosh arrived during the spring term of 1877 in time to teach a singing class well enough to perform at commencement; and musical programs featuring vocal soloists, instrumental music, and ensemble singing directed by him were favorites with the commencement audiences for nearly twenty years thereafter. Bishop Pierce agreed to the innovation partly because McIntosh had begun to teach at Emory's rival, Vanderbilt, and because the emphasis in the classes was in learning to read *hymns* by note. McIntosh discarded, while at Oxford, the shaped-note method and developed one of his own in which the students sang numbers to indicate scale relationships. He continued to write songs and edit songbooks, and in 1887 had published by J. W. Burke & Company of Macon his singing method.[26] As a truly secular spirit, McIntosh was a fresh addition to the closed Oxford society. While he became in the 1880's an outstanding conference layman, on the other hand he encouraged Atticus in his increasingly evident abandonment of the manner and mentality of the preacher. The Haygoods had reason to be indebted to the music professor: he taught both Wilbur and Mamie to sing exceedingly well, and Wilbur became an accomplished pianist.[27]

As president, and as professor of mental and moral philosophy, and further, as his denomination's outgoing Sunday school secretary, Haygood brought to Oxford a determination that the Bible should be the center of Emory's curricular studies. He was acutely aware of the decline of literacy in Southern Methodism in men of his own generation and of the need for teaching Emory graduates a theistic philosophy of life. As a preacher, moreover, intent on proving Bishop Pierce's thesis that ministerial students need not be cooped up in a seminary, he was aware of the necessity for the preservation of the Arminian heritage of Wesleyans. It would serve the Baptist students as well as the Methodists to believe in an overriding Providence in the affairs of history, a world-plan which nevertheless did not predetermine human decision or relieve the educated individual from the duty of developing "moral sensibilities."

After the first year Haygood realized that he must limit his teaching to the series of lectures for the seniors, on "Evidences of Christianity." He gave these weekly in his home, and it is significant that after 1882 he restricted the lectures apparently to those who would take them seriously, the pre-theological students.

Nevertheless, the serious lay students believed that no one anywhere could be more profound than the beloved Dr. Haygood, and the school paper said, in 1881, that his lectures "Can't be surpassed . . . North or South" and ought to be published.[28] Ironically, the lectures had by then come to be taken somewhat less than seriously by the rapidly changing president, who had written them originally in an effort to convince himself of the truths he so eloquently taught others.

President Haygood suffered, in a sense, because of his wide reading. He had read, or read about, the spectrum of thought from Spinoza to Goethe, from Lucretius to Spencer. He also read, primarily in periodicals, about the new biology, about physiology, and mechanics. The fact that he was afraid of the challenge of Darwinism indicates that he recognized the premises and possible validity of the arguments. He must have known that his Paleyesque argument that the "design" of the universe posited a carpenter-God was antiquated. He had a prophetic insight into what the inferences from Darwinian materialism would do to Protestant teaching about the "soul." The sphere of Grace was now shadowed by a sphere of Nature which was governed by Chance, by demons. Could the Providence which governed Biblical events continue to hold the leash on a dynamic natural history?

While beginning his lectures on evidences of Christianity with delineations of pantheism, materialism, and agnosticism, in that order, he concentrated in the final sessions mostly in warnings to the students to be on their guard against the insidious adoption unawares of atheistic ideas. The fascinated, alarmed, secretly delighted students sat silently by as the bearded professor warmed to his warnings. They would not have dared to challenge, even had they been sophisticated enough to do so. Tragically, there was no one in his church, in his section, with whom he could dialogue. He had been "playing the pope" so long writing the exegeses for the *Sunday-School Magazine* that only occasionally did he sense the need for a censor, a moderator, a devil's advocate outside. Unchecked he switched arguments bewilderingly, appealing to history, the authority of ministerial tradition, personal observations, indulging in flights of logic and sentimentality, all in an indiscriminate amalgam.[29] To the students, of course, the chaos was unnoticed; Dr. Haygood's lectures were far superior to any sermons they had ever heard.

No one outside knew that a new seriousness came to the campus of Emory College by 1879 or 1880, derived partly from the intellectuality of the president and from the esteem in which the students held Dr. Haygood. The lay Trustees learned, through a report by Alfred H. Colquitt and John J. Floyd of Covington only that there was a determination to teach modern languages, a change the two approved, remembering with pain their own recitations. The benefit of Greek and Latin, their report said, was "in the refinement of taste, rather than in more solid results." Since it took "little reflection to see how small a part of education founded in college . . . passes down . . . into the future . . . life," Colquitt and Floyd advocated further that a special curriculum leading to a bachelor of science degree was desirable; students in such a course would be excused from the study of both ancient languages. The report, made in 1880, showed some ignorance of the fact that Emory had given a number of B. S. degrees since the Civil War and complete unawareness of the fact that Haygood in four years had so de-emphasized the special course that the B. S. was practically non-existent.[30]

It is not easy to state the effect of residence at Emory between 1876 and 1880 on the lives of young Georgians, Alabamians, and Floridians attending, since many of their values had been determined before arrival. The difficulty of assessing Haygood's influence is complicated by the fact that few students had an uninterrupted course of study with its cumulative effects. There seems enough evidence nevertheless for some analysis. Most of Emory's first-year drop-outs were sons of Emory Trustees and of Hancock County planters, the friends of Bishop Pierce. Emory College in the late 1870's obviously did not provide a congenial atmosphere for the casual seeker after the prestige of its diploma, in a manner more common before the war. The scarcity of money and the increasing presence of marginal-subsistence students, (courtesy of Dr. Haygood's co-operative boarding houses) undoubtedly contributed to a barebones vocational evaluation of a college education.

The tracking of the professional choices of the five classes, 1876-1880, leads to the same conclusions about the influence of Emory, and inferentially of its president. There is a notable proportion of future public school men, these outnumbering the preachers produced. Haygood was during this time an active member of the Georgia Teachers' Association, being president one year. There is, moreover, a trend toward the choice of the law, the Class of 1880, an especially ambitious and well organized group of twenty-odd students, having the highest proportion. The same class produced two men who became outstanding in their states (Georgia and Alabama) in public school work.[31]

Another area of influence by Haygood was in the teaching of discipline. There was undoubtedly an enormous improvement of behavior over that during the five years of O. L. Smith's presidency, and the excesses of the lackadaisical students of the 1850's were clearly reduced. In the early 1870's the rules were evaded, even the longstanding requirement of compulsory chapel and church attendance. Students were excused from classes "to witness some importance cases" in court, and until Haygood came a midspring vacation was allowed for anyone interested in attending the stockholders' meeting of the Georgia Railroad. After 1876 the boys were more willing to go to chapel, since they liked to hear Dr. Haygood preach. The main factor in producing adherence to the rules was the President's institution of a demerit system which, to the literal mind of adolescents, was "objective" and did not reduce their affection for Haygood. Five demerits were recorded for missing any class, chapel program, or church service, and two for being tardy. A student with seventy-five demerits before the term ended would be expelled, unless mercy was shown. The system worked so well that Haygood had to expel only a few students.[32]

This was not a regime of fear. Haygood had established respect for himself, which was not reduced by his great cordiality—both qualities being absent heretofore. The boys had frequently bedeviled Smith by forming a military column in front of the President's residence, armed with pots and pans, challenging a show of authority. Smith would run out and chase the "column" until it disintegrated far down the road in paroxysms of laughter. Smith did not know what to do even with the boys whose faces he saw; there were too many. When in the spring term of 1876 the trick was tried on Haygood in front of the new President's home, he marched out, armed himself with a washpan and a tin kitchen spoon, and calmly established himself at the head of the procession, asking as he marched away, "Why don't you come on, boys?" One of the chagrined students recovered voice enough to object that "It's not any fun unless you object."[33]

The new respect, and the threat of "0 to 150 demerits" for "Entering into combinations to violate College order" had a quieting effect. The townspeople complained that the students still fired off pistols at night, but Haygood insisted that most of the noise came from local boys who were trying to get their rivals in college in trouble. After 1880 the fraternities, which had caused

.. *Emory College*

so much of the ruckus until 1857, were revived, but were directed primarily to adding to the social life of the commencement week.[34] It must be observed that the greater seriousness of the student body was matched by a reduced revivalistic spirit. After all, Haygood had early in his career turned his back on manufactured unctuousness in the pulpit. There would never be, in his presidency, anything like the orgy of the revival in the spring of 1858. In this determination he remembered the effective words and example of Lovick Pierce.

Despite the restrictions on out-of-bound pranks, there returned to the life of the college some of the playful and inventive atmosphere which had begun to develop up until 1871, when O. L. Smith's administration began. Until that time the Emory boys had organized a baseball team which traveled as far as Augusta; in fact, Atticus's brother Willie had been on the first team.[35] Athletics of the impromptu variety were much in evidence after 1876, although the "town ball" contests were now intramural and restricted to Oxford. In 1880 the school acquired a vacant house which was named the "gymnasium," but it was not until the 1890's that real supervision of physical recreation was inaugurated. The main extracurricular activity was, between 1876 and 1880, what it had been in the 1850's—debating in and between the two literary societies. Phi Gamma and Few. Both groups made special effort to attract Covingtonians to their special debates, and Few began to hold a mid-year "anniversary." Both societies of course still provided the arena for preparation of commencement speeches.

The flavor of postwar rhetoric is shown in the speech given to the Few Society in 1879 by the preacher-father of one of the officers:

Five years ago, when the Civil Rights Bill hung like a cloud upon the horizon of politics, it was a Georgian, an Emory Alumnus, and a Few [Lucius Q. C. Lamar] who . . . held it up before the country in all its hideous deformity, and exposed it . . . as a vile and loathsome resort of a ruined and bankrupt party.[36]

The speaker was unknowing of the fact that Senator Lamar had helped to establish the important liaison in Congress between the Southern Confederate Democrats and business-minded Northern Republicans.

Atticus was a good president because he was young—in absence of dignity younger than he had been at seventeen—and showed an interest in the students' whole round of activities. Also he made obvious efforts to make it possible for any deserving Georgia or Florida boy of Methodist connections to get a college education at Emory. A visitor from Nashville in 1879 considered this concern Emory's outstanding feature:

> The College has scarcely any endowment and yet it educates about one-third of its students free. By rule, the sons of all preachers (and there are many), and two sons of laymen from each presiding elder's district in the three patronizing Conferences, are admitted free. Besides these, the President and Faculty are active in providing especially for others unable to pay their way, and, if all other arrangements fail, they divide the expenses among themselves. No student has ever been turned away or denied admission . . . for the want of money.[37]

In 1876 Haygood rented a house, later paid for, and after careful screening—to avoid any kind of trouble since no adult would live within—he converted the house into a "Helping Hall," a co-operative dormitory or "mess," in which the boarding cost was limited to $10 a month. In 1878 he began to keep boys in the President's home under the same plan, with the cost of board reduced because the boarders helped in the kitchen and garden. A second hall, unsupervised except for a boy manager, was secured in 1879, there being eventually five including his own home. It was well known on the campus that the costs of the messes were such that Dr. Haygood had to subsidize out of his meager salary in order to keep the price per resident down to $10 a month. In the early 1880's he bought coal for all the halls in one order. Other students continued to live with old-time residents of Oxford, notably the faculty, but in the democratic regime established by the son of Greene Haygood (who had moved from Clarke County to Atlanta in order to teach his children to care for themselves), those who paid up to $20 a month for board were placed in the position, almost, of having to apologize for their luxuries. Haygood helped along this inverse snobbery by publicly protesting that *all* of the remaining discipline problems came from the minority who had "pocket-money."[38]

It would seem at first inconsistent with his policies that the president asked from the Trustees, and had approved, a raising of the matriculation fee from $1 to $5 and an increase in tuition to $60 a year, $35 of this being for the longer spring term which began in January. He believed, though, that a higher matriculation fee would discourage students from coming to Emory to see how they liked it and to please their fathers, such students causing much of the trouble. The tuition increase was slight—and in the emergency atmosphere of the 1870's it was known that payment would be accepted at the end of the term, or when cotton money came in in the fall, or never. Dr. Haygood felt justified in these changes when, during 1878-1879, there were about 140 college students, a number considerably strengthened the next year with the inclusion of the college preparatory in the enrollment as "Sub-Fresh." But with a movement begun to eliminate tuition costs at the state University in Athens, Haygood knew that Emory's income problem had still no prospect of being completely solved.[39] Certainly he remembered his collaboration with the bishop's wishes in 1874-1875 and wondered whether denominational pride was worth the price of its maintenance.

A strong-willed man like the energetic doctor was free to control Emory College as he saw fit—so long as Bishop Pierce had confidence in him. The president was accountable to the Trustees, but their knowledge of the campus was indirect, and the records of their meetings during the four or five days of the commencement season in July show the limited degree of their concern. Their main business during their meetings, which were sandwiched in between the public functions of a hot and exhausting schedule, was to pass on the seniors' degrees, approve M. A. degrees for outstanding graduates of three years before, decide which ambitious preachers should receive the coveted doctor of divinity distinction, approved automatically any new plan for a financial agent to gather the uncollected notes, and make a hasty inspection of the six buildings, some of which were not even unlocked.

The Board was divided between the outstanding preachers and the affluent or influential laymen, chosen in the hope that they would increase the endowment and/or patronage of the school. The lay Trustees dominated deliberation only during the financial discussions, such as decisions about whether to retain the bonds of the Memphis and Charleston Railroad upon maturation. The preachers, all presiding-elder types, thought of the school primarily as a training ground for future presiding elders—especially since the Pierce-McTyeire controversy of 1872.

During the 1870's four ante-bellum preachers, Uncle Billy Parks, Josiah Lewis, E. H. Myers, and O. L. Smith, died, to be replaced by Clement Evans, the Confederate general; Haygood; and Charles E. Dowman, a Floridian born in England who would be president of Emory after 1898. In 1871 the leading lay Trustees were John Floyd of Covington, Dr. Henry Gaither of Oxford, and

T. M. Meriwether of Newton County; John J. Jones of Waynesboro and W. H. Goodrich of Augusta; James Jackson of Macon (until he moved to Atlanta to become a judge on the state supreme court); the Bourbon J. I. Wright of Rome; and E. E. Rawson and Governor Colquitt, residents of Atlanta. In the early 1870's J. S. Stewart of Oxford, and politicians Hiram Bell, Warren Akin, and Judge E. H. Pottle replaced older men, there being several resignations during the depression. Between 1875 and 1880 E. E. Rawson resigned, his brother W. A. Rawson taking his place and proving a gem of a Trustee, since he gave generously to Emory. The Rawsons were in-laws of Haygood's sister, Myra Boynton of Atlanta. Some of the lay Trustees (Jones, Stewart, Jackson) were alumni; others (the Rawsons, Bell, Akin, Goodrich) were not.

They were all men of statewide reputation. Jones, of a famous Burke County family, had married the niece of Robert Toombs and served in the United States Congress in the 1850's. Bell was a Congressman from the mountainous Ninth District, losing his seat in 1880. Governor Colquitt had served a Congressional term in the mid-1850's. As a lay preacher and devout Methodist layman who outlawed gambling and horse-racing at the Georgia State Fair, Governor Colquitt was to the young President of Emory the ideal Trustee even if he did nothing except adorn the Board.[40]

Undoubtedly a majority of the lay Trustees served on the Board for the prestige it gave them, especially at commencement time. Such prestige, observable in the context of a social event which attracted hundreds of people, was of obvious political benefit. From Haygood's point of view, the standing of the Trustees was a factor in the acceptance of an invitation to be a commencement speaker, whether those invited were state politicians or out-of-state preachers. In general the success of the commencement was gauged by the importance of the speakers. By this standard 1879 was a poor year, the Address to the Alumni being delivered by a gentleman named Henry Perry of Gainesville, who "gave some pretty hard hits at the innovations of modern times and the good old way of our fathers in running colleges . . . for nearly two hours."[41] Disappointment was especially felt since the year before the chief speaker was Henry W. Grady, brilliant writer and editor of the *Atlanta Constitution,* who chose the rostrum of the old church in Oxford and the Emory commencement as the occasion for his last public appearance on the commencement circuit (he refused his Alma Mater, the University, in 1879). Haygood was excited and somewhat fearful as he introduced Grady, warning him that he should feel "no legitimate cause of discouragement if . . . certain ill-bred fellows . . . should get up and walk out," since that was likely to happen for any controversial speaker. Grady beamed knowingly, got up, and launched forth on a non-controversial subject. After wiping his perspiring forehead, he deposited his handkerchief on the pulpit and spoke for two hours on the importance of the pursuit of happiness: "I know that life is good."[42]

Despite the occasional appearance of men like Grady, Emory commencements were still marked in memory by the addresses and sermons of Methodist ministers. The rise of Nashville as a center of the church had not diminished Georgia Methodists' belief that Oxford was the shrine of Southern Methodism. Dr. Haygood was thus reassured of the drawing-power of the old pulpit in the town church when for his first commencement the chief speaker was Alpheus Wilson, a Baltimore minister slated for certain election as a bishop. Wilson used the platform to give an "overwhelming refutation of infidelity and an utter confutation of infidels."[43] In 1878 Grady's glamor had to be shared with Young J. Allen, missionary to China, who returned to the United States for the first time in nearly twenty years. His dramatic appearance had such an effect on three sophomores that they decided they would also be Chinese missionaries. Dr. Haygood was puzzled at his failure to be excited by his former idol, the cause of *his* missionary zeal and his decision to be a preacher, and he began more openly an appraisal of his life, an activity already begun since he was nearing the mid-mark of forty years.[44]

Eighteen Seventy-Nine was an off year at Emory commencement. The banality of Mr. Perry, Esquire, was particularly oppressive since Bishop McTyeire had to cancel his appearance as baccalaureate preacher at the last moment (Haygood sat up all night writing a sermon for the occasion). The new additions of wings and an enlarged choir area (for McIntosh's concert and for the seating of dignitaries), a project completed by the collaboration of the president and J. S. Stewart, kept the July event from being entirely a disappointment.[45]

The 1880 commencement redeemed the tradition. Emory College's enrollment had increased so that the number of graduates— over twenty—was once again impressive. With the prospect of momentous choices ahead in state and national election campaigns, Dr. Haygood sensed also that 1880 was a watershed in his career as president, and since he was forty, in his own life. He was elated with the graduation of three boys whose education he had personally subsidized, the three boys who two years before had given their lives to their Lord for use in the Chinese mission field. It was as though he, Atticus Haygood, was discharged through their decisions from any further obligation to Young Allen and Young Allen's example. Dr. Haygood spoke twice at the commencement, giving besides the president's address after the delivery of the diplomas, the baccalaureate sermon. For the sermon, he returned to the theme of his lectures to the seniors, reminding the graduates that they were "going out into a world whose very air is tainted with unbelief." They could not avoid reading and hearing "all sorts of theories of the universe, of man, and of God, in place of the grand old gospel which you first learned at your mother's knee." If they had recall of his lectures, however, they would be safe; be reminded, he said, that "Our mistakes and misconceptions ... are due not to our science ... but to the lack of the indwelling Spirit."[46]

On Wednesday morning he listened with unwonted involvement to the speeches of the best seniors. On the program beside the title of the speech of his favorite he wrote: "Ressonating voice hansome man will exemplify the doctrine he teaches."[47] After delivering the diplomas, he gave his own speech, as outside above the oaks "A bluer sky never over-hung Middle Georgia." Since the President was not expected to give a major speech, the audience's mind wandered in anticipation of the conventional old-time oratory of Augustus O. Bacon that afternoon. But the words of Atticus Greene Haygood were worth listening to; he was exhorting the South to put behind it its bitter 1870's, its tragic 1860's, its poorly remembered 1850's:

We do the illustrious dead no dishonor to look forward. . . . I protest . . . against the pessimistic folly of the whole race of cowards and croakers, . . . forever harping over what they call the ruin of the South. . . . I wish to say, deliberately and emphatically, the South of to-day has excellencies of character that were impossible to her twenty years ago . . ., the cotton-crop, made with free labor, in 1879, was never equalled in the history of our people.

Of all people, in the civilized world, we of the South have the least reason to lament the overthrow of slavery. I, for one, do not lament it. . . .what the new South needs, is not so much money, or manufactures, or commerce, or political power, but whole-hearted men and women. . . . *The War is over.* . . . It becomes our duty, no less than

.. *Emory College* 109

our interest, to take an intelligent and active part in the general government.... Intense and over-done sectionalism defeats itself....

Young gentlemen, the man who puts allegiance to party above allegiance to country, cannot be a true patriot.[48]

The significance of his words, and of a changing direction of his life, he himself could not fully sense. In the next few months he would understand his mission in part. Within the next three years or four he would know all. Providence had given him the mantles of several men. One was that of Lovick Pierce; on Sunday afternoon he had preached in the place of the dear old crotchety doctor, who had given the afternoon sermon after the baccalaureate for decades until his death in 1879. In this hallowed tradition Atticus consciously tried to keep alive the doctrinal interests of the preacher-giant. Haygood preached in July 1880 on the distinction between the "new man" and the "inner man," as a first step in the direction of challenging the "second blessing" doctrines for the first time being preached in Methodist pulpits in North Georgia, as close by as Eatonton.

The speech to the seniors about the requirements and responsibilities of idealists in a "new South" was a new voice for Haygood; the mantle was that of the "great editor," the voice that of the editorial exhorter. The voice was an evangelical echo of Grady's, and he had found it while writing the weekly column of the *Wesleyan Christian Advocate*, which in two years had come to sound more and more like the editorial columns of the *Atlanta Constitution*. The spring of words with which he spoke at commencement had yet a greater meaning. Self-anointing, Atticus Haygood was that summer declaring himself a man. He would thereafter be his own kind of Southern Methodist preacher. No more would he be the agency for fulfilling the wishes of the Bishop of Georgia Methodists, that croaking old George Pierce, the Bourbon of the decayed Hancock County gentry, the semi-literate autocrat—and the symbolic figure in a slave society which Haygood now counted good riddance. The "new man" in Dr. Haygood accepted wholly the egalitarian prejudices of his father and the optimistic nationalism of his grandmother. He looked forward to the progress of a classless South, led by an aristocracy of the ethical, a section which would resume its role in the purification of American society begun a century before by the public men of 1776.

SEVEN

The Editorialist and the *Advocates*

FROM THE SUMMER of 1880 on, Dr. Haygood's exuberant self-confidence marked him as an extraordinary man. It is true that the mood of many Georgians in 1880 was exuberant—a reflection of the new market strength of cotton. But those who had known Dr. Haygood since he was a boy sensed within him a new poise and a new strength. Major credit for this transformation was obviously to be attributed to his successful management of Emory College through the difficult years before 1879 and his own awareness that he had done a great deal already to save Emory, the charge given him by Bishop Pierce in 1875. Fewer people knew how rewarding were his two other major roles: "head of household" for the Haygood and Yarbrough families, and editorial tribune for both the *Southern Christian Advocate* and the *Wesleyan Christian Advocate,* the latter a successor to the former for Georgia and Florida Methodists. It is to be remembered here that in 1861 young Atticus had declared that "a great editor is a very great man."

From the time Dr. Haygood took the presidency of Emory, beginning with the spring term of 1876, the office had great bearing on the speed and completeness of his maturing. It allowed him a means to grow free from Bishop Pierce's influence, his debt to the bishop for past favors being more than repaid by the administration of Emory. In his own mind, moreover, the fatherly relationship he had with the students, especially those to whom he gave money out of his pocket, ended completely his thinking of himself primarily as "the son of Greene Haygood." The difficulty of this achievement in a society still remarkably patriarchal was eased by further solicitousness toward young men such as Warren Candler and Lundy Harris. Not least important was the prestige in the town of Oxford which being president gave him. He was the admired object of the "howdying throng" at the post office, where Mrs. Mary Henderson presided, and in the aisles of the general stores—Brantley's, Harwell's, and Branham's.[1] As an employer of the college janitor and cooks for the helping halls (and as the son-in-law of their preacher, John Yarbrough), he enjoyed a connection with the Negro populace of the town analogous to that of a slave-holding aristocrat twenty years before.

The late 1870's reordered his family life. He was the loving master of his own house, of Mollie and the four children. Living in Oxford once again made Mollie so healthy that when Bishop McTyeire saw her in 1878 (having last seen her that dreadful autumn of 1874 in Nashville), "she was fixed up so fine, & so improved in health" that "She had to introduce herself!"[2] Her father died in 1879, and she was reduced to her normal state of poor health thereafter; but for approximately four years of her middle thirties, she was a warm, happy woman.

In patriarchal fashion, Papa had his family favorites, preferring the young son, his namesake, to Wilbur, and becoming almost the soul-mate of the older daughter Mamie. (There is a striking parallel here with Greene's attitude toward his family, for Greene preferred the healthy younger son, Willie; and his favorite daughter, Laura, was in stature and solidity a copy of her father.) On her ninth birthday, during his second year as president, Atticus gave Mamie a saddled pony, and thereafter allowed her to ride with him during his late afternoon constitutional.

In the years when Mollie was healthy, the whole family camped out for days at Snapping Shoals in the southwestern part of the county, during the summer vacation, and Atticus passed on to Mamie some of the woodlore that Uncle Jim had so expertly given him. The main activity of the camp-outs was fishing, which was almost a fanatical solace to the president's wife. After she decided that she could not tolerate tramping through the underbrush any longer, her loving husband built her a fishing pond behind the president's house, by damming up a small stream. This was the first of several ponds he built for her thereafter, though the expense was a severe drain on their meager purse. Dr. Haygood was almost as fond of fishing as Mollie, but did most of his alone or with a single faculty member, in Haynes Creek in Oxford, or in the Yellow River three miles away.[3]

There is indirect evidence only about Haygood's preference for his younger son. Atticus Greene Haygood, Jr., inherited, or learned, his father's skills with tools, knife, hammer, and axe, and, like his father, found joy in manual accomplishment. He was somewhat like his father in appearance, but he was much quieter, and had dark, somewhat expressionless eyes. His father, in contrast, had a facial expression, even behind his glasses, that was dynamic almost to the point of nervousness. Wilbur, whose middle name was the same as Mollie's—Fletcher—was his mother's boy. He entered the preparatory classes of Rufus Smith in 1875 when he was eleven and was prematurely pushed up to the freshman college class when he was thirteen. Wilbur rewarded his father for his determination to have a scholar by specializing in failure. He became proud of his mischievous accomplishments: in his first college year he had more demerits for being late than anyone else. He was a freshman for three years. His later failure to become a sedate Georgia Methodist Layman, and the circumstance of his marriage, suggest that insofar as possible in the climate of Oxford Wilbur became in his adolescent years addicted to the sensual pleasures, perhaps taking his father's disapproval as a mask for envy. But Atticus could be proud of Wilbur's musical attainments, as pianist, harmonium player, and singer.[4]

The Haygood family circle was not limited to the children, Mollie, and Atticus. Atticus assumed a protective role toward Mollie's sisters, especially after the death of John Yarbrough. One was married to Dr. W. W. Evans, who became the college physician. A younger, unmarried sister, who eventually became a preacher's wife, had to be housed. The Yarbrough home was only four blocks away, and Mollie spent much time with her sisters, especially after her residence and kitchen were made communal in 1878, as a "helping hall." In the early 1890's there was some Yarbrough visiting when the Haygoods moved three thousand miles away to California; Dr. Haygood apparently accepted his obligation to his wife's sisters quite cheerfully. There was less need for his care within the Haygood family. Laura, living with their mother, became principal of the new girls' high school in Atlanta. Willie was a successful young businessman, and Myra had married into an affluent family.[5]

The self-assurance given to him by his success in his roles as responsible family man and college president was more than matched by his pride in his career as a journalist. Between October 1875 and the end of May 1878 he was the editorial correspondent of the *Southern Christian Advocate,* and after June of 1878 he was for four years the editor of the *Wesleyan Christian Advocate.* The two offices allowed him a visible control over public opinion, the kind of "exhorting" which had delighted him since at least 1861, when he wrote for the *Educational Repository*. More important, being his own boss as to subject matter and tone of expression in the editorial columns allowed him a necessary Dionysian outlet for his inner self, the "shadow" of the outwardly proper Southern Methodist preacher.

His language in most of these columns, which he wrote rapidly at night and seldom corrected, was a tongue alien to his ordinary daytime conversation. When the occasion required, however, his written expression could be and was carefully disciplined. His early books and his articles for Northern periodicals, for critical Northern eyes, have not the least hint of abandon. The same is true for his sermons, for which he wrote outlines and key sentences. His contemporaries noted his self-discipline in the pulpit. As he grew older, Dr. Haygood became less and less "unctuous" in the pulpit. He always started off in a low key. However, his intensity nearly always got the best of him and he frequently reached unplanned climaxes, during which his musical baritone voice fairly thundered—a characteristic which appealed to students. Nevertheless, his homiletical ideal was to maintain control. It was derived from his admiration of Bishop Pierce when the bishop was young, impressive, and dignified. Later Bishop McTyeire replaced Pierce as Haygood's model until Haygood heard Henry Ward Beecher in 1881. A statement about the desirability of self-control was fittingly worked into the sermon President Haygood preached at the 1879 baccalaureate service at Emory in lieu of Bishop McTyeire:

> In this way we reached the idea that the will measures a man's power. And the common sentiment is right. It is *will*—& not merely knowledge, or opinions, or emotion, or desire that makes the difference between men; it is will. . . . The doctrine of the text . . . is about this: Its highest exercise is in self-control; its supremest triumph in self-conquest.[6]

Though Haygood preached self-control and restraint, he did not practice them in his writing. Although his addiction for straightforward sentences and "Anglo-Saxon" words makes his written prose easy to understand, his preferred style must be considered "undisciplined." He enjoyed his extensive personal correspondence; and both in volume and lack of restraint he was truly a "promiscuous" nighttime letter writer. His long letters betray haste and excitement; he contracted words, misspelled others, and reduced his sentences to phrases separated from each other by dashes. Clearly he thought of his editorials in the *Advocate* as letters to Methodists. There is in them the same evidence of haste, lack of restraint, and helter-skelter organization. He without hesitation leapt into irrelevant reminiscence. Those meeting the mild-mannered amiable Georgian in person must not have recognized him as the same man who in his writings was strident, often petty, and even for the age embarrassingly sentimental. As he grew older, his bifurcation of language became less pronounced: his sermons, articles, and books became more like his letters and his editorials. He lost the capacity for tight organization. It was as though a demon had established himself in Haygood's study, separated by a narrow porch from the main building of the President's home. Since he wrote everything in the same room, it was easy for the demon's voice to dominate whatever he wrote.

The letters to the *Southern Christian Advocate* began in 1862 when he wrote about the revivals on the Watkinsville circuit. During 1864 he sent accounts of his travels and duties as a missionary chaplain; and after 1868 he wrote "Letters from the Country," which were begun when he was presiding elder of the Rome District. These sharp criticisms of the failings of loyalty of Georgia Methodists significantly were written by "John Tryon." The desire for relative anonymity suggests the development of the demonic personality. During the winter of 1875 in his articles destroying hope for the Reverend Clark's university plan, he wrote under his own name, but then as the agent for the bishop. Even though disciplined to a degree, he wrote with the kind of "racy" language (a favorite adjective of the day) which would mark his columns later, contrasting markedly with the dull pietistic prose previously characteristic of the *Southern*. It is not surprising that after his resignation as Sunday school secretary was announced in September 1875, F. M. Kennedy, editor of the *Southern*, invited him to be a regular weekly columnist, his name appearing on the masthead in October, with billing equaling that of Kennedy and John W. Burke—his family's old friend—who was assistant editor and printer of the journal. A consideration, besides his uniquely zestful style, was the fact that he was a Georgian. Kennedy as a South Carolinian felt somewhat alien in Macon.[7]

Haygood's columns were by far the liveliest part of the *Southern* until it returned to South Carolina by permission of the General Conference held in Atlanta in 1878. Burke wrote on the back page about books which preachers should buy, and terse accounts of places he had gone and people he had seen. Kennedy's editorials were seldom concerned with social matters; once he referred gingerly to "the alienation of the confidence of the colored people with the white Churches of the South."[8] In comparison, the Emory president's language was almost scandalous; he made sarcastic comments about the minor idiocies of Northern Methodist editors in discussing the South, indicated his political support of Governor Colquitt, and condemned the un-Methodist aspects of behavior of laymen as recklessly as an exhorter of a class of Emory students in the 1850's. The only restraint visible was in his reviewing of new books.

In 1878 the South Carolinians, who perhaps found Haygood's articles less appealing than did the more homespun Georgia and Florida Methodists, demanded the return of the *Advocate;* it had been a "temporary" refugee in Georgia (first in Augusta, then in Macon), since 1862. But the three Georgia and Florida conferences had become so used to an *Advocate* in Macon that the bishops agreed to a successor. Haygood was the obvious choice for editor, and it was he who chose the title of *Wesleyan Christian Advocate* (rather than *Georgia-Florida*) since this name "will help to delocalize us."[9]

After 1878 the Nashville *Advocate* became the official organ of all the conferences, with only the *New Orleans Advocate,* because of its age and wide influence in the lower South, rivaling it in any official sense. The *Southern* lost influence by becoming purely a South Carolina paper. Haygood's writing ability and the social relevance of his columns made the *Wesleyan* prominent from the beginning and possibly the Southern Methodist periodical most read by Northern Methodist editors.

The *Wesleyan* was modeled consciously on the style of the daily newspaper; from the beginning Haygood used a "Page One" for each issue, rather than copying the *Southern's* continuous pagination throughout the year. Haygood encouraged polemical correspondence and announced that he was happy that the epistolaries were "fast losing their sensitiveness to Editorial criticism."[10] Controversy reached its peak during 1880 over whether the public schools were a menace or a blessing to Georgia. One of the more frequent contributors from 1878 to 1882 was Weyman H. Potter, who signed his articles "***" and became Haygood's successor, from 1882 to 1890. He continued the policy of forthright editorial pronouncements which included political matters within their scope. After 1890 the *Wesleyan* ceased to recognize the existence of the great contemporary issues involving Southern society; that is, the *Wesleyan* thereafter was indistinguishable from a dozen other badly written, monotonous conference journals which catalogued church meetings.[11]

Paradoxically, despite his bravado of style and subject, Atticus Haygood's editorials between 1875 and 1880 mark him from the viewpoint of church society as a conservative in the manner of Bishop Pierce—he was, of course, until 1880 not truly an independent agent. Editor Haygood continued to express his preference for the atmosphere of the rural church and his distaste for town airs. Like Bishop Pierce, he bemoaned the loss of the habit of obedience and deference formerly given the clergy by loyal members of the sects in the South. This loyalty had not depended on the observance of a strict code of behavior, for the Methodists had made considerable compromises with the life of the plantation South. Both Bishop Pierce and Haygood smoked, and Bishop Pierce came from a county where syllabub was enjoyed at Christmas. Haygood's medicine cabinet contained a bottle of "bitters," and this was not an unusual circumstance—until the 1880's.

Nevertheless, since lay loyalty in the towns seemed to Haygood not to be the total involvement which the Wesleyan tradition sought, he apparently accepted as a best substitute for loyalty an emphasis on behavior. He thus editorially chided Methodists for not observing the Sabbath, for carrying pistols, and for attending theatricals. He clearly opposed the growing prominence of women in the church, probably believing this to be a factor in the loss of interest on the part of the men. He wrote sarcastically about a missionary meeting at Salem campground where "The sisters" arranged for an address, "and it was long enough. . . . There was not a man present. . . . But the sisters reported harmony, zeal, unction, enlightened interest—progress."[12]

The same year, 1878, he praised the Atlanta General Conference for "its splendid conservatism and its almost monotonous 'non-concurrence' in propositions to change the polity of our Church."[13] There is a possibility of sarcasm here, given his later open objection to a strong episcopacy. About the same time he ridiculed a proposal to democratize the church by allowing preachers to elect their presiding elders and district conferences to set the bounds of the circuits. As an amendment in the spirit of the suggestion he mockingly proposed that "The Church Conference . . . select their preacher, determine his text, and the length of his sermons."[14] Editor Haygood did have some perspective on his conservatism, admitting that "our fathers were not perfect," and confessing to imagining them with a "sort of halo . . . as the artists painted about the head of saints."¹⁵

At no point was he closer in concurrence with Bishop Pierce's conservatism than in his contempt and disrespect for most of Northern Methodism and its works. In 1875 he wrote that "the Methodist Episcopal Church has esophagal capacity for every emergency. We saw a snake once in the act of swallowing a live and kicking frog, yet strange to say the unreasonable frog did not seem to enjoy it"—this comment in reply to a proposal of "organic union" of the two episcopal Methodisms. Nothing riled him more than statements in Northern Methodist journals (principally *Zion's Herald*, of Boston; the *Western Christian Advocate* of Cincinnati; Chicago's *North-western Advocate;* and the *New York Advocate*) such as: "under the staunch . . . leadership of godly ministers [the Southern Methodists] could have created a public sentiment as would have rendered Kukluxism an impossibility"; or the statement that there were in the South "whole parishes or counties where a Protestant sermon is seldom or never heard."¹⁶

In reciprocal fraternity he in 1877 exclaimed with delight when New Hampshire failed to lift the voting restrictions against Catholics and Jews. The Georgian thundered: "Where are the champions of human liberty? Where is the North-western . . . ? . . .Let President Hayes try his 'prentice hand' on insolent New-Hampshire."¹⁷ The longest apologia for Southern Methodism and the South appeared in September 1877, in response to what he called the "Unbrotherly Sneers" of the Northern church press:

> Why did the surrender of the Southern armies . . . estop, to a large extent, the work of the Church, South, among the negroes? We answer . . . the Church . . . was pushed aside . . . by carpet-bag politicians and Northern Methodist missionaries . . . by appealing to the prejudice, the ignorance, and the fears of the . . . negroes. . . . The negroes were told that the Church, South, would attempt to re-enslave them. We affirm . . . that these white men, in the employment of the Mission Board . . . made every possible appeal . . .: incited every passion . . . calculated to alienate them from their old masters, to get them out of the Church, South, and to keep them from the Democrats.
>
> Moreover . . . hundreds of churches built and paid for by white Southern Methodists were used . . . for Union League Meetings, in which hatred of the whites was kindled into a blaze that, but for the conservative power of the pure Gospel the Southern Church gave them before the war, would have flamed into a conflagration.
>
> Last November, when it was believed that Mr. Tilden was elected President . . . Our old colored nurse, noticing the gladness of the

Democrats, said to our family, that she believed . . . the negroes would be "put back into slavery."[18]

In a rare use of the disciplined tongue, however, Haygood expressed his approval of the custom of exchanging fraternal delegates. James A. Duncan, of Randolph-Macon College, and Landon C. Garland, of Vanderbilt, were the South's delegates in 1876 to the Northerners' General Conference.[19]

In analysis of the Methodist Episcopal Church, South, Haygood was what may be described as a romantic primitive. Even though he was training himself away from a level of excitement in the pulpit, he was ready to defend the elder generation in its high valuation of love-feasts and preaching with the incandescence he associated with prewar campmeetings. Thus, in his editorializing of the 1870's he defended Dwight Moody, the archetypal postwar evangelist. The college president said that Moody was "not a learned, but . . . a well-informed man." His failure as a "profound exegete" was not disturbing since he was a "forcible expounder of the great gospel facts." His legitimacy was not hampered by his "defective and inconsistent" theology—it not being totally Arminian—for Moody's integrity was endangered only by the possibility that a "herd of imitators may spring up," that is, mere manipulators of emotion, without Moody's "divine vocation."[20] The decline of "gospel-preaching" was the result of the search for learned pretense in the pulpit. Haygood told the story of the pastor who wrote the Publishing House: "Send me another book: I've done preached through 'Five Hundred [Sermon Outlines]' and I want a new book."[21] He shared Pierce's aversion to the aristocratic mannerisms of town churches, attacking the pew doors, which he lampooned as "entrance-stoppers . . . for ladies and fat people."[22] He regretted the transferring of memberships by prominent gentlemen farmers, whom he described as "kings" in rural churches, to town churches—church loyalties following the postwar transfer of central economic interests.[23]

Haygood was a keen observer of the new campmeetings, and in this more a progressive. He approved of the physical improvements: " a new camp-ground in Heard county" had "seats . . . 'as comfortable as . . . in Oxford church.' " And in Campbell County, southwest of Atlanta, a Presbyterian named Alfred Austell had installed "a large hall [kerosene] lamp that when, by cord and pulley, he raised it to a certain height it gave light to every room in his large and well-arranged tent." Tents were houses at campgrounds, which in the old days had been quite primitive shacks.

At some places there were kerosene lamps in the arbor itself, "to make it practicable to read one of Dr. McFerrin's '72 mo. Hymn-Books."[24] Preachers like Haygood who smoked appreciated especially the custom of building washrooms near the arbor for the preachers, for prayer or nicotine consumption.

Not so favorable were Haygood's comments on the excess enthusiasm of the younger generation for the tangential values of gospel preaching at the campgrounds. Sunday meetings especially were bothered by gay young men who "made a show of their fine horses —the drivers suffering in comparison." Sometimes these " 'lewd fellows of the baser sort' " were encouraged on the strength of whiskey to overdo "the rowdy bit." As a result "splendid campground police" were necessary to maintain the evangelistic demeanor on Sundays.[25] However, the impressionable addle-pated youngsters who behaved their parents and loved campmeeting time were at times as bothersome. Haygood did not approve the

eccentric, bodily gyrations, leapings, tumblings that, to put it mildly, do not edify. . . . We saw . . . a woman jump up and down with amazing quickness and then run backward and tumble over a man who was lying on his back, kicking the floor. We saw a stout young girl . . . 'take a through' in a camp-meeting altar till she shook her high back-comb loose. Pausing an instant, she took out her comb and handed it to a friend saying: "Hold my comb while I shout."[26]

In another place after a group of young men, apparently sincerely, indicated their joy at the gospel message, a woman shouted, and "Preachers, exhorters, spectators crowded around her and they all 'had a good time' for perhaps an hour"—the young men being left to God's graces alone.[27]

Also the young people furthered the abandonment of the sedate hymns of the prewar meetings, which were sung now only by "a few old people, with quavering voices . . . in several times." As soon as they broke down a young leader sitting in the choir would show off the vitality of the young by breaking in with the first phrase of " 'Bear me away on your snowy wings,' " or some other of the fast, verbally nonsensical "gospel songs." There would resound a "rush of voices if not of wings that . . . hushes Wesley, Watts, . . . Toplady . . . for . . . half an hour." Pointedly noting the theological rubbish implied in the words to the new gospel songs, Haygood editorialized that "to be 'borne away . .' is about the last . . . thing these precious young choristers want."[28]

The habit of exhortation to live the good life, given the Arminian insistence on the absolute dependence of achievements upon the correct choice of the will, had been extended by Haygood to preaching to children even before he became Sunday school secretary. Haygood, the editorialist, in a sense both a progressive and a traditionalist, during 1875 and 1876 elaborated a "modern" statement of the Southern Methodist position on the "techniques" for leading children into the desired maturity and holiness. The result was a carefully worked-out book, entitled *Our Children,* which was so helpful and clear that it reached its third edition in 1877, a year after publication. In the main, it is a studied rebuttal of *laissez-faire* child-rearing advice and of deterministic psychologies, such as Spencer's, which de-emphasized the crucial importance of parental teachings. Haygood particularly disliked Spencer's pessimistic dictum that "the defects of children mirror the defects of parents . . ., therefore, the general practice of any ideal system is hopeless: *parents are not good enough.*"[29] To a Southern Methodist such a position was as reprehensible for its denigration of the family as for its "Calvinistic" resignation to the likelihood that not all Sunday school scholars would grow up to be loyal, moral church members. Haygood insisted that *all* individuals could be induced to reformation "through the redeeming and saving power of the Gospel" as made known by earnest exhorters.[30]

Haygood's book obviously owes much to the writing of Horace Bushnell, whose earlier importance, however, was in liberalizing the high Calvinist position on the original nature of children. Since the Southern Methodists had *started* with a belief in the unlimited range of possibility of holiness in the flesh, the importance of Haygood's statement was in increasing to the point of mortal anxiety the fear of some parents that their moral teaching had been insufficient. The "clarification" which Haygood's book afforded thus was in consonance with a denominational culture and its "logic," not with a true ground of spiritual harmony. He was confused completely for instance, in his delineation of the norm of Christian adulthood toward which the child should be directed. Sometimes maturity was spoken of in terms equivalent to the modern idea of "adjustment" to the best of secular society; less often it reflected the spirit of Wesley's General Rules with their assumption that Methodists should be a people apart. In latter-day hindsight the book is valueless because of its pedagogical nonsense, in its unexamined acceptance of the psychic value of rote-learning, of "drill."

Haygood continued to assume, as he had as Sunday school secretary, that the memorization and transmission of precepts—from exhortatory author to pastor to parent to child—would automatically result in the transformation of will. This long-held rationalist faith of the Wesleyans must have been the source of frequent parental discomfort: their children simply ignored the "truths" to which they so easily had given their verbal assent; the failure of transformation of will must have been interpreted by parents as the result of their own failure in a chain of rational communication. (Surely Atticus felt like the weak link between Greene and Wilbur.) The concern Methodist parents had because of their highly developed conscience must nevertheless have been socially valuable: Methodists responded to the kind of social criticism found in Haygood's editorials in the *Advocate* because they had been trained to feel that social imperfections were *all* the result of a lack of diligence on the part of preceptors. A moral "progressive" society would be the inevitable result of correct child-rearing.[31]

The greatest spiritual faults of the Methodist way, given as a reference point the life of Atticus Haygood, was the impossibility of ever being certain of having reached the threshold of spiritual maturity. That this was widely felt as discomfort at the time that *Our Children* appeared is shown by the phenomenal development of new interpretations of "the great doctrine of 'holiness,' 'sanctification,' 'Christian perfection' " so gradually restated as to sound traditional.

At the time Haygood wrote his book, a leading "speculative theologian" in the denomination was J. M. Boland of Kentucky, who had asked for, but not been granted, an honorary degree from Emory College in 1874.[32] Boland's proclamation of the literal possibility of reaching total holiness, given a "sound conversion," seemed close to Lovick Pierce's emphasis on the constant groping *toward* holiness. Boland provided a promise of certainty at having crossed a threshold which would be buttressed by "Second Blessing" teachings in the 1880's.[33] A second answer to the problem of knowing one's standing was a rapid re-definition of Wesleyan holiness, during the 1870's, in terms of external marks of behavior rather than of spiritual rewards.

By far the most relevant proof of this postwar debasement of Wesleyanism was the clarification at the 1874 General Conference of the prohibition against "drunkenness." The resolution that the

General Rules required abstinence from spirits was openly opposed by so prominent a minister as A. P. McFerrin, brother of the missions secretary, who called the new interpretation a repudiation of the traditional Southern Methodist position. It was obvious, he said, that Christ Himself made wine and sanctioned its enjoyment.[34] Here then were possible solutions for those who did not want to live with the problem of continued groping: an emotional experience of "real conversion" (or "second blessing") would serve as the mark, or a scrupulous observance of taboos would suffice as a sign of arrival.

Atticus Haygood would eventually reject the extremes of either of these routes. At the time he wrote *Our Children,* however, he assumed that parents could teach salvation as successfully as they did behavioral prejudices. He attributed the cause of spiritual *shallowness* in people whose behavior did not offend their parents to that nemesis—the customs of life in towns and cities! It was the town laity which demanded "not . . . more than . . . forty minutes in the morning" as the limit of a sermon's length. Town pastors, in an effort to retain the interest and loyalty of their parishioners —those "superficial people"—were calculating the success of sermons in terms of their "emotion-producing power" or their shock value, thus opening themselves to "the first doctrinal vagary" which would attract attention.[35] Ironically, it was in the towns that the financial strength of the Southern church continued to be centered, and it was the human products of their Sunday schools (using the Nashville literature) which, in ignorance of Wesleyan doctrine, were open to "the first doctrinal vagary," from any source inside or outside the denomination so long as it was attractively packaged.

The editorial voice of the *Advocate* frequently lectured adult laymen on their behavioral imperfections. The tone was unlike that of the understanding college president; only once did it register any humor: "A correspondent in this week's issue says severe things about croquet."[36] Haygood was not amused at the " 'tableau,' 'charades,' and such 'amusements' " that were being added to the commencement programs of the female colleges. He objected to the attempt by laboring people in the towns to dress their daughters "like princesses." He registered, in that shrill editorial voice so untypical of his conversational manner, real horror at a "Sacred Concert" in Savannah held on a Sunday, which included the singing of "Grandfather's Clock." And he chided Atlanta citizens, most of them Protestants, for using passes given by the

Central of Georgia Railroad for a Sunday excursion to Savannah to honor a new ocean steamer named after Atlanta the "Gate City."[37]

The exhorting voice acted as though it did not expect town behavior to improve. However, at least twice his editorials registered on readers of the *Advocate* to the extent of producing observable results. For years Haygood had objected to the "Continental Sunday," introduced into the United States by Roman Catholic immigrants in the South, mostly Irish and German. He had observed in Atlanta that "Sunday evening [parade] music [at U. S. military posts] has led thousands to spend Sabbath afternoons in a manner as little conducive to morality as religion"; frequently those who attend the parades would complete their Sabbath evening in a "German beer garden." The Georgia Independent Congressman, Emory Speer, in response introduced a bill to outlaw Army parades on Sunday. Speer was the son of a well-educated Georgia Methodist preacher, a professor at the University of Georgia.[38]

Haygood also harped on the danger of the carrying of pistols, many times concealed in special pockets in the trousers. Two weeks after one of these editorials appeared in the *Wesleyan Advocate* the Atlanta chief of police issued an order for increased vigilance in finding those offenders who illegally carried concealed weapons. Most of the guilty ones in Atlanta, he said, were those who attended "obnoxious parties" in upstairs rooms in the business section in the company of "lewd women."[39] Many of the *Advocate's* editorials discussed the dangerous results when liquor bought by young men (illegally when under age, or openly off the shelf of stores) depressed the inhibitions against wild shooting of the pistol. Haygood's indignation here seems directed at the resulting violence rather than at the consumption of "bitters."[40]

Occasionally Dr. Haygood's columns showed his growing humanity and his increasingly ambiguous attitude toward the kind of lay behavior he generally advocated. In 1877 he made a memorable trip to the Florida Conference, and on his return enjoyed indirect association with a rough group of young men. He wrote:

we left the Atlantic and Gulf Road at Jesup and started Macon-ward by the Macon and Brunswick. . . . The smoking car (we beg Dr. Summers' pardon) was packed full with a rare and racy, if not rich crowd of lumbermen. They were returning from Brunswick, whither they had taken a large raft of timber . . . spending several days on the river. . . . They were of all colors; white—under the dirt—yellow, brown, black. They were a motley, ragged, greasy crowd. We never saw the like . . . at least in their complete 'acceptance of the situation. . . .' We saw a very black negro and a fair-haired youth drinking alternately out of the same black-bottle. They sat promiscuously and drank, smoked, laughed, sang, whistled, and danced together. One young fellow knew the potent notes and they sang 'fa, so la' while he beat time. . . . He sings a sort of wild tenor we used to hear at camp-meeting. . . . Perhaps we ought to be ashamed . . ., but we did enjoy their songs. Once they sang one of Sankey's tunes. . . . The contractors may have made money on the raft, but these men . . . got home with a very few dollars. . . . A smart young drummer . . . said . . .: 'When . . . I look at these men I feel rich.'[41]

By 1877 the editorialist with the bitter tongue was subject to some perspective on his editorial positions. But he would never be free from the habits of the exhorter; he would never be able, like the rowdy lumbermen, merely to "accept the situation." His healthy tendencies toward tolerance of behavior that would not meet the test of holiness would be checked because of a vital friendship with Warren A. Candler, which had begun its course in 1875 when Candler as a young preacher boarded with the Haygoods. During part of 1875 and most of 1876 President Haygood gave the promising Emory graduate the same kind of careful guardianship given him by Lovick Pierce, even to requiring that Candler learn to paraphrase Watson's *Institutes,* as he had. The years 1875 and 1876 were crucial in Candler's life. Later he kept, without change, all of Haygood's prejudices—enmity to "un-Methodist" behavior, hostility to Northern Methodism, and violent disrespect of the University of Georgia. Except for the last named, Haygood's own positions moderated as he grew older and more humane; Candler on the other hand kept Haygood's unmatured positions for life.

Eventually Warren, the "born riser," would obscure the career of the older man. In the 1870's there was no comparison. Externally attractive, Candler quickly became the darling of an Atlanta pulpit and a favorite speaker at female college commencements. The young Candler was concerned with any activity which would attract attention to himself. He produced a poorly written book on the Sunday school movement, modeled on Haygood's book on the missionary movement but far inferior in craftsmanship and thoughtfulness. He flirted with the coterie of "Holiness" preachers for a while until their expected political triumph in the North Georgia Conference after the death of Bishop Pierce did not materialize. Candler then took on the role of oracle to his denomination; and before he was thirty he was the chief enumerator of the sins of Georgia church people. His specialty was lambasting the theatre and dancing. Tragically, all of Candler's considerable mental powers were diverted from self-analysis. He never had any doubts about his being a giant, about being a chosen prophet. He delighted in the eccentricity of his own judgments—and with popularity and political power coming to him he retained until old age the limited insights of the precocious, self-assured adolescent. He did not develop a capacity for self-criticism. So long as Haygood lived, Candler was a caricature, the worst expression, of the editorial personality of his early model.[42]

It is strange that the two men remained so close, from 1875 until Haygood's death in 1896. Haygood was customarily cordial in conversation, and concerned with people; Candler was customarily abrupt, with the lack of concern for other's feelings usually found in the born manipulator of people. Haygood, trained in the habit of spiritual groping, was a searcher after wisdom; Candler, of the postwar generation, was a storehouse of conventional knowledge, and an expert in giving the appearance of wisdom. Haygood was a reader of everything from good novels to the *Popular Science Monthly*, from the poetry of Tennyson to the theology of Charles Hodge. Candler's distaste for imaginative literature is proverbial. (It should be recorded that when he attended Emory Professor Callaway was teaching Latin rather than English literature.) Candler did not escape the influence of his ministerial generation: the prime attention given to the *effect* of sermons—and he was a fantastically successful orator. Haygood, like Pierce, had greater respect for the sensibilities of his hearers, and consequently came to be considered—by the younger generation—less skillful a preacher than Candler. Nevertheless, Haygood was known to be a genuine lover of the Bible *as literature,* rather than exclusively as a starting point for theatrics. And in the 1870's, as an editorial writer, Haygood was effective in his editorial register of unhappiness in the decline of intelligent Bible reading. Bibles, he observed, were used in some homes primarily to add height to piano stools or to prop open windows.[43]

Through his reading Haygood emancipated himself from his own lack of perspectives—on himself, preacherly society, and the South. Whereas editorializing gradually weakened his self-discipline in communication, reading in effect allowed him imagined conversations outside his milieu. Between 1875 and 1880 his most important reading was Atlanta's progressive daily newspaper, the *Constitution*. There were special reasons for its influence, which extended to prompting direct editorial comment in the *Wesleyan*. Henry W. Grady, one of the paper's editors in the 1870's, and by far its most brilliant reporter, fulfilled Haygood's boyish ideal of the "great editor" who captured the public's attention by his literary skill. The publisher of the paper was W. A. Hemphill, a fixture in Trinity Methodist Church. A rising reporter was F. H. Richardson, son of that other fixture of Trinity, F. M. Richardson.

Beyond these personal reasons for favoring the *Constitution*, Haygood experienced vicariously through it the excitement of political power during the governorship of A. H. Colquitt, elected in 1876 to a four-year term. Colquitt was an outstanding Methodist layman, a local preacher, and an Emory Trustee. The *Constitution* was the administration's "house organ." The paper's hopeful progressive tone about the state's future appealed to Dr. Haygood, who was wearied by the Bourbon bemoaning of the good old days of slavery and sectional isolation. Three of the *Constitution's* editorial positions had an enormous influence on the preacher-editor's thought: its advocacy of industrialization and commercial growth; its recommendation of friendliness with the industrially expanding North; and its willingness to encourage Negroes in their aspiration for full citizenship.

In Georgia in the election year of 1880, secular evangelists for a "new South," more concerned with progress than with tradition, were not classed with the backward-looking Bourbons. Ironically by 1890, with the farm-based decline of enthusiasm for a capitalistic South run for the benefit of an elite of businessmen and investors, the progressives of ten years before were called Bourbon Democrats. By then Colquitt, Gordon, and Brown had lost their reputations as progressives. Dr. Haygood could not be labeled a Bourbon at either date, despite an uncritical admiration of Governor Colquitt. Haygood wanted Georgia to be economically progressive, but as a sort of proto-Populist he early sensed something insidious about the national "syndicates."[44]

Haygood's cautious approval of the booster spirit of the late 1870's was grounded in a complex ideal for Georgia society. Although in manners himself a "proletarian," Haygood held no brief for the "average man" who conformed to the requirements of his environment rather than to his own demands on himself. Haygood's ideal man was not exactly a disguise for a prewar Whig. He did not confuse high economic status with character, and he respected Colquitt for his character, not for his wealth or political power. His respect was always given to any man who accepted *work* as "a primal law of man's nature"[45] He did not count it progress, therefore, when fastidious young men sought clerkships in stores in order to avoid manual labor. Georgia needed farm laborers, and anyone with a stout body—"and there are more stout bodies than most people suppose"—could support himself as a farmer if willing to start as a hired hand.[46] He expressed pleasure that the passing of slavery had reduced the prejudice against female labor, and joined the *Constitution* in praise of the new Atlanta Cotton Factory, which hired women.[47] He also pronounced as admirable the increasingly important occupation of the "drummer," the traveling salesman. These men, he said, outdid practically everyone else in their hard work, their general store of information, and their "national vision."[48]

In spite of his sympathy for workaday callings, Haygood believed that intelligent choices and a sense of social morality must undergird all commercial activity. He felt, for example, that Georgia needed wagon roads more than she did railroad lines to every county seat:

We dream . . . about the "development of Georgia's great physical resources," but what is the use . . . unless we could get a market. . . . How can we have good roads? Make them. How? With convict labor. . . . There must be . . . nearly a thousand. . . . It was always wrong to insult honest mechanics by teaching convicts their trades. We can't build a railroad to every man's house. . . . We need the roads, and don't know what to do with the convicts.[49]

He criticized Georgia farmers for poor management as the cause of their difficulties: they bought

guano at a ruinous price, keep their smoke-houses in Cincinnati, their corn-cribs in St. Louis, their stockyards in Kentucky, mortgage their farms to brokers (breakers) to pay for things that they can do without or provide for themselves, wind up each year head over heels in debt, and then cry "hard times."[50]

He did not attack the profit motive, but found the "grasping, speculating spirit" a cause of subsequent economic recession.[51] His enthusiasm for women's work in the cotton mills was tempered by finding out that pregnant women were not allowed to sit down and that one girl was fired for going to get a drink of water.⁵² Equally doubtful to him was the choice by stockholders of corporation officers "without regard to [their] moral worth and religious life and charitable conscience."⁵³

His advocacy of public use of convict labor put him in the camp of Governor Colquitt's enemies. Joseph E. Brown and Senator John B. Gordon were both prominent lessees of convicts. Public consciousness of the frightful living conditions of the convicts and of the fact that the lessees benefited by a heavy-handed administration of sentences in the state courts had a part in the campaign of 1880, and reached a crest in 1881. In that year Haygood printed a letter from his old teacher, Gustavus Orr, now state superintendent of schools, sharply critical of sentences to labor under private contract, especially since Negroes did not receive their share of an education which might have forestalled commission of misdemeanors.⁵⁴ Not until 1887 did Haygood openly attack convict leasing on moral grounds—by then Governor Gordon's public position was one of embarrassment for the system. During 1880, the *Wesleyan's* silence on the question exceeded that of the *Constitution*. The *Constitution* defended lessee Brown in a journalistic controversy with a Miss Lillie Barr, who wrote a letter about her discoveries after visiting one of Brown's camps. Her horrified report of nakedness, filth, and degradation appeared in the *New York Christian Union,* a liberal Congregationalist paper. Typical of Brown's reported rebuttal was his statement that the irresponsible convicts, thieves "by nature," would not put on the nightshirts which their solicitious owner had provided for their comfort and dignity.⁵⁵

Haygood's editorials in praise of Colquitt during 1879 and 1880 were doubtless of great political value to the governor. He admitted that it was a mistake for a preacher to be "partisan," but considered that holding the kind of opinions he had was not political partisanship. Preachers had a duty to make strong public pronouncements, in both editorial column and the pulpit. It was beyond his control, he said, if his "criticisms . . . of putting . . . drunkards, blasphemers, and other bad characters in office" were taken as personal attacks by Colquitt's enemies.⁵⁶ He countered openly the charges that the governor's appearance at Sunday school celebrations and in the pulpit of Negro churches was undignified. He ridiculed the reaction of an editor of a Fort Valley paper to Colquitt's speech at a Sunday school assembly at Chautauqua, New York. The paper was quoted in the *Advocate*:

Gov. A. H. Colquitt . . . has been up in Yankeeland and made them a speech at Chautauqua, N. Y. We haven't had time to read it, but from a hasty glance, we suppose he spoke on politics, law, religion, Sunday-schools, the nigger, legislation, a little about the South and more about the North. . . . We don't think Georgians are much on the "I tickle you and you tickle me" game, but Colquitt seems to be running it sharply "way up thar North," eh!⁵⁷

Such attacks were obviously politically dangerous, with the state less than ten years away from military government during Reconstruction. Bourbon Democrats benefited from a strong Confederate identification which they did not care to lose. Both Gordon and Colquitt were Confederate generals, and Brown of course, despite his unorthodox role during Reconstruction, had been Georgia's governor during the Civil War. Certainly Colquitt was grateful to Haygood for pointing out how legitimate it was for him to be a lay preacher—he had been one for thirty years—to speak at camp-meetings, Negro churches, and Sunday school meetings. The governor otherwise did not enter into controversy with his opponents. He confined himself to pleading that he was "innocent of all charges" of misrepresentation of the will of Georgians.⁵⁸

The appearance of the governor before Negroes, primarily in churches, was part of calculated politics. It seems likely that Dr. Haygood failed to analyze properly the political motives of the governor. The aim was to corral Negro votes in the direction of the "Confederate Democrats," the former slaves having previously since 1867 voted for the Republicans. The *Constitution* praised Georgia Negroes for owning 341,000 acres of land, announced that Negro children had a "capacity" for school work equal to that of the whites, and boasted that the Georgia Negro was a model of civilized industry compared to his South Carolina counterpart. The paper insisted that the "educational interests of the colored people in democratic Georgia are more closely looked after . . . than in any state north or south," and also maintained that "Practically, the color line does not exist," admitting, however, that the situation did not support the "dream of social equality."⁵⁹

In July 1880, Joseph E. Brown, soon to be U. S. senator, gave a campaign speech in the Atlanta city hall in line with Colquitt's politics. Brown declared that

> Whenever any constitutional amendment is proposed by the people of the north to take back the ballot from the colored men you will find the democracy of the whole south rallying to the colored man. He gives us power and he shall ever exercise the elective franchise! [Great

Applause.] He shall no more be a slave: and he shall ever more be a voter. [Applause] I am willing at all times to submit to my part of the burden, to raise whatever sum is necessary to educate the children of the whole state. [Applause][60]

Haygood's editorial position on the political capacity of the Negro meanwhile was considerably "Bourbon." At one time he said that the relationship between Negroes and whites had not changed since the war; they "nursed us, cooked for us, cared for us; and truer, more loving friends we never had. . . ." On his Florida visit in 1877 he expressed approval of "redemption" of the state from Reconstruction, believing that Negroes "as well as the whites will reap the benefit" from the return of Confederates to political power.[61] He did not admire the Negroes' habit of voting Republican, once mentioning that when "The College janitor voted the Democratic ticket," in 1878, he "had his life threatened . . . and did get a fight" on account of his show of independence.[62] To a great extent he shared the Southerners' belief that they alone loved the ex-slaves. He was slow to drop his prejudice that Northerners were incapable of intelligent philanthropy in the South. The enormous Northern subsidy of Negro colleges in the South he considered a token retribution for their idiocy when they "flung five millions of negroes into the responsibility of full citizenship and the whirlpool of political excitements." Nothing shows better his unremarkable position before 1880 than an article excoriating Northern agents who enticed Negroes away from parts of Louisiana where "negroes were doing better" than almost anywhere else. The exodus from the Delta plantations was the result equally of the "artful lies of designing men" and a "certain little-understood fanaticism in the negro mind that leads him to imagine himself in the case of Israel in Egypt."[63]

The first appearance in the *Wesleyan* of any positive statement about the possibility of political and social reform for the Negro appeared in 1879, an article attributed to "Matheney," probably written by Gustavus J. Orr.

> The "negro problem" cannot be ignored. . . . The late elections [1878] in Georgia suggested some very unpleasant facts and forebodings. Issues were mainly personal . . ., and the contests . . . were very close, . . . the negro was regarded as holding the balance of power. Ignorant and poor, thoughtless and impulsive, taught in a bad school of politics since the beginning of his citizenship . . ., no wonder that he is sought by corrupt men as the means of elevation to office. . . .

Public morals are at stake. . . . Each citizen, black or white, helps to determine the moral tone of the State. . . . We cannot afford for the negro to remain in ignorance and vice. . . . We must furnish white Southern teachers. (We stand on this platform.—Ed.) [64]

Between the appearance of this article and the Emory president's great, hopeful "New South" sermon of Thanksgiving 1880, radical events moderated his pessimism, and rekindled his earlier dreams for the social achievements possible in the South.

The factors involved in his change of attitude were twofold: his own growth into self-confident adulthood and the growth of a small but influential progressive core of citizens in Georgia, and other Southern states, a growth speeded up because of political exigencies. There was now a new audience receptive to the unbounded dreams he had kept locked away from consciousness since the destruction of the Confederacy. The *Atlanta Constitution* had provided the key to this renewal of hope.

The Atlanta paper was influential further in the development of other new enthusiasms of the *Wesleyan* editor, the prohibition movement and cordial relations between North and South. Both of these new attitudes Haygood shared with the Colquitts and other politically prominent Georgia Methodists. (Grady was during the 1870's a member of the First Methodist Church of Atlanta, as was H. I. Kimball, the *bête noire* of Georgia's Reconstruction, who became probably the chief liaison between Atlanta's business community and the North.)

The *Constitution* in general reflected the current interests of respectable Atlanta Methodists. During the fall of 1879 the paper advertised the organization of a prohibition group among members of the First Methodist Church, through the efforts of a visiting attractive young New England zealot for the cause, who left Mrs. Colquitt and Kimball in leadership when he left Atlanta. During the winter of 1880 the group circulated pledges among respectable Atlantans, in and out of their church, in order to promote total abstinence.[65] Until 1880, Haygood's most serious comments on the revitalized anti-saloon movement were approval of a pamphlet written by a preacher friend in 1879 (entitled *Wine and Blood*) and a vitriolic expression of his own Arminian displeasure with the argument by scientific authorities that some drunkards " 'can't quit.' "[66] In March 1880, nevertheless, Haygood wrote a long and skillful pamphlet arguing for local elimination of the saloon, entitled *Close the Saloons*. Since it drew heavily on quotations from three Atlanta judges, and since Haygood had written nothing before in this vein, it must be inferred that the pamphlet was in effect commisioned by the First Methodist leaders. During the election campaign of 1880, Haygood's pamphlet was widely circulated in support of local option votes, and the hint was spread afar among church-oriented Georgians that those opposed to prohibition were the enemies of Colquitt. The kind of men who bought the vote of the Negro with a drink of whiskey became "public enemies."[67]

After Colquitt's re-election a state prohibition convention was held in Atlanta, which no important Methodists attended; but in December 1880 the North Georgia Conference by resolution initiated statewide Methodist leadership of the movement. Haygood was voted chairman of a temperance committee. One of its members was the defeated "Colquitt" candidate for the Ninth District Congressional seat, H. P. Bell. The report of Haygood's committee, adopted by the conference, called for enforcing existing laws such as the one forbidding the sale of liquor to minors, and urged new legislation which would allow counties and cities to hold prohibition elections without a special act of the legislature.[68] This local option measure passed the legislature four years later, with Georgia Methodists, chief among them Haygood, being in the forefront of agitation. In July 1881, Dr. Haygood spoke to an Atlanta audience, "composed of the best citizens."[69] The *Advocate* during his two last years as editor, 1880-1882, was full of the issue. The most radical editorial statement Haygood ever made was that "it is the Church's business to fight the liquor power" as much as "to have Sunday-schools, preachings, revivals, or funerals.[70] Since Henry Grady was not totally sympathetic with the elimination of social drinking, the *Constitution* played no major role in the spread of prohibitionist sentiment. However, its news stories about the initial organization of Methodist sentiment in Atlanta aroused Haygood's interest.

More direct and more active was the *Constitution's* open advocacy of friendliness with the North, since the commercial development of the South was dependent on Northern resources and investments. North and South both had succumbed to railroad-expansion fever in the mid-1870's. This common interest was the basis of political liaison between Northern Republicans and Southern "Confederates."[71] The *Constitution* was a booster of additional railroads for the "Gate City," and during the early 1880's recorded in frank detail the politics of competition between rival syndicates. Colquitt's trip North, in 1878, to attend the

Chautauqua (following the holding of the Second International Sunday School Convention in Atlanta that spring) allowed him entree into economic as well as Sunday school circles. The idea began to be current, through his and other contacts, that the white Protestants of the North and the white Protestants of the South had a community of interest in the wise use of both the almighty dollar and the stewardship of Protestant Christian civilization. In a lecture trip South, in 1879, Henry Ward Beecher, of a famous abolitionist family, was warmly received. On his return the Brooklyn preacher said that "The conduct of the Southern people since Appomattox is 'without a parallel' in the history of subjugated peoples . . .; they have shown the best qualities of the best Christian civilization."[72]

The thawing affected Northern Methodist publications which Haygood only three and four years before had found detestable. In 1880 a reader could still find statements such as the generalization in Northern Methodism's *Quarterly Review* that the Southern Methodist preacher was " a dealer in intellectual abstractions, or an apologist for a shameful institution." But the new tone of church journals is found in the *Advocate* printed in Chicago: "There is another Church holding the same doctrines, having substantially the same polity and methods as ours. . . . Why should we invade their territory?"[73]

In the improved climate, extra effort was made to welcome the fraternal delegates of the Southern church to the Northerners' General Conference in Cincinnati, May 1880. Since the city was bubbling with excitement over the recent completion of the city-financed Cincinnati and Southern Railroad—linking the Queen City of the Ohio with Chattanooga, and hence directly with Atlanta—the cordiality in the conference was genuine. The delegates benefiting from the friendliness were two Southern Methodist college presidents, James H. Carlisle of Wofford and Dr. Atticus G. Haygood of Emory College—whose Board of Trustees, it was buzzed about, included the progressive Governor of Georgia. Haygood's fraternal address warrants close reading.

The different sections . . . are being brought close together by steam and electricity. May they be brought together in affection also.

The opening of your great . . . railroad was counted a very notable event by the business men. . . . A wise and energetic city does not spend twenty millions . . . that her people may go on excursions to Lookout Mountain. Cincinnati seeks not a better view, but a broader field. And these States bid her "Come on."

But a few weeks ago the Southerners, by the thousand, came to see your "Queen City," . . . and the hospitality . . . and brotherhood . . . quite took their hearts away. Recently a large delegation from this city visited my own State. The Georgians received them as brothers. . . . I fell in with some of them, and I thought them very pleasant people to know. . . .

A Georgia lady told me that there is serious apprehension Georgia and Ohio are about to lose some of their children. (Hear!) I wish one hundred thousand of your best Northern girls were married to one hundred thousand of our best Southern boys. (Applause) and that 100,000 of your best boys were married to 100,000 of our best girls. (Applause and laughter). Then we would beat the politicians. Moreover, we would beat the editors—especially the church editors—of whom I am one. And when we beat the politicians and the editors we will have a union and peace that will be a joy for the sun to look down upon. (Applause).[74]

This visit to Cincinnati, and the commercial and political climate of North Georgia which made the trip so meaningful, had opened "broader fields" for Haygood. Not only did he envision a new relationship with the Northern church editors, but he could think now what his new contacts with the wealthy, philanthropic Northern Protestants could mean in the building up of Emory. He experienced that spring and summer of 1880, moreover, the feeling that the closed society, the narrow life he had lived since 1865 had been opened, liberated by historical chance. His *will*, his self-discipline, his years of exemplary service to his church had won him or his people nothing in comparison to the large movements of the time—which were beyond his control. The theological effect of the context of 1880 was to liberate him from a literal belief that an Arminian life was the proper road to salvation. The liberation allowed him the declaration of independence from Bishop Pierce that summer. In the future, Providence rather than his own planning would guide him. *His* part in his destiny still lay in the use of his writing talents. Henceforth he would give his writing talent over to the demon he encountered in his study in Oxford. The bishop's obedient servant, Attie Haygood, was dead. The "new man" had still his baptized name, but his character bore no sign of a Georgia preacher's personality.

EIGHT
◊ ◊ ◊
◊

Northern Philanthropy and Southern Profits

ON THANKSGIVING DAY, 1880, Haygood preached in the church at Oxford a sermon on "The New South." Seven years later, when the Emory president's national reputation was at its peak, a Methodist preacher in Maryland, J. C. C. Newton, who used "The New South" as part of the title of a book, speculated that either Haygood or Carlisle had originated the by then shopworn phrase.[1] Newton was in error, however. It seems certain that Haygood borrowed the phrase from the *Atlanta Constitution,* from Henry W. Grady. Grady used the phrase in an editorial in 1874 (for the *Atlanta Daily Herald*), saying at the time that Georgia's statesman Benjamin H. Hill originated it.[2] The *Constitution* used the term several times during the 1870's—on February 11, 1879, it was used in a headline over a column about an interview with General Sherman on the occasion of a return visit to the "Gate City" which he had destroyed fifteen years before. It was also used in a headline in the Atlanta paper two weeks before the Thanksgiving service of 1880.[3]

Haygood's close following of the *Constitution* and its progressive tone can be shown through the editorial concerns of the *Wesleyan Christian Advocate*—even though he occasionally disliked what he called its "raciness." The optimism about the South's progressive development which he shared with the Atlanta editors was strengthened by three events during 1880. In the summer Chautauqua, Gustavus J. Orr delivered a moving address for his New York audience on "Education of the Negro" in the South. Haygood read in the February issue of the *North American Review* an account of the origin of the Emancipation Proclamation which started him on an important train of thought about the developing destiny of the slave. And the peaceful presidential election of 1880, so in contrast to the Hayes-Tilden controversy of 1876, convinced Haygood that the wounds of the Civil War had in the main been healed.[4]

Legend, transmitted orally in the ranks of Georgia Methodist preachers, some of them students at Emory in the early 1880's, has simplified the circumstances of Haygood's "conversion" to a Negrophilia considered extreme, especially in retrospect. One account dramatically relates Haygood's instantaneous emergence as a spokesman for this exotic cause upon reflection on the cash value of some work done on his house by a Negro handy man. Another simplification of this crucial activity in Haygood's life is possible if the biographer accepts as standard the most important human motivation allegedly at work in the Gilded Age—uninhibited ambition. Haygood might thus be characterized as a rational egoist. It might be argued, on the basis of his activities during 1880, 1881, and 1882, that he wrote the "New South" sermon to attract the attention of the Northern press and Northern philanthropy to Emory and to himself.

If an oversimplification is needed, as it seems to be for this complex man, it should not emphasize his conscious decision to write something spectacular. This new passion for the Negro's cause, and the desire for a wider audience, may satisfactorily be attributed to a "daemon," in modern parlance an unconscious fragmentary personality which used the occasion of the sermon to destroy completely Dr. Haygood's external, preacherly personality. It is true that Haygood had his address, once it was printed, broadcast in a wider circle than his prohibition pamphlet of the same year. But it is inconceivable that he *planned* the response when he outlined his sermon for an Oxford audience in a quite traditionally serious local occasion. Furthermore, it was sheer accident that the New South pamphlet fell into the hands of a Brooklyn banker and philanthropist at the precise moment that he was expanding his investments in the direction of Georgia. This coincidence only a "daemon" could arrange. The banker, George I. Seney, gave Emory during a few months of 1881, $50,000 in cash and an endowment of more than $50,000 in railroad securities.

The organization of the important sermon with the radical statements saved for the last suggest convincingly that Haygood's preoccupation in preparing it was with his Southern audience. Publishing was the result of its favorable acceptance in Oxford, on motion of Professor Callaway—and this kind of motion was not unusual for an exceptional sermon.[5]

The sermon began with conventional Thanksgiving expressions of gratitude to the Deity: for the South's good cotton crop of 1880, making it possible for Southern homes to have "parlor organs, pianos, and pictures, where we never saw them before"; for good order during the election campaign and electoral vote counting; for good will between the races (partly because of Colquitt's desire to win the approval of Negro voters, but attributed by Haygood mostly to a common Protestantism). But he went further, further even than his commencement-time expressions. He was satisfied, publicly, with Garfield as President of all the people. He was glad that Providence, by means of a Confederate defeat, had ended slavery. He agreed that the South's cause had been the "Constitutional" one, but his position came close to defamation of the Confederacy. He claimed that Southern whites were "more civilized and Christian," more industrious, than they had been twenty years before. He advised a continued copying of the business-mindedness of Yankees. He looked forward to a day "twenty years from now" when "the words 'the South' shall have only a geographical significance."[6] The impact of this sermon, as reprinted in a pamphlet, and in the *New York Advocate,* can well be imagined.

Most of the notice of it came from the North. Strangely, less attention was paid in the South to the Thanksgiving sermon than to one preached at Trinity Church in Atlanta in January 1881, after a tryout in Oxford earlier the same month. This latter sermon, entitled "The Christian Citizen," was reprinted in the *Constitution.* The daily declared it to be founded "upon the line of his great Thanksgiving sermon . . . which was so extensively published and read throughout the union, but more particularly in northern and eastern states."[7] The paper had not carried the Thanksgiving sermon, and the January reproduction of the Trinity sermon was only a capsule of the entire address. Interestingly, the December 11, 1880, issue of the paper carried an article reprinted from a Republican periodical, in Washington, with the title "The New South." The January sermon was printed on a Tuesday following a Sunday issue featuring an article by Grady, forwarded from New York, with the headline "The Atheistic Tide Sweeping Over the Continent. The Threatened Destruction of the Simple Faith of the Fathers by the Vain Deceits of Modern Philosophers.") Haygood's January message accepted the blessing of peace and order, being an almost scholastic sermon on the necessity of civil obedience to duly constituted authority. Unlike his frank admonishments in his book, *Our Brother in Black*, (completed that January), and in the earlier sermon, he did not criticize Southerners for their civil disobedience to *national* authority. He expressed the idea that "The Christian men of Atlanta, of Georgia, of the United States, can carry any election," referring thus vaguely to the commonalty of interests newly found between Northern and Southern Protestants.[8]

Haygood's pamphlet came to the attention of George I. Seney during the winter of 1880-1881. The father of George Seney was in his day one of three college-educated Methodist preachers in America. The preacher's son had a well-developed habit of philanthropy, including the subsidy of Abel Stevens' four-volume history of (Northern) Methodism.[9] Since 1877, when he became President of the Metropolitan Bank, Seney had demonstrated a speculative fervor for railroad building and consolidation, at this time possible for a man of his secondary rank in the capitalistic structure of the country. Before this time, railroad speculation in the Southeast centered around the extension of the Pennsylvania system; between 1876 and approximately 1887 the withdrawal of the Pennsylvania syndicate allowed for greater competition in the building of rival sectional systems.[10] With the entire Southeast open for investment in railroads, Seney, considered a conservative banker theretofore, could not resist trying his hand. He first acquired at foreclosure in 1878 the Ohio Central Railroad, moving to extend it in two directions—into Virginia and also through Kentucky and Tennessee into the Deep South, initially tapped from Ohio by the Cincinnati road then being built. Seney chose to buy into a competitive route, that of the East Tennessee, Virginia, and Georgia Railroad, centered on Knoxville, a line which the Pennsylvania interests had temporarily controlled. The other major North-South competitor in the eastern South was a complex of "Coast Lines" centered on the Richmond and Danville road in Virginia.[11]

Speculation was a kind of game to many Eastern investors, no doubt, but it had serious implications for the economy of both the South and the Midwest. Midwest equality with the East depended greatly (as before the Civil War) on the section's maintaining its commercial ties with the Southeast. If by means of cheaper transportation the Midwest became the chief supplier of processed goods for Southern as well as Midwestern consumers, the section's storing-up of capital might eventually free it from dependence on

Eastern and foreign sources of credit. The South of course stood to gain from any Midwestern competition with the East, especially if it resulted in the lowering of freight rates. In 1880, because of agreements made by Eastern-dominated railroads, rates into the Deep South from Cincinnati were higher than from the much more distant Baltimore. Seney, an Eastern banker, was one of many investors fearful of the Midwest's potential. (The Easterners within a few years controlled the transportation ties between the Midwest and the South to the extent that the plan to make the Tennessee River a route for barge traffic competing with the railroads was buried for fifty years.)[12]

In 1876, with the outcome of Eastern capitalism's ambitions still uncertain, both the City of Cincinnati and two Tennessee entrepreneurs believed that new Midwestern-Southern railroad links would enhance local and sectional prosperity. The two Tennesseeans, C. M. McGhee, a banker in Knoxville, and E. W. Cole, a Nashville citizen whose railroad activities included a vice presidency of Georgia's Western and Atlantic, joined their ambitions in plans for expansion of the East Tennessee road. In February 1880, they acquired the Macon and Brunswick line—with the cordial good wishes of many Atlantans, the Colquitt administration, and the *Constitution*. In order to complete a "system" which would extend from the Ohio River, through Kentucky, Tennessee, and Georgia to an Atlantic port, the East Tennessee needed a link between Macon and Rome via Atlanta—Rome being at the end of the East Tennessee line. Such a link, however, would destroy the monopoly of the Central of Georgia in Atlanta-Macon shipping, and the Atlanta-Rome-Chattanooga link would reduce the volume of traffic on the state-owned line to Chattanooga. Cole lobbied during 1881 for a charter from the legislature for the Macon-Rome link.

Atlanta business leaders, believing the competition would benefit them, on May 26, 1881, gave Cole a testimonial banquet. Atticus Haygood reported the occasion in the *Wesleyan Christian Advocate*:

> Our readers are doubtless familiar with the great railroad movements that have been recently inaugurated. They have heard of the "syndicate," headed by Mr. George I. Seney, with capital of sixteen millions of dollars, of the purchase of several lines . . . and the projection of others, as the "Extension" from Macon to Atlanta of the Macon & Brunswick road, the "extension" further . . . to Rome. . . .

On Thursday night ... Atlanta, through many leading citizens, gave Col. E. W. Cole, the President ... a complimentary banquet. ... During the evening the following telegram was read and answered with thunders of applause:

New York, May 26

The Empire State of the North desires to join the Empire State of the South in developing its railroads, commerce, manufactures and in kindling a fraternity that shall never die.

George I. Seney.

There is true gospel in such a telegram.[13]

Seney was already a dominant voice in the East Tennessee's plans, which incorporated schemes for further railroad dominance of the Southeast. A month after the Atlanta banquet he gained control of two railroads leading from Ohio into Virginia, and plans were made to tap the commercial strength of Alabama—ahead of the push of the Coast lines, the major competitor, which through the agency of General Gordon were building west from Atlanta at the same time. The securing of the Georgia link that summer, 1881, was vitally important in completing the syndicate's network. Building up a favorable Georgia opinion which would approve the granting of a charter for the Macon-to-Rome extension was a necessity. Seney's philanthropies to Georgia during 1881 (to Emory, and to Wesleyan College in Macon where sentiment in favor of continuance of the Central's monopoly was strong) were obviously the results of a calculated beneficence.[14]

To the President of Emory, a meeting between Seney and himself seemed the result of "Providence." The banker saw it differently. Haygood was in New York, February 1881, to see about the printing of his new book, *Our Brother in Black,* by the Northern Methodist presses. He was given an invitation to Seney's bank after visiting the headquarters of the American Bible Society. Having no foreknowledge of Seney's direct connection with railroad competition in Georgia, and no awareness that Seney had been impressed by the Georgia Methodist's "national vision" as shown in his Thanksgiving sermon, Dr. Haygood was staggered upon admittance to learn that the Brooklyn banker wanted to help in the establishment of a Methodist fraternity with the South by giving Emory College a $10,000 endowment (in railroad securities). In a later communication Seney raised this figure to $15,000. This single gift dwarfed the small collections by the "Financial Agents" of Emory College since its reopening after the Civil War. The securities were holdings in the Ohio Central and another Ohio road, and in one of the Midwestern routes to the Southeast, the Nashville, Chattanooga & St. Louis.

In March, Haygood was invited back to be royally entertained in Seney's home, strewn with art treasures, and to preach in Seney's church. The Northern Methodist increased his deposit of faith in Georgia Protestants by leveling off the endowment at $25,000 and pledging $20,000 in cash, so that Dr. Haygood's dream of a new administration and classroom building for Emory, complete with museum and library, could become reality at once. Also $5,000 in cash was pledged to take care of what supposedly remained of Emory's debt—the President being so stunned and careless as not to include in his hasty calculation obligations still remaining on the helping halls.[15]

Construction on "Seney Hall," the administration building, began in May, after the arrival of a check for $10,000 of the pledge. At graduation Haygood in the presence of the Trustees amended his old hostility to the "syndicates," and separated Seney from those "bad . . . railroad directors" who took malicious advantage of the invested savings of widows and orphans. Nevertheless, the cautious Trustees refused, despite the motion of L. D. Palmer of Nashville, to sell all of the college's longheld securities in the Central of Georgia.[16] On August 1, as the time neared for decision on a state charter for the railroad extension sought by Seney, the banker wired Dr. Haygood that he wanted to add yet another $50,000 to his contributions to Emory's endowment. The new gift, making a total of $75,000 transferred that year, was in securities of the East Tennessee and one of Seney's Virginia roads.

On August 6, Haygood published in the *Wesleyan Advocate* an impassioned editorial favoring the charter; the title he used was "Will Georgia Act in Bad Faith?" Haygood mentioned that the lobby of the Western and Atlantic was working overtime against the charter. He declared that competition would be healthful for the state's development and registered once again his confidence in any enterprise supported by Colonel Cole, the important Nashville Methodist layman. He was convinced that "our Legislators" would not be "so shortsighted as to arrest the inflow of the millions that are setting in to build up every interest of Georgia and the whole South."[17]

Five days after this editorial appeared, the East Tennessee, Cole, and Seney had their charter. Since it is certain that Brown opposed the charter, Governor Colquitt's influence in favor of this decision may be labeled "Methodist." The editorial support of the church paper may not have been crucial, but it was certainly an important reminder to Colquitt of the Methodist respectability of the Brooklyn speculator who was also a benefactor of Emory College.

From Dr. Haygood's perspective, the charter and Seney's gifts to Emory were related in no untoward way. His excitement over the transformation of Emory's prospects allowed for no suspicion, and neither he nor his successors as president could tolerate suggestions by outsiders that Seney's philanthropy was born of guile and greed. It is true that the first meeting with Seney was puzzling, but as good fortune bred continued fortunate occurrences, Haygood by the summer of 1881 had ceased to wonder about the magnificence of Northern philanthropy.

Haygood's beneficent attitude toward the North was influenced also by the fact that his book, *Our Brother in Black*, published in the spring of 1881, had such favorable reception in the North. Perhaps the most favorable of the reviews was that written by D. D. Whedon, editor of the Northern Methodists' *Quarterly Review*. Whedon found the book "epochal" and believed it would "initiate the transition to a better understanding between the two sections." He admired Haygood's ability to "see that even his beloved South can err."[18] The influential *New York Advocate* called it "one of the most important volumes issued in the United States since the war."[19]

The *Atlanta Constitution*, however, did not find the book so important. It considered itself the organ which "has been the pioneer in coaxing and breaking down the lingering prejudices of the past, so far as Georgia is concerned." The daily therefore felt it not remarkable, in the climate of 1881, that Haygood's book would "receive the warm approval of those . . . whose approval is worth gaining."[20] One of those Southerners who did not accord the book warm approval was Warren Candler. The young Bourbon remarked in the Nashville *Advocate* that

The Old South, which is the South of to-day, had quite too many virtues to be scandalized by an omnibus confession of guilt. She does not need a baptism of tears over crimes that she never committed in order that she may be christened 'New South.' . . . She feels no occasion to call herself 'New.'

Haygood's delight in candor required that he reprint this rebuke in the *Wesleyan*, allowing himself the editorial comment that he still rejoiced in "that 'new South.' "[21] Candler's non-participation in enjoyment of the dropping of sectional prejudice was symptomatic of a "Bourbon" disenchantment, especially among Southern Methodists, with Dr. Haygood's new cause. It was the liberal *Constitution* itself which compared Haygood's book to *A Fool's Errand*, by Albion W. Tourgee, the semi-autobiographical novel by a Union veteran who had had to leave Greensboro, North Carolina, because of his criticisms of "redeemed" government in that state.[22]

The justice of the *Constitution's* comparison depends on the unarguable fact that *Our Brother* is, while not a novel, a combination of autobiographical events associated with Southern Negroes and the statement of a social philosophy. The Negro anecdotes, some forty in number, must have added greatly to the readability of the book in the eyes of Northerners—they did not need to be instructed in social philosophy. Seven of the anecdotes are about Negroes who were slaves. The most interesting is a tale of a Negro mechanic in Oxford who refused to buy his freedom, although he had saved up enough money from hiring out to do so; he considered the cost of buying his freedom a poor investment of his savings. About ten anecdotes deal with Reconstruction times, and in these Haygood gave vent to his old feeling that Northerners were foolish in their earlier philanthropic ventures—a perspective which Northern Methodists could now share. The most unhappy experience mentioned occurred on a train in 1867 (no doubt when he was riding the Western and Atlantic for a round of overseeing the Rome District). A Federal judge who shared the car dogmatically announced that Southern whites would have to give up their opposition to the amalgamation of the races. The final group of anecdotes delineates the character of the Negroes of Oxford—Bristow Maxwell, the "bachelor cook" who helped pay a supplement to the teacher of the state school in Oxford for Negroes; the saintly David Cureton; the pillars of Yarbrough's congregation, "Judge Levi" and "Aunt Amie"; and Daniel Martin, who every winter burned the fence dividing Haygood's property from his instead of chopping down trees aforetime.[23]

In the statement of his social aims for the South, Haygood did not advance an enormous distance beyond his editorial position of the previous years. His book is full of criticisms of the part played by Northerners and amounts in areas to an extended apologia for the inactivity of the Southern whites. There is veiled contempt in reference to the limited understanding of the Northern Methodists Haygood met in Cincinnati in 1880 as a delegate to the General

Conference. He praises the Southern people, a folk "of strong character" for "the modifications of opinions" since 1865. He is less radical than in his Thanksgiving sermon, absolving himself and Southern slaveholders of any guilt for the historical contingencies producing slavery. He considers that Providence kept abolitionist influence to a minimum until the prelude of the Civil War in order to allow American civilization to reach a point where amalgamation would not take place.

Nevertheless, his acceptance of the unity of the human race, though biologically uninformed, must have startled even some Northern readers in a Darwinian age. He recognized that the "black race" had a kind of "psychic integrity" (this is not his language), but he brilliantly understood the distinction between inherited and culturally ingrained characteristics. His use of the term "stronger race" in talking about the Southern "Anglo-Saxons" was not meant to be derogatory to Negroes. He seemed, in 1881, to be uncertain on the inherited patterns of the Negroes as factors in their obvious failure to conform to "Anglo-Saxon" mores. In the main he seemed to believe that the habits which whites considered primitive—the tendency to solve problems by the whim of a moment rather than with attention to future developments; the propensity to drink too much and to ignore Western marriage traditions; the debasement of "worship" services; and a disregard for the sanctity of other men's property—as habits which Southern whites could in time teach their former slaves to abandon or modify.

In order to create a "brotherhood" of the races in the South, immediate efforts should be made to educate him, teach him a trade so that he would acquire the conservative attributes of the property-owner, and impress on him the importance of literacy in the choice of elected officials. Abandoning his earlier attitude of criticism, Haygood praised the Northern Protestants for their efforts to educate the Southern Negro, and suggested that Southern Methodism ought to support an institution above the elementary level for their education. No doubt, this unusual praise from a Southern white man did much to commend *Our Brother in Black* to Northern readers.[24]

One of the Northern clergymen who admired the book was Leonard W. Bacon, an eccentric, liberal Congregationalist preacher in Norwich, Connecticut, a town in which the richest parishioner was elderly John F. Slater, an owner of textile mills. Bacon knew that Slater planned to establish some major philanthropy, having already set upon the figure of "one million dollars" as suitably large. In the fall of 1881, Bacon, with the aid of Slater's friend Moses Pierce, began to argue that the most needy cause in the nation was the support of Negro colleges in the South. Haygood's readable book provided arguments for them in their visits to Slater's mansion. In their favor was the fact that the best-known philanthropy in America was the Peabody gift, devoted exclusively (most people mistakenly thought) to the improvement of the education of whites. Bacon won his point by persuading ex-President Rutherford B. Hayes (whose family originally was from Norwich) and Chief Justice Morrison R. Waite, both Peabody Trustees, to let Slater know that they would serve on any Board directing an endowment to aid Negro education.

In late November 1881, Dr. Haygood was in New England on a lecture trip of three weeks in prominent churches, one Monday afternoon appearance being at "the People's Church" in Boston, where the Southern preacher was introduced by the Governor of Massachusetts. His lecture was the "New South" sermon reworked to suit the Yankees—with statements like this:

The multiplication of small farms, the increasing railroad facilities that Northern money . . . is bringing us, the development of manufacturing interests, and the common school . . . and, above all, *free labor*, will bring . . . that which . . . we have sorely needed . . . *the habits of small economies*.[25]

These lectures were noted in Norwich, and although Bacon failed in an attempt to get in touch with Dr. Haygood in New England, when the Emory President got home to Oxford in mid-December, he found a wire from Bacon. Three days before Chrismas he was back in New England, and was introduced to Slater in his home by Bacon. The Southern preacher made a favorable impression on the textile man by telling him about his helping halls, where college students worked at menial tasks in order to pay their board. Bacon's interest in Haygood was enlarged by the visit, and he devoted himself to convincing Slater that Haygood was the ideal person to work for the cause now certain to be endowed. In January, Haygood cautioned Bacon: "Now, my dear Doctor, I no more offer myself for the Agency than you nominated me in your letter."[26] But Bacon could read between the lines, and Haygood was pleased that he did. J. L. M. Curry, Agent of the Peabody Fund for about a year and a Baptist preacher and educator, was also lobbying for the job. Slater's preference during early

1882, despite his approval of Haygood as a good man, was Joseph E. Roy, a Congregationalist home missionary working in Atlanta.[27] With that unerring instinct of successful capitalists, Slater sensed that Dr. Haygood was not entirely at home in the management of money matters.

The official choice of an Agent would be entirely up to the Trustees, among whom Bacon had influence. Besides the distinguished Hayes and Waite, Daniel C. Gilman (President of Johns Hopkins University), and the outstanding Wall Street lawyer with Southern investments on his mind, Morris K. Jesup, were the most consequential. Gilman was primarily concerned that academic distinction should be a major point in selecting those Negro colleges where "industrial education," Slater's interest, would be endowed. Jesup was particularly interested in the investment of the principal. Other Trustees were John A. Stewart and William E. Dodge, who deferred to Jesup's judgment; Slater's son; Governor Colquitt of Georgia; Phillips Brooks, the low-church Episcopalian, who was fairly inactive; and James P. Boyce, a Baptist minister from Louisville's theology school (Haygood had suggested to Bacon the propriety of naming a Southern Baptist, especially since, they hoped, Curry might not be the Agent.) All the Trustees had accepted by March 1882, and in April a charter for the foundation was secured from the State of New York.

The first meeting of the Trustees, in May, illustrated the influence of the business-minded members of the Board; and Hayes feared that Slater's anxiety to "get a good income" would lead the Trustees to make "unsafe investments." He was unhappy that $500,000 of the gift was "in the bonds of a railroad from Louisville to Chicago."[28] It was agreed that the principal would be protected against the dangers of speculation by setting aside each year a portion of the income as a reserve. The income in normal times would rise to approximately $40,000 a year. After June, the main concern of the Trustees was the choice of an Agent who would recommend the proper institutions as recipients of the income; and Hayes, who was President of the Board, was in favor of a Southern white man.

The decision in favor of Dr. Haygood made before July 15, probably was partly the result of Hayes's awareness that Curry was openly lobbying for the job. Waite, Boyce, Dodge (a prohibition advocate), Gilman, and Slater's son immediately agreed with Hayes's decision. Haygood's freedom to accept had been cleared during the meeting of Emory's Board of Trustees, held that year in June. Colquitt's assurance was needed to convince Bishop

Pierce that the Agent of the Slater Fund could also continue as President of Emory College. (Haygood had previously resigned as editor of the *Wesleyan Christian Advocate,* effective at the end of May.) Bishop Pierce was not so much concerned about the survival of Emory without Haygood at its helm as he was with the public impression which a resignation would make. Dr. Haygood had refused to be consecrated a Bishop of the Methodist Episcopal Church, South, in May 1882, giving as his chief reason the unfinished nature of his work at Emory, primarily in expansion of the helping halls. Resignation to accept a secular job with a Northern foundation would be an insult to the General Conference which had elected him bishop.

Haygood became Agent of the Slater Fund in November 1882, at a salary of $3,000 a year. His first appearance as agent was at the annual meeting of the American Missionary Association in Cleveland, Ohio, a philanthropic organization supported mainly by Northern Congregationalists which had founded the most distinguished Negro colleges in the South: Fisk in Nashville, and Atlanta University. On this Ohio platform, Dr. Haygood called the dead Garfield a true friend of Negroes and promised a fruitful harvest for money given to Southern education of the Negro. From this time until his death, ex-President Rutherford B. Hayes, who shared the platform, was certain that Haygood was the ideal choice for the Slater Agency. For Haygood, President Hayes became a patron, a most important correspondent, and it might be said a secular bishop and substitute father.[29] Dr. Haygood was agent of the Slater Fund from 1882 until 1891. During those eight and a half years, letters poured into Oxford from all over the South—from Negro universities, colleges, normal schools, seminaries, "institutes"—seeking a portion of the Slater largesse, $20,000 being available during 1883. Haygood's new office in Seney Hall became the clearing-house of a substantial business operation.

By 1883 an understanding of Seney's motives in giving Emory money for the grotesquely fascinating administration building (and its companion in Macon for Wesleyan) and the endowment, must surely have been known by the Trustees of the two colleges. To Emory's Trustees, or some of them, Seney Hall was a monument to Seney's reckless speculation, for in 1883 he was in serious financial difficulty. That year his roads in both Ohio and Virginia defaulted and went into receivership. The East Tennessee expansion, maneuvered so skillfully in Georgia, was proved to be an unwarranted risk, based on miscalculations as to the amount of traffic that would pass from Tennessee through Atlanta and Macon to the minor Atlantic port of Brunswick. The East Tennessee issued debenture certificates, but was forced to consolidate with the Richmond and Danville syndicate in the hands of a new holding company, which J. P. Morgan later acquired. In May 1884, while Haygood wrestled with disposal of the first $20,000 of Slater income (from railroad stocks), Seney's Metropolitan Bank failed, as did other New York banks in a short panic. The East Tennessee was reorganized in 1885 under a receivership headed by Seney's son-in-law, but the owners of common stock were left out in the cold. As a result of Seney's speculative adventures, Emory College's income dropped disastrously. The income for 1884 was not quite $10,000, down 22% from the previous year, there being no income from the Ohio and Virginia roads. In 1885 East Tennessee dividends declined, and it was not until 1887 that Emory's income approximately equaled that of 1883.[30]

In 1887 the disgruntled Trustees of Emory College sold some of their bonds in the Ohio Central, investing part of the money received in the East Tennessee, which was already consolidated with the other railroads held by the Virginia holding company. Cole in 1887 was back in Nashville, his financial energies partly dedicated to the Southern Methodist Board of Missions, of which he was president. McGhee, who had enticed Cole into the East Tennessee expansion, was in New York, where he would become in 1892 by appointment of J. P. Morgan senior receiver of the road. Seney in 1887 had begun to recoup his fortune, fill his home up again with art treasures, and re-establish his reputation for philanthropy. His reputation in Georgia generally was untarnished. Dr. Haygood by 1887 had cut his ties with Emory College, and was a full-time agent for the Slater Fund. Even the Trustees forgot their indignation of 1883-1884 when the Seney endowment seemed a liability. The only monument in Oxford of Seney's ambitions of 1881 was Seney Hall, a structure physically dominating the campus of Emory.[31]

Until he left Oxford in the fall of 1887, Dr. Haygood continued to use Seney Hall as his office for Slater activities, and there he would write far into the night, by the feeble reach of kerosene light. Sometimes it would be daybreak when Haygood clumped on his stumpy feet northward toward the "President's House." On such mornings he must have occasionally turned to look at the monument to Seney's generosity. If he by the late 1880's understood better the motives of Northern men, he may have likened Seney's massive brick tower to that of many a railroad terminal and the cobbled floor of its foyer to the pretentious interiors of many a bank. But his new life had been caught up in the involvements of the nation, and more often than not his many activities drained from him the capacity of acute observation.

NINE

The Church in the Wilderness

BETWEEN 1884 AND 1890 Dr. Haygood's principal activity was as agent of the Slater Fund, a position which increased his number of appearances as a lecturer and preacher outside his home state. But he continued during these, his busiest years, to have many other important though secondary occupations. One of these was his undiminished wardship over Emory; he remained an active member of the board after resigning the presidency in the fall of 1884. His activity as a lecturer extended far beyond the confines of exhortation for Negro education in the South. And his contributions to the Methodist Episcopal Church, South, were never more far-reaching than during this six-year period when he continued a member of the North Georgia Conference (and briefly of the North Alabama) out of his colleagues' courtesy. His refusal to be ordained a bishop, after election in 1882, made the courtesy of some preachers most perfunctory, for Haygood's manner and other involvements were hardly preacherly. So long as he lived in Oxford, until the fall of 1887, he was the assistant pastor of the village church. Between 1887 and 1890 he lived in Decatur, Georgia, and Sheffield, Alabama, but his "appointments" during these three years were even less related to pastoral assignment that before 1887. Without an extended inquiry into his church-related activities in the 1880's, his second selection as a bishop, a choice in 1890 which was followed by ordination and a return to the Methodist fold, is incomprehensible.

The years of freedom from control by an episcopal superior were enjoyed by Dr. Haygood, who felt he was fulfilling his call and calling in his own way. But such an anomalous membership in a Southern Methodist conference was not unusual in the 1880's. In fact, the most prominent men in the largest conferences were often the editors of church papers, college presidents or professors, and officers of boards (missions and church extension) in Nashville. It was these men who dominated the field in the selection of new bishops in 1882, 1886, and 1890. John Keener, Linus Parker, and Charles Galloway, for instance, had been successive editors of the *New Orleans Christian Advocate*. John Granbery, R. K. Hargrove, W. W. Duncan, and E. R. Hendrix, elected bishop either in 1882 or 1886, were college men. O. P. Fitzgerald, chosen in 1890 when Haygood was elected for the second time, was editor of the *Nashville Christian Advocate*.[1]

None of these other bishops, however, had detached themselves from conference ties so completely as had Dr. Haygood. It is true that all were in effect free of domination by a supervising bishop, in their earlier tasks. This freedom was possible because of the death in 1884 of Bishop Pierce and also of Bishop Kavanaugh, in their prime both "strong" bishops. The influential Bishop McTyeire lived on until 1889, but McTyeire had been a leader in democratizing the church, and besides, as a former editor and college man, had a natural understanding of the younger generation's desire for independence. It was he who had proclaimed the progressives' ideal: free men, both ministers and laymen, though susceptible to moral suasion, should be responsible for their individual spiritual and moral growth.

Haygood surely felt that he had episcopal sanction for his ignoring of episcopal authority, particularly at the time of his break from Bishop Pierce, after 1880. It is not surprising that he considered McTyeire his church's leading "statesman." In his forties, though, Haygood was emboldened to go far beyond McTyeire's position. In 1881, when several bishops attended an ecumenical conference of Methodists in London, Haygood editorialized in the *Wesleyan Advocate* that some of the conferences that fall would have to do without a bishop as presiding officer. His implication was clearly that the business of presiding would not be harmed at *any* time if the man with the gavel lacked episcopal ordination. There is no direct evidence, but it may be assumed furthermore that Haygood accepted the premise of most if not all presiding elders that they could arrange appointments more satisfactorily than any bishop; it was they who knew best who deserved promotion and demotion.[2]

In 1896 D. C. Kelley, an independent-spirited minister in Nashville (and a consistently unsuccessful aspirant for the episcopacy) wrote in private correspondence that Haygood had taught him "my first ideas of over much Episcopal power," pronouncing the Presbyterian doctrine that the non-apostolic ordination of Methodist bishops following heated election campaigns in general conferences "the source from which sprang lines of portentous division between the bishops and the brethren."[3] It may be argued that Haygood's position was a logical extension of McTyeire's ideal of self-government. Since the progressives after 1866 destroyed the elaborate overseeing of parishioners' behavior by ministers—and of the preachers' performance by the bishops—the role of the bishop had logically been reduced to that of a presiding officer at conferences, at bishops' meetings, and at appointment conclaves of the presiding elders. The influence of the Northern Methodists confirmed Haygood in his opposition to a sacrament of ordination of bishops, with its implications that elders thereby achieved a higher spiritual rank.

Atticus's problem was that he did not fit into either the prewar or postwar generation. He felt close to Lovick Pierce's generation, now all dead, with its awareness of the importance of a distinction between Arminianism and Calvinism. Such niceties were not important even to leading ministers any more; since the war the preaching in low church Protestant pulpits was much less denominational. And certainly there was no need felt among laymen for emphasis on doctrine; the "progressive" Sunday schools after 1870 produced a generation totally ignorant of the Articles of Religion from any kind of coherent theological viewpoint. Unread in matters of faith, Southerners by the 1880's were even more unread in general cultural matters than they had been in 1861, when Atticus had made the comment that his people were not readers. Pulpits of prominent churches were filled with attractive personalities who had no strong sectarian intellectual guideline. Furthermore, intellectuals in their editorial and college positions were isolated from the run-of-the-mill preachers. And the country people, once patient hearers of long and difficult sermons, were beginning to protest the near monopoly of the bishops' seats by the intellectuals. Shortly before the General Conference of 1886 a Tennessean wrote the *Nashville Advocate* that what the church needed was "A Field Hand for Bishop."[4] One of the new bishops that year, Joseph S. Key, a non-intellectual politician-type from South Georgia, came near filling the Tennessean's bill. But Key did not emerge as a "strong" bishop.

Atticus Haygood, not fitting categories by which other candidates were judged—he was in a sense both an ecclesiastical traditionalist and a secularist, both a democrat and the logical heir to the autocratic Bishop Pierce—might have been able to provide the kind of strong leadership many laymen felt that the church needed. In 1882 his prestige was high, despite the recent publication of *Our Brother in Black*, the conference somewhat reluctantly agreeing to the book's suggestion for the establishment of a Southern Methodist training school for Negro teachers and preachers of the C. M. E. church.[5] This prestige overrode some valid objections to his election. In protecting his own reputation, Dr. Haygood had in 1878 tactlessly added to the disgrace of A. H. Redford, the former Nashville Publishing House book agent, then under fire for falsifying his accounts.[6] Redford's fellow Kentuckians felt unkindly toward Haygood for deserting his former associate so ruthlessly. At the time of the 1882 conference, moreover, Haygood was working for the appointment as agent of the Slater Fund. Had it been generally known, he would surely have lost votes. As it was, when Haygood refused ordination after receiving the necessary majority for election as a bishop, his puzzled contemporaries judged the action as a shirking of duly delegated responsibility.[7]

To a few influential men who knew Haygood's private view about the episcopacy, however, his refusal to succeed Pierce, his sponsor, as the "Georgia autocrat" of the church must have been seen as an act as praiseworthy as it was unbelievably self-effacing. After Pierce died in 1884, Dr. Haygood's hostility to succeeding him obviously softened. He returned to an earlier view that bishops were valuable as leaders of church opinion, even though he continued to disagree with the Southern Methodist contention that episcopal ordination was as much a sacrament for Methodists as for Anglicans. In 1886 Haygood rebuked D. C. Kelley for derogatory remarks about the bishops' jealous determination to keep their ranks thin. And there was at least one report that Haygood by 1886 wanted to be re-elected to the episcopacy, to leave his quarreling North Georgia brethren, and to move to Texas.[8]

Only a few members of the General Conference of 1886 voted for Haygood in the elections of new bishops, and his relationship to his annual conferences remained tenuous for three years. A book produced in 1889, *The Man of Galilee*, delighted everybody from the intellectuals to the politicking city pastors and immediately restored much of Haygood's prestige. The book was a candid effort to spell out the very real problems raised about the "dual nature" of Christ, settled for all time in the fourth century until the nineteenth-century Biblical scholarship of Renan and others reopened the issue. Haygood did not really answer the new questions, but his book seemed to protect the Biblical personality of Jesus familiar to Southern Methodists. Therefore, even in Louisiana, a state unfriendly to Bishop Pierce and to Haygood's work with the Negro colleges, *The Man of Galilee* was called "chief among the few books of the day worthy of deep study."[9] At the St. Louis General Conference, 1890, Dr. Haygood was given a phenomenal vote of confidence when nearly two-thirds of the delegates elected him a bishop on the first ballot, an unprecedented act, especially since he was not present.[10]

This vote indicated the confidence of rank-and-file leadership in Dr. Haygood. The time had nevertheless passed when anyone could be as influential in the church as Bishop Pierce had been into the 1870's. In 1890 Bishop John Keener was the "Senior Bishop." Haygood was in a sense returning to the fold after his secularist activities of the 1880's and therefore not of a temperament to challenge Keener's position. Ironically, he had many times in the 1880's acted like Bishop Pierce's successor. It had been said of him that "his utterances bear a sort of official stamp which gives them . . . with many, almost ex cathedra authority."[11]

He accepted the lowliest episcopal appointment, in his strange new diffidence, and in 1891 moved to California to become superintendent of the two weak California conferences and the mission conferences in Mexico. There was some gallantry in the move, for he had long demanded that the church appoint resident supervisors of its missionary activities. His service on the West Coast was generally hailed as truly idealistic, but his absence from the main arena of the church nonetheless reduced sharply his influence in Nashville. Twice during his short episcopacy he was overruled on missions policy—a concern he considered his special province. In May 1893 only Bishop Hendrix stood by him when Haygood asked for an enthusiastic support of Southern Methodist expansion in California and Mexico.[12]

His removal to the Coast also resulted in the diminution of his bishop-like authority in Georgia, built up after Bishop Pierce's death. Especially after 1885 he was the chief force in counteracting the ambitions of preachers in Georgia susceptible to the Holiness movement. Haygood's rapid decline in authority in his home state was exactly paralleled by the meteoric rise of his young friend and "political deputy," Warren Candler. In 1888 Haygood influenced the board's selection of Candler as president of Emory College, and his acquisition of the degree of doctor of divinity.[13]

As president, Candler was in a position to further his own career. He built a personal reputation for managerial strength by enlarging Emory's endowment. He attracted attention in the state, and a defensive loyalty among Georgia Methodists, by his willingness to speak boldly on controversial questions, but unlike Haygood his boldness never flaunted public opinion of the Populist era. In 1893, the year Haygood returned from Califonia to Oxford, for instance, Candler was engaged in a two-front war, vehemently attacking the University of Georgia as un-Christian and "exposing" the W. C. T. U. as a "front" for the woman's suffrage movement.[14] In 1889 Dr. Candler would become Bishop Candler, reviving the tradition of a "strong," autocratic Georgia bishop. From 1893 until 1896, Haygood's personal, political, and spiritual strength dwindled, until all could see that he was living in Oxford as no more than Candler's ward. Outside North Georgia this loss of leadership was not widely known during Haygood's lifetime, and he apparently retained a great amount of the rank-and-file's affection and respect which had made possible his election in 1890.

The gradual domination by Candler of a relationship of twenty years' standing, so important to his successful emergence as the political power of North Georgia Methodists, is intertwined with the story of the rise and fall of the Holiness movement and with the continued weakening of Southern Methodism as a healthful spiritual force. Between 1882 and 1885 Haygood and Candler were estranged, the younger man allying himself with the leaders of the Holiness movement. Candler apparently made his decision for two reasons. He believed that the Holiness preachers would succeed in their aim of dominating the conference. On a less pragmatic basis he admired the spellbinding preaching methods of traveling evangelists who brought the Holiness doctrines into Methodist pulpits. Although Candler never subscribed to the "Second Blessing" theory, he was, like many other young ministers of city churches, addicted to the practice of haranguing respectable congregations on their sins. Dr. Haygood's position was that pretension to righteousness—by the Holiness preachers' definition, the equivalent of Christian virtue—was by far the worst sin of all, more unforgivable than even drinking or sexual impurity. Candler may be called an exponent of a "New Puritanism" which was strengthened in Georgia from Holiness roots, and as a result, in intellectual direction he parted company with Haygood. Their cordiality was nevertheless renewed in 1885. If the friendship was, from Dr. Candler's point of view, slightly strained, it is almost certain that Haygood never stopped loving his "Dear Warren."[15]

The emergence of the "New Puritanism" in the 1880's is best centered around the phenomenal success of those who determined to turn American Protestant denominations into "prohibition" churches. The campaign began in earnest about 1880 and was completed by the mid-1890's. The movement was the cumulative result of the activities of many individuals, of enormously varying motivations, theological viewpoints, and social philosophies. In the first stages, most of the prohibitionists shared a genuine humanitarian concern for those victimized by drink. Atticus Haygood's participation was limited to this phase of the movement. By the 1890's three large organizations, the Women's Christian Temperance Union, the Anti-Saloon League, and the Prohibition Party dominated individual efforts and enlisted persons whose talents were often organizational rather than humanitarian.[16]

The success of the prohibitionists in the South paralleled the program and philosophy of the Populist era. Anti-liquor appeals capitalized on the common notion that the Negro drunk was a menace to white womanhood and, at the ballot box, to a broadly based state government. In 1890 a Georgian, Sam Small, a former newspaperman newly converted to Methodism, wrote that "The men of the two races stand in such relation . . . that slight inflammations cause general disturbances. . . . One gallon of whiskey . . . is enough to raise 'a race war.' "[17] Moreover, prohibitionism fit well into the Populist crusade against the alleged conspiracy of rich men and the city dwellers to undermine the farm. A prohibitionist could be hostile to (1) the pleasure-loving and callous rich, (2) the whiskey trust, and (3) that anti-American menace, the Roman Catholics, all in one fell swoop. In the South especially, where as elsewhere the saloons were located adjacent to town red-light districts, Protestant penance was often satisfied in the shedding of tears for "fallen women," whose initial steps toward degradation were thought always to have begun on the dance floor or in attendance upon the theatre. Growing resentment against the millionaires of the East, shared by the farmers with the business leaders of small Southern cities, was warmed by prohibitionist propaganda which contrasted the lenient treatment given the drunken top-hatted playboy with the certain imprisonment of the drunken workingman. In 1888 a Methodist preacher in Georgia claimed that eliminating the availability of liquor would strikingly reduce "the mistreatment of the lower and more dependent classes by the upper and more independent."[18]

The most advanced prohibitionist church was the Northern Methodist. Between 1882 and 1884 the denomination's scholarly magazine printed a series of articles conclusively proving, to the author's and editor's satisfaction, that the wine Jesus had used in the Last Supper and at the wedding feast was unfermented grape juice.[19] The General Conference of the church, in 1884 and 1886, condemned the "social glass" and endorsed the secular prohibitionist movement to end all legal sale of spirits.

Southern Methodists were followers of their Northern brethren. In the rural South the conversion of peaches into brandy, scuppernongs into wine, and corn into ardent spirits was so much a part of the country folk culture that the city-based condemnation was slow to effect embarrassment among Baptists and Methodists. In 1854 the Southern Methodists in their General Conference had repealed a clause in Wesley's Discipline which forbade preachers to "distill or vend spirituous liquors."[20] The 1874 clarification of the church rule against the use of light wines aroused, therefore, loud protest—notably from Tennessee. But commitment to abstinence did not embrace the favoring of the church's engagement in political campaigns to outlaw the sale of liquor in saloons. So late as 1882, Charles Galloway, who would after 1886 become the church's leading prohibitionist, as editor and then bishop, refused to join the Prohibition Party of Mississippi. As a Georgia layman expressed it in the *Wesleyan Advocate,*

The coercive principle is a stranger to Christianity, and it is a mortifying shame to all who have an anxious concern for the purity . . . of the ministry to see the sacred robes of the Gospel dragged into the filthy scum of politics, in order to accomplish that which the Church failed to do.[21]

The General Conference of the Southern church, by 1894, made it church law that none of its members could sign a petition asking for the sale of liquor, or become a bondsman for anyone seeking a license to sell, or rent property to tavern-keepers. Non-compliance could subject the delinquent member to a church trial, the means for correction which had taken the place of the prewar class and probationary systems. By this new means, a church member might be impeached of charges drawn up by a special committee investigating his behavior and, after trial by a church court, might be excluded from membership.[22]

Governmental prohibition of the sale of liquor in local political jurisdictions began in the South in the 1870's. In Georgia the first legislation specifically calling for a local election on the question occurred in 1878. Special legislation thereafter was so rapid in coming that by the end of the Colquitt regime, in 1882, eight-tenths of the counties were legally dry—these being rural counties where the church influence could not be openly challenged.

After 1881 the Methodists were at the center of the campaign to dry up Georgia. When Frances Willard of the W. C. T. U. visited Georgia in 1881 and again in 1883, her biggest welcome was in Atlanta, where Governor and Mrs. Colquitt and H. I. Kimball were the leading spirits. In Oxford, Haygood presented her to the student body of Emory. The Greek professor there, Henry Scomp, became the historian of the "Temperance Movement" in Georgia, his ponderously statistical *King Alcohol in the Realm of King Cotton* being published in 1888.[23] The Baptists in the state by the mid-1880's were mostly prohibitionist, but during the 1884 convention a Baptist preacher was still moved to inform the other elders that the Lord's Supper demanded the use of real wine.[24] Urging by the two major Protestant denominations induced the state legislature to make it possible to hold prohibition elections without special act. The movement reached an early apogee in Georgia in 1886-1887, when Atlanta became, briefly, dry, the evangelist Sam Jones adding laurels to his crown in this achievement. Even Henry Grady, a somewhat tepid Methodist, supported the anti-alcohol campaign—primarily because his opponent, Hoke Smith, was heading up the anti-prohibitionists.[25]

Dr. Haygood's participation in the prohibition campaign began in 1880 and ended abruptly in 1887. His motives grew out of his sympathy for those people he called "The Neglected Classes." Unlike some prohibitionists his concern for the victims of drink was not matched by an animus against the victimizers. In 1885 he preached in Candler's pulpit in Augusta and spoke movingly of an Army friend "who occasionally flung himself into a drunken debauch. . . . How he writhed in spiritual agony when he came to himself." The argument of the sermon was that "the occasional drunkard" was "unspeakably" better than "the self-contained self-satisfied Pharisee." He warned his Augusta audience of "the folly of trying to be Christians by merely trying to get to heaven."[26] No doubt Haygood's sermon was unsettling to many who heard him. They were accustomed to hearing Candler's "stirring sermons" on the wickedness of drinking, dancing, theatre-going, card-playing, swearing, "even wine on family tables." More than once they had heard Candler in ringing climaxes like this—"The light of the millennial morning will not fall upon the earth to arouse from unholy slumbers a world of debauchees and drunkards."[27]

Haygood's appearance in Candler's church re-established a friendly relationship between two men whose pulpit style was as dissimilar as were their temperaments and ages. The friendship had been under a severe strain since the preceding October. Articles by both in the *Wesleyan Advocate* broadcast the open challenge Candler was making of Haygood's use of his influence against conference exponents of "Holiness." At the Conference of 1884, they openly clashed. Candler, from the Committee on Sabbath Desecration, presented a list of specific items of Sunday behavior which should be taboo for Methodists. Haygood, feeling very keenly the decline of emphasis in Georgia Wesleyanism on inner values, jumped up and proposed an amendment which would have eliminated enumeration of specifics.[28] As a result of Candler's renewed friendship with Haygood in 1885 and after, his attitude toward drunkards and fallen women was considerably humanized, and when a meeting to establish an Augusta home for women of the streets was held at St. Johns, Haygood was charitably invited back as a fund-raising speaker.

The rebuilt friendship was aided by their mutual interest in Lundy H. Harris. Harris was adjunct professor of languages of the "Sub-Fresh" Department at Emory until the spring of 1882, when he scandalized Oxford by succumbing to the influence of liquor and, it was commonly thought, of narcotics. Haygood allowed him to resign, but for a year or two Lundy resented the president's refusal to vouch for his story that Dr. Evans had prescribed liquor for him for his psychosomatic ills—liquor, he claimed, first spooned out to him by Mrs. Atticus Haygood from the family medicine cabinet. Feeling despondent and outcast, Harris came under the influence of his former classmate, Candler, who gave him "gloomy books" to read and left him unhappy until he felt that God forgave him. With his "experience" and a satisfying marriage, Harris regained composure and much later became a preacher. During Candler's presidency he returned to Oxford as a language professor at Emory, Candler favoring his advancement over the eccentric Scomp. When Bishop Haygood came home to Oxford in 1893, Lundy Harris became his intimate friend. This strange communion between the two suffering souls—Haygood being by then a sick, defeated man—was seemingly crucial in the spiritual descent of both. Two years after Haygood's death, that is in 1898, Professor Harris left Emory College for the second and final time, a despondent man, having fallen again into excessive indulgence.[29]

Between 1884 and 1887 Dr. Haygood was an outstanding lecturer on the prohibitionists' platform, having graduated from the role of mere writer of pamphlets. His first appearance was in September 1884, at Salem Camp Ground at the inauguration of the unsuccessful campaign to dry up Newton County. In 1885 he spoke in a gospel tent set up on a vacant lot in Atlanta, sharing honors with Sam Jones, then on the threshold of his national reputation as an evangelist. In 1887 Haygood spoke in Raleigh and Concord, North Carolina, and during July was the chief speaker for the W. C. T. U. in a hot and arduous campaign (also unsuccessful) in Texas. His children Mamie and Wilbur accompanied him on this sawdust trail, as musicians. In December 1887 he was one of two prohibition lecturers invited to speak at a "social gospel" convention in Washington, D. C., a meeting of distinguished Protestant humanitarians organized by W. E. Dodge, Jr., a trustee of the Slater Fund.

There were surely other invitations, but Haygood did not make a single appearance after 1887 on behalf of the prohibitionist movement. His disinterest may have been strengthened by Candler, with his special dislike for the W. C. T. U. Neither of the men was a sympathizer with suffragettes, many of whom were prominent in the W. C. T. U. Haygood probably was offended furthermore by the scandal in 1887 of a Mississippi debate between the prohibitionist Bishop Galloway and Jefferson Davis. Davis was still a Southern hero, and many Southern Methodist preachers may have shared his embarrassment that "a dignitary of the Methodist Church, South, should have left the pulpit and the Bible to mount the political rostrum and plead the higher law of prohibitionism—the substitution of force for . . . moral responsibility."[30]

Haygood's seven-year league with the prohibitionists was but one aspect of his quasi-episcopal activities in Georgia Methodism in the 1880's. Between Bishop Pierce's death in 1884 and his own in 1896, his major theological and political encounter was with the preachers leading the Holiness movement in North Georgia, men who had made Bishop Pierce's last two or three years miserable. In July 1885, at the Oxford District Conference, Dr. Haygood preached a sermon on "Growth in Grace," a well-wrought doctrinal sermon designed to dispute categorically the Holiness preachers' contention that the Wesleyan tradition contemplated the possibility of the *attainment* of purity, of perfection in this world.[31] The sermon was a brave move calculated to put on the defensive those conference lights who had "captured" the Gainesville District—adjacent to the Oxford district—by the appointments of late 1884, following the death of Bishop Pierce.

Haygood was emboldened to speak ex cathedra for North Georgia doctrinal orthodoxy because of the stand taken in 1884 by Wilbur F. Tillett, Vanderbilt University theologian, who called all varieties of the Holiness teaching "semi-Pelagian." Tillett meant by this that, in contrast to the orthodox Augustinian tradition which emphasized the helplessness of sinful man and his utter dependence on the Trinity for the action of saving grace, Holiness theology placed a large faith in the human capacity for self-improvement. Tillett and Haygood both felt that the effect of the Holiness teaching was to convince Methodists that they could attain salvation through willing it.[32] Haygood, though his teaching influence was limited in the 1880's to the pre-ministerial students at Emory, was as good and orthodox a theologian as Tillett. The theme of his anti-Holiness argument is that the realm of Nature is separated from the realm in which Grace saves. Man could control nature and could to some extent discipline his body, but he could not control the destiny of the soul—salvation being a phenomenon in the spiritual rather than in the natural world.

Holiness "do-it-yourself" doctrines of salvation appeared in Georgia Methodism first in the pulpits of town churches where the congregations refused to listen to long sermons and were, as Haygood had frequently observed, doctrinally illiterate. In the late 1870's Holiness evangelists came into Methodist pulpits during the revival season. Their point of origin was most frequently Kentucky, a state well known for its inter-denominational tendencies. Within Southern Methodism they made the greatest inroads in Mississippi and Georgia. At first they taught only that the good Methodist should seek "heart purity." Even to older Methodists this sounded like Wesleyan doctrine. J. E. Evans, one of the oldest preachers in northern Georgia, had been preaching the possibility of total conversion since before the war, when he became a convert to the teachings of Mrs. Phoebe Palmer. In 1854 Evans suggested that George Pierce should not be elected a bishop because he denied the "Wesleyan" teaching that a man could become totally holy.[33] In the late 1870's Evans still wielded considerable influence and was admired by Haygood and others as a man genuinely interested in the spiritual development of the Negro.

The younger men in the North Georgia Conference, some of them college educated but none of them as well trained in doctrine as was Haygood, were understandably confused as to the true Wesleyan orthodoxy on the possibility of earthly holiness. Most susceptible to the traveling evangelists' teachings were W. C. Dunlap, A. J. Jarrell, and Asbury Dodge. Jarrell and Dodge were Haygood's associates on the Watkinsville circuit in 1862. Open confrontation between the position which Haygood maintained, having been taught it by Lovick Pierce, and that of Evans and the younger men was delayed. Haygood waited until after Bishop Pierce's death in 1884 to challenge the political clique grown up around Jarrell and other Holiness exponents.[34]

Between 1880 and 1884 the Holiness preachers were on the offensive. They accused Bishop Pierce and other "secularists"—meaning Haygood, Clement A. Evans, and W. H. LaPrade—of setting a sinful example among Methodist laymen because they smoked. Dunlap was the most persistent critic on this score. He loved to testify to his own failure to conquer the tobacco habit, though an ordained preacher, until his will to conquer had been strengthened by a "second blessing," the final experience of grace needed for the attainment of purity. These charges against such prominent Georgia preachers—accompanied by whispers that Bishop Pierce showed signs of never having had a *first* blessing, salvation from eternal damnation—were accompanied by a political power play within the North Georgia Conference. Haygood's own political role was confused until 1885 because he too was challenging "overmuch episcopal authority."

The Holiness challenge was well organized. A district Holiness association emerged to match each district conference, and a conference-wide association made it possible to build a hierarchy among the Holiness preachers and laymen. The conference associations met in the churches where the congregations were most enthralled by traveling non-Methodist evangelists. These were all town churches—in North Georgia the cities of Dalton, Gainesville, Athens, and Milledgeville, and in South Georgia primarily Waycross. The church in Gainesville, which may or may not have been typical, had only "one college man" in its membership, but "some very excellent and deeply pious women."[35]

There was little tendency among Georgia preachers before 1884 to dismantle the Holiness structures within the conferences. Many preachers who did not subscribe to the Holiness demand that all Methodist laymen devote themselves to receiving a second blessing felt that sermons emotionally exhorting congregations on the importance of "heart purity" were spiritually beneficial. In this group were the elderly S. P. Richardson and Haygood's brother-in-law, George Yarbrough. To young quick-witted alumni of Emory, like James W. Lee and Warren Candler, moreover, the Holiness preachers were brothers in arms in their cries against smoking and other aspects of behavior which the "New Puritanism" found abhorrent in its own rigid way. Lee was a "simple hearted sincere emotional" and pretentiously serious young man. Even his friends said that he was "too fond of Theodore Parker and Emerson." His "philosophical" sermons delighted congregations in Dalton and Atlanta, and in 1892 he published a pompous book, possessing all the accidents but none of the substance of thought.[36]

Both Candler and Lee, in their search for prominence, felt that the political prospects of the Holiness preachers were as sound as their teachings on correct Methodist behavior. It would be advantageous to be friendly to the challengers of Bishop Pierce. The bishop died in September 1884. The North Georgia Holiness Association met at Candler's church in Augusta in October, no doubt using the occasion to plan strategy for influencing conference appointments. By no coincidence the visiting bishop concentrated Holiness preachers in a single district centered on Gainesville, thus providing them an ideal base during 1885 for furthering their domination, political and doctrinal.[37]

The Holiness doctrines, as taught in their "pure" form by evangelists, required that a man seeking salvation be uneasy until he attained through some emotional experience (long after he had become a member of any church) a *certainty* that he was totally pure. *Uncertainty* was a symptom of only partial salvation. In the charged atmosphere of revivals, of course, almost any sympathetic hearer could remember moments of doubt and depression, and many lapses of behavior, if only to the extent of thinking of profane words and licentious thoughts. If his regular pastor followed up the revival with similar warnings that the man was not yet saved, he could be easily convinced that radical new experiences in church were necessary for him to attain a complete blessing and a seat in heaven. The "new experiences" were offered in new liturgies for the worship services, the use of special songs (in songbooks sometimes sold by traveling evangelists), acceptance of "speaking in tongues," and to a limited degree acts of faith healing.

During the 1870's and 1880's many books were available to the Holiness preachers as authority for their claim that the teachings were directly derived from John Wesley. Foremost among the writers who were Southern Methodists were Albert T. Bledsoe, J. M. Boland, Thomas N. Ralston, and C. W. Miller. Bledsoe, with a background in both Calvinistic and Anglican theology, on conversion to Arminian principles exaggerated the power of will. Miller was his disciple and delighted in refuting the Calvinist doctrine of original sin to the point where he said the activity of the undirected will after birth created all evil. Ralston published an *Elements of Divinity* in 1875 which maintained that "Christian perfection is attainable in this life."[38] Boland, who did not demand experience of a second blessing, sounded so much like Lovick Pierce that, in a doctrinally ignorant age, his cry for heart-purity was especially helpful to Holiness preachers in Georgia. All these theologians were influenced by the climate of Tennessee or Kentucky, the latter state being the site in the early 1870's of interdenominational camp meetings. The leading Holiness preacher in the Ohio Valley was J. A. Wood, a disciple of John S. Inskip, who moved into western Pennsylvania in the 1860's. The most popular evangelist in Georgia Methodist churches in the late 1870's was J. D. Godbey from Kentucky, apparently not a Methodist.[39]

Dr. Haygood's sermon before the Oxford District Conference in 1885 began an attack on the political influence of the Holiness preachers in Georgia and a determined assault on their claim that they were in the clearest line of heritage of the Wesleyan tradition. His leadership encouraged others, both preachers and laymen. One sermon pointed out that the Holiness men appointed to churches in the Gainesville District had taken over the camp ground near Dahlonega. At one of their meetings there, a visiting non-Holiness pastor could not "stop [the people from] rejoicing and testifying long enough to hear the cause and cry of the orphan." When he tried to get his congregation to be quietly seated "a coldness come [sic] over the meeting and many scattered to their tents."[40] Two articles to the *Wesleyan Advocate*, written by H. P. Bell, Emory Trustee and a lawyer-politician from Cumming, describe the schismatic aims of the Gainesville District presiding elder and his chief subordinates:

They have changed the name of our meetings, substituting Holiness for Methodist. They preach a different doctrine . . . ; they sing different songs; they patronize and circulate a different literature; they have adopted radically different words of worship. . . .

A sanctified light was asked a short time ago why Dr. Haygood and other distinguished ministers were not invited to their meetings? He replied that "they did not want those opposed to them at their meetings."

Bell said their teachings in North Georgia were these:

1. That entire sanctification can be claimed "right now. . . ."
2. That the Lord will give new lungs to consumptives. . . .
3. Faith cure is a progressive work; no instances cited. . . .
4. That the hundreds of thousands of non-holiness people are saved if at all on same basis as children and idiots.[41]

Haygood's action to destroy Holiness respectability was in part "episcopal" displeasure at the threat to the "polity" of the church. More personally, his unyielding opposition to the Holiness movement grew out of his longtime commitment to intelligence in the pulpit and trained understanding in the pew. His early distaste for "loud preaching" had become an ingrained prejudice after hearing the Northern Baptist preacher, Dewitt Talmage, in 1881. He was also profoundly aware that the traveling evangelists and their stationed imitators (including Emory graduates like Jarrell) were capitalizing on illiteracy. In several *Advocate* articles of the 1880's he spoke his alarm at the widespread feeling among pre-ministerials that the "call to preach" made a college education supererogatory. Haygood maintained that the call was a "call to get ready." He registered shock at the postwar generation's narrow reading. In 1881 while still editor of the *Wesleyan* he expressed concern when he was criticized for advocating the reading of imaginative literature—"Robinson Crusoe, Arabian Nights, and such like"—strongly defending the proposition (so alien to the spirit of the "New Puritanism") that reading good novels for pleasure was "not to be classed with dancing, diceing or drinking."[42]

On the question of reading, as on the Holiness politics, Haygood found himself at outs with Candler, who seemingly believed that the reading of plays was equivalent to attending the theatre and that the main calling of playwrights was to make depravity attractive. During a brief residence in Nashville Candler vilified an actress, who gently rebuked him at the end of a vicious antitheatre sermon, leading D. C. Kelley to observe that "It was hard to believe that a boy who has completed the curriculum of a high school could . . . speak" so derogatorily about the dramatic heritage of Western civilization.[43]

After 1890 Bishop Haygood was in a position to use appointments so as to demote those preachers who persisted in the political aspirations of the 1880's. In 1893 he gave "permission" for J. W. Lee and A. J. Jarrell to transfer their membership to a Missouri conference.[44] With their most aggressive leaders intimidated, the Holiness associations in the two Georgia conferences continued to meet, but every year in less and less important churches. In 1894 the North Georgia Holiness Association met in the sanctuary of the Methodist church in the little town of Harlem, outside Augusta. In 1895 no congregation would approve of their meeting in a Southern Methodist church, and so the Association had to use a tent on Edgewood Avenue in Atlanta. Asbury Dodge was the only member of the North Georgia Conference to persist in his allegiance to the movement, despite demotion back to the appointment of city missionary in Atlanta, a position he had held twenty-five years earlier. Dodge was a leader in the development of the interdenominational Holiness Camp Ground at Indian Springs, between Atlanta and Macon, in 1895.

Haygood's campaign had been successful for several reasons. First he had influenced appointments made in 1885 and 1886 by Bishops McTyeire and Wilson. After 1889 his friend John W. Heidt became an influential deputy in the conference, and Bishop Haygood imported the Reverend W. B. Stradley from Los Angeles in 1893 as another deputy. In the 1890's Haygood had Dr. Candler's co-operation, since Emory's professional future was tied in part to the education of a greater proportion of the ministers of Georgia. Haygood also enlisted influential lay support in the demeaning of Holiness excesses. An Elberton editor on hearing Bishop Haygood preach in 1894 commented in an editorial column:

> We had always considered Bishop Haygood an intellectual giant, but somehow there was woven into our admiration . . . a dark thread of prejudice that marred the beauty of the otherwise splendid character. . . . It grew out of the mere name of a book of which he is the author, "Our Brother in Black," and was strengthened by the gossip of an uninformed public criticism. We are free to acknowledge we have never read the book, but we intend to do so now since listening to the splendid sermon. . . .
>
> The doctrine of finite perfection dispelled before his clear analytical text and exposition. . . . He said the idea that some people entertained that there was a line beyond which God refused to grant mercy

to the culprit was against all attributes of his divine Master, and that the line was drawn by man and not by God.[45]

The General Conference of 1894 heard the bishops denounce those doctrines, falsely purporting to be "Wesleyan," which had infiltrated Southern Methodist parishes. John J. Tigert, Tillett's successor at Vanderbilt, and Haygood led in the clean-up campaign of 1894-1895. The Georgia bishop lampooned traveling evangelists as "tramps" and in his last book, *The Monk and The Prince*, made as unattractive as possible emotional "messianic" preaching. The Florentine monk, Savonarola, was portrayed in the mold of a Georgia Methodist Holiness preacher four centuries later.[46] It would seem that unintended results of this episcopal interdict against the second blessing scourge were progressively less doctrinal preaching and an intellectual timidity in the pulpit, which Haygood especially would have found pitiable by his own standards. In July 1895, W. F. Quillian, an established North Georgia preacher, chose as his sermon topic for a Rome congregation the now dangerous matter of "Sanctification." The sermon is platitudinous, and the good Dr. Quillian defined being holy as affecting docility, living like a child.[47]

The Holiness movement was truly a doctrinal vagary, but it served the purpose of making townspeople excited about their church affiliation. Less commendably, as Haygood feared it would, in its separatist tendencies it reduced a consciousness of "being a Methodist" to the vaguest kind of denominational loyalty. It would seem that its insistence on behavioral manifestations furthered the "New Puritanism" and for many Georgia Methodists in the 1890's reduced religion to anxiety-ridden observance of the sacred "dont's." With the development of unique individual inner values discounted, the relationship between the preacher and the layman became a mockery of what the progressives of 1866 had intended in their repudiation of the ante-bellum ideal of supervisory responsibility. The Southern Methodist preacher of the 1890's had to sermonize in an intellectual void; he was expected to act as a kind of policeman who only rarely could exert a sort of parental guidance over his timid flock. In 1893 the old preacher George G. Smith mourned the fact that it was "generally conceded that a vigorous execution of the laws of the Church, rigidly interpreted, is . . . impossible."[48] The 1890's were not gay times; a widespread spiritual depression accompanied the economic anguishes of a people whose center of life had shifted from the barnyard lot to store vestibules in town.[49]

Bishop Haygood in his declining years was troubled by the unhappy role of pastors, but had no training for the analysis of social change. He did know that too much was being said by ministers and everyone else about the need for "refined feminine sensibility." He had no sympathy for the growing influence of ladies within church congregations, but there is no record that he realized the desperate quest for manhood on the part of white males of the younger generation, who had lost the mastery of their fathers over both slaves and wives. As he grew older, Haygood saw more clearly that his own spiritual development, as aberrant as it had been, was partly the product of an ante-bellum Methodism which encouraged healthy introspection. It was distressing to recognize that not even an exceptional man like himself, of Candler's generation, could launch so bravely as he had on a private spiritual quest into God's mysteries.

TEN

The Uncommon Schoolman

DESPITE the significance of his role within the Methodist Episcopal Church, South, Dr. Haygood himself felt after 1880 that his new calling was in behalf of a constituency larger than his church, his state, his race. His professional career during the 1880's was that of a professional advocate of the recognition by whites of the potentialities of the American Negro. Less professional—after 1884 when he resigned from the presidency of Emory College—but perhaps more hearty than his interest either in church polity or the Negro cause was Haygood's passion for education, its availability and relevance. In his Slater work, of course, he was fighting a losing battle in his attempt to sharpen the Southern white man's conscience about his obligation toward the former slave. In the long, successful doctrinal war against the Holiness movement, and the futile stand against the pharisaism of the "New Puritanism," Haygood was a striking anachronism.

The work in behalf of education was another matter. Here he was completely in step with his times. The 1880's produced a peak of national interest in the new ideas of the vocational relevance of education and of the need for the Federal government to underwrite the efforts of the common school, especially in the South. Furthermore, in Georgia the 1880's was the decade when the common school became truly accepted as an integral institution of Christian civilization. Such was not the case at the beginning of the decade. State financial support in 1880 was feeble, and many Georgia Methodist preachers condemned elementary education in secular institutions as immoral. The weight of Dr. Haygood's influence in the dramatic transformation is far more evident than in any other of his endeavors. Supported by his continuing admiration for his old teacher, Gustavus J. Orr, until 1887 superintendent of Georgia's public school system, Haygood "singlehandedly" modified the attitude of Georgia Methodism. His influence as president of Emory, and as elder statesman during the presidency of his immediate successor, though more restricted in its effects on Georgia education, was timely and vitalizing. Emory College engaged in experiments in higher education between 1879 and 1888, some of them abortive, some leading to important growth. Ironically, Dr. Candler received in hindsight credit not only for the viability of Emory's curriculum of the 1890's but also for much of Haygood's accomplishments as an advocate of the public schools.

The common school system in Georgia was authorized by the Reconstruction constitution of 1868. Opposition to its inauguration was quite open. In 1869 the editor of the weekly paper in Covington frankly said that the attempt to equalize educational opportunity (an ideal of Greene Haygood in 1858) was "socialism":

The proposition ... for the establishment of a State School system will doubtless become a law, and the first notice of its enactment which will attract the attention of the people, will be the discovery that the control of education of their own children has been taken out of the hands of parents, and transferred to strangers whose interest only leads them to train the rising generation to be subservient to the directions of a central oligarchy. A State religion is scarcely more at variance with a free government than a State educational system.[1]

This conservative position comes from the ancient belief, dominant in Southern white society, that the social order is a federation of families. The revolutionary idea of the eighteenth century that the individual has a "liberty" and purpose outside the family was logically at war with family loyalties. Education, to the Covington editor, as the common schools conceived it, was a rebuke to parental responsibility.

Despite such hostility, a Georgia school "system" was in operation by 1872; the result was that the sometimes excellent schools of the major towns were joined by new structures in some backwoods areas of counties where, before the war, there had been neither academies, poor-schools, or "field schools." These miserable classrooms, given the limit of state financial support, could be operated about three months of the year, during the season when children were not needed to work on the farm. The inconsequential results, especially among the Negro children who had few literate adults to encourage them, added criticism during the 1870's to the whole idea of the common school. In 1874 the Committee on Education of the Methodist North Georgia Conference reported that "The prevailing theories of secular education are full of perils to the best interests of society" and advocated that the Methodists, if they could afford the expense, should establish their own primary schools.[2] In 1880, in the columns of the *Wesleyan Christian Advocate*, a similar report, signed by a committee of the Macon District of the South Georgia Conference, declared:

> The people must be educated. . . . They must be religiously educated. . . . We cannot hope that private effort can compass the end required. It is irresponsible, unsystematic, unequal, . . . unreliable. . . . Nor do we feel justifiable in relegating the matter to the State. . . . The State is incompetent and even pernicious.[3]

A rebuttal to his hostility to state-financed education was printed in the *Advocate*. Appropriately, the author was the Methodist preacher, Eustace W. Speer, a professor at the University of Georgia. Speer averred:

> It is not only the right, but the duty of Georgia to educate her youth; and . . . such education will contribute, not only to their material advantage, but to their *moral* and *religious* improvement.
>
> Without a system of public schools, free to all, the majority of our citizens will become ignorant and venal voters; and an oligarchy of profligate and flagitious men will rule the State.[4]

In 1880 in Georgia it is probable that the majority of Methodist preachers felt, with S. P. Richardson, that "as a general thing" it was "a very great disadvantage to the general progress of education in Georgia" to have a public system of education separated from training in family or church loyalties; however, it was "impracticable" for the Methodist conferences to support a system which would reach all Methodist children.[5]

The *Advocate* controversy in the fall of 1880 cleared up Dr. Haygood's mind on the issue. In January 1881, he wrote his first statement in favor of Federal financial aid to the state school systems. It is a paraphrase of a speech made in the Senate by Joseph E. Brown, in December. Haygood wrote that "There is no consistency in resisting help from the nation after receiving proceeds of the 'land script' to help 'Agricultural Colleges' as Georgia and other States did years ago." Besides, "If the remaining public lands are not used to help educate the poor and illiterate they will be gotten up by land speculators."[6]

Haygood's radical move from the logic of his position in 1874 (when he killed the possibility of association of Emory and the University of Georgia out of fear of secular education) was aided by other factors. He knew of the growing national esteem of Gustavus Orr, Georgia's school superintendent, who became president of the National Education Association in 1881. Haygood's sister, Laura, was principal of Atlanta's Girls' High School and had attended the N. E. A. meeting at Chautauqua in the summer of 1880. She, brother Willie, and Attie all were members of the Georgia Teachers Association, of which Dr. Haygood was president for 1880. Haygood's personal interest in pedagogy went back to the years immediately before he became Sunday school secretary, when he came to admire John H. Vincent's training of Sunday school teachers. In July 1879, Haygood invited Bernard Mallon, superintendent of schools in Atlanta, to hold a "normal institute" for public school teachers at Oxford, the sort of institute that the Peabody fund was beginning to subsidize.[7]

Orr's presidency of the N. E. A. brought the Association to Atlanta during the summer of 1881 for its annual meeting, the first in the South. And in February 1882, Orr called a special meeting of delegates from the Southern states in Atlanta to word a memorial to Congress in favor of legislation giving Federal aid to state school systems. Five thousand Georgians signed the petition, which was given publicity in the *Wesleyan Christian Advocate,* three of these being the children of Greene Haygood.[8]

The idea of Federal aid had first been stated in 1866, growing out of the Republican Party's Civil War premise that "republican democracy requires universal education." James A. Garfield, Radical Republican from Ohio, was chief sponsor of legislation establishing a department of education in the Federal government, the commissioners of which—Henry Barnard, John Eaton, and, in the 1880's, A. D. Mayo—worked hand and glove with the N. E. A. The first bill proposing the establishing of a national educational fund was thrown in the hopper by George F. Hoar of Massachusetts; but, significantly, a similar bill was introduced by a Mississippi congressman in 1872. The N. E. A. in 1881-1882, however, felt that the Blair Bill (for Senator Henry W. Blair of New Hampshire) had the best chance of passing. It was an "emergency measure" designed for a ten-year subsidy of schools in the poorer states, most of the money to go for building schools. It received the powerful support of Southern "Bourbons" like Senators Brown of Georgia, L. Q. C. Lamar of Mississippi, and Wade Hampton of South Carolina.[9]

The Senate passed Blair's bill three times during the 1880's, first in 1884. Dr. Haygood spoke in Washington in both 1883 and

1885 in favor of the bill, and at Chautauqua in 1883, this appearance following by one month a politically influential speech by Rutherford B. Hayes in Ohio. The key sentence in the Slater agent's Chautauqua address is: "It would be hard to prove that the capable ought to endure being voted down by the incapable."[10] In 1889 Dr. Haygood gave what he considered his "most telling blow" for Federal aid, an article on "The South and the School Problem," published in *Harper's* magazine.[11] The budget-minded opposition to Federal aid in the House of Representatives (more Northern Democratic than Republican) killed it three times in the 1880's, and in 1890 the Blair Bill failed even in the Senate.[12] Haygood by then had come to consider the Roman Catholic hierarchy as the chief opponent of the "American common school."[13]

On November 18, 1888, Haygood preached a sermon entitled "The Cry of a Half Million Children" to many members of the Georgia legislature, in Atlanta for the opening of the legislative session. He used the pulpit of Trinity Church, almost within the shadow of the new million-dollar state Capitol, to exhort the representatives on their responsibility toward public education. The "Cry" of the children, relayed by him, then at the peak of his national reputation, was that a three-months term was more harmful than no school at all, and unless the legislature increased its appropriations for the state system, only the strongest city schools could fulfill their obligations. Using language keyed to the Populist ear, Haygood said: "If our law should remain as it is, the commissioner's last hope for an increased fund must be in the increased use of imported fertilizers, more whisky drinking, and more convicts."[14]

No other appearance on the platform by Haygood was ever so successful. The demonic force of his natural eloquence was enhanced by his and his congregation's awareness that he was speaking in behalf of the labors of Orr, dead for just a year. For once his eloquence was not futile; he knew that he had "raised a breeze." A Milledgeville journalist agreed: "The agitation of the school question, so mightily revived by Dr. Haygood, of late seems to have caught the popular ear, and even to have shamed . . . the 'watch-dogs of the treasury.' "[15] Within a few days a bill was introduced in the state legislature to give a portion of the property tax to the schools, enough to expand the term to five months, effective within two years. On December 10, two days before the state house was to debate the appropriations bill with this property-tax arrangement included, Haygood dominated a meeting of the North

Georgia Conference. He asked his church to go on record supporting a resolution which would favor legislative financial support for a six-months term. The resolution passed, 107-54, a tremendous achievement, since the presiding bishop openly expressed his opposition to such obvious meddling in affairs politic.[16]

During 1889 and 1890 the partisan involvement of the North Georgia preachers in the matter continued. Dr. Candler spoke at least twice before Alliance groups, and used the opportunity to get in licks at the University of Georgia: "Building up the common schools," he said, "is the shortest route to higher education."[17] As a result of the pressures, the Georgia legislature enacted the proposal of 1888, and in a second action raised the mill appropriation slightly.[18] The transformation of opinion among Georgia Methodist preachers is indicated by the tone of a defensive article by the Holiness leader, A. J. Jarrell, during the period of this legislative action. Jarrell said that the Holiness people did not dishonor the cause of education in their high valuing of "experience."[19] An indication that the Southern Methodists had altered severely their view of the 1870's that moral influence should be confined to the home, the church, and the church school is found in a statement, in 1890, in the *Southern Methodist Review*: "Christian character, while it is chief, is not all."[20]

The general acceptance by 1890 by Georgia Methodists of both the necessity and the value of the public schools may have reduced suspicions about the air of iniquity and infidelity alleged to pervade the state university in Athens. Dr. Haygood's prejudice against secular higher education was still strong, however, and in this Dr. Candler was a faithful disciple. Haygood raised a public cry in 1881 against the proposal to make tuition free at the University—his opposition being on the grounds that it would hurt Emory. Indirectly he argued that poor boys would receive a "proper philosophy" of life only at a church school. Candler, in 1884, likewise wrote in the *Advocate*:

I can explain why the University don't turn out both better spellers and more preachers. It's located in a social atmosphere where there is too much dancing, social wine-drinking, political excitement, and theatrical diversions.[21]

Following the lead of Haygood and Candler, Emory alumni and students of the Populist era turned their school pride into a kind of inverse, proletarian snobbery. Candler spoke to the Populists in favor of heavier subsidy of the public schools as a way of decreasing financial support of the University of Georgia. In 1893 he engaged in public debate with a prominent Atlanta alumnus of the University, N. J. Hammond. Since Hammond was a Methodist layman, Candler was able to indulge in such irrelevant remarks as the statement that "in the ninety-three years of the University's history it has had eight Calvinistic chancellors and [but] one Arminian."[22] Methodist denigration of the University inspired a premature overvaluation of Emory's intellectual climate.

Surely some of Candler's language must have been understood for what it was: platform rhetoric. However, his warning to Christians that "a Mussulman or an agnostic may now be a professor at Athens" gave even "Calvinistic" (Baptist) parents pause before sending their children to the care of a faculty not dominated by preachers.[23] In the South generally, the age was one of almost unrelieved narrowness about the dangers inherent in higher learning. In 1884 the Presbyterian Synod of Georgia censured, as did other synods, the Presbyterian seminary in Columbia for "allowing the teaching of evolution." The seminary had failed to respond to criticism of Professor James Woodrow by firing him. Woodrow taught "that the world is very old . . . and that Adam was created from organic . . . not inorganic dust."[24] Even in state-supported colleges, a young teacher would be "in danger of losing his place because it was known that he read Huxley and Darwin, and it was supposed that he held a liberal creed in religion."[25] Many Methodists still distrusted Vanderbilt University (a university was supposedly more dangerous that a college) even though it had abolished its chair of zoology. Even Dr. Haygood got letters from parents who feared that a *college* education would pervert their sons' faith. Such concerns about Emory were unwarranted: Lundy Harris's wife found Oxford in the 1890's to be a "narrow-minded little community . . ., pigeon-breasted morally."[26]

These extremes of alarm disturbed Haygood, who understood perfectly that moral excellence could never justify intellectual slackness. His touchiness about Emory's deficiencies is suggested in his opposition to a proposed classifying of Southern Methodist schools, for the guidance of parents. He knew that any classification would put Emory in a category below Vanderbilt.[27]

It was good for Emory that Haygood was touchy about its limitations. His desire to improve the college's reputation was exceeded only by his desire to make the hard-earned tuition money of working students a sound investment. These devotions were strong enough to modify his pronounced and limited ideas of the mid-1870's about a proper college curriculum. During his own administration, and that of his successor, Isaac Hopkins, 1885-1888, Emory engaged in radical curricular experimentation. Some of the developments of the 1880's were necessary precedents for the accomplishments of the 1890's, when Candler was president. The new bachelor of philosophy degree which exempted its earner from studying Greek and Latin is an example. Dr. Haygood observed, in concurrence with such gentlemen as Charles Francis Adams, that the bachelor of arts degree was designed "for the wants of the few unhappy gentlemen of fortune who want a liberal education with no special end in view— . . . for the honor of it and for what is called 'culture.' "[28]

Haygood as president persuaded the Trustees, over the objections of Bishop Pierce, to require the study of one modern language. In 1882 he hired Otto Cohahn, a Jewish immigrant in Atlanta, to teach French and German to the sophomores. The sophomores were delighted that the language study was subtracted from the time for "reciting Philology." The juniors were indignant, since they "had enjoyed no such privilege." Cohahn taught also at the female seminary in Covington—now a Methodist school by donation of the Georgia Masons—but Emory could not afford his meager salary during 1883-1884 because of the collapse of the Seney empire. When language teaching was resumed, Dr. Candler's faculty included Julius Magath, also a European Jew—but unlike Cohahn, a "Hebrew missionary" and a Methodist preacher.[29]

Haygood's administration laid the basis for the professional and specialized study of the 1890's—for which Candler received most of the later honors. One of the needs Haygood specified to Seney in 1881 was a well-lighted room for a college library and museum. A two-story reading and browsing area was incorporated into the plans of the building. Dr. Haygood gave most of his personal collection to the library, consolidated the Few and Phi Gamma libraries with the small college collection, and named one of the young adjunct professors custodian. The library was enlarged during Candler's regime by the collection of W. P. Harrison, but Bishop Haygood had a part in the securing of this valuable addition.[30] It was Haygood who, himself adept at research, first showed Emory boys how to use books of different kinds in collating information on a single subject. It was he more than anyone else who regretted that there was not a single library in the South where a "large subject" could be investigated.[30]

It was Haygood who suggested to the Emory Trustees a radical stiffening of requirements for the master of arts degree. Hitherto given automatically to literate graduates if they lived honorable lives for three years after receiving the bachelor's degree, this honor hereafter required the writing of a thesis. In 1882 Haygood inaugurated Emory's first professional school by adding to the faculty James M. Pace, a Covington lawyer. Emory's law department flourished so that in 1887 a second lawyer was hired for part-time teaching. The law school was in direct competition with the Lumpkin School of Law in Athens, which was training fewer than twenty students. The date usually given for the founding of Emory's theological school, a "Biblical department," is 1894. This was the year that Dr. Candler found a few hundred dollars to pay Haygood and E. E. Hoss, of Nashville, for lectures on the evidences of religion and pastoral theology, respectively. Authorization for the department was given by the Trustees in 1887. And it was Haygood who had restricted the traditional lectures to the seniors on the evidences of Christianity to those students of 1880-1884 who planned to be preachers.

Justice therefore would seem to demand that Haygood be considered the father of Emory's professional and graduate schools. His claim is bolstered by an examination of the post-graduate careers of Emory College students. A higher percentage of graduates during Haygood's administration, 1876-1884, went on to professional schools than under Candler's regime, although economic conditions were in a roughly equivalent condition of depression under the two presidents. Most of the early post-graduates went either to Vanderbilt's professional schools or to the University of Virginia.[31]

In fostering the professional schools—in competition with Vanderbilt's—Haygood acted along lines established in mid-century in schools like Yale. His own limited educational experience and his admirable flexibility led him into many experiments at Oxford, some of them abhorrent to the traditionalists among Emory's alumni. In 1877 he had sponsored McIntosh's music classes. He held the Normal Institute in 1879. He decided to attract bright, poor, hard-working students to Emory by the boarding hall experiment. And he dropped his experimental curriculum of 1876-1877 planned to use the Bible as a means of teaching a theistic world-view.

In 1881, influenced by the vocational emphases of the National Education Association, he introduced at Emory a "Department of Bookkeeping and Accounts," taught by A. S. Hough, to which for a short time was added a "Department of Telegraphy." By 1886 there were thirty students taking the commercial courses.[32] Lay Trustees like Governor Colquitt approved of the success of the bookkeeping instruction during 1881-1882, and that summer the Board resolved to investigate "attaching . . . a . . . department for Handicraft Education."

Dr. Haygood was now an enthusiastic supporter of the idea that academic training would not be demeaned by a teaching of the trades. His revision of his position of 1874 had come about gradually. At the N. E. A. meeting in Atlanta, 1881, C. O. Thompson, of the Worcester (Massachusetts) Institute, spoke of the benefits of a familiarity with wood- and metal-lathes in an expanding industrial economy. That fall Dr. Haygood was enchanted by the Yankee shop skills he found so widely distributed in New England, particularly at Willimantic, Connecticut. By June of 1882, the Emory president was expectantly hopeful of being the Slater agent—and the Slater Fund was specifically designed to subsidize industrial training at Negro colleges.[33]

Emory's committee to investigate the teaching of industrial crafts consisted of Colquitt, Haygood, Potter (Haygood's successor as editor of the *Wesleyan*), the old Holiness apologist, J. E. Evans, and a new lay Trustee from Savannah, whose interest was primarily in railroads. This committee deputed its authority to Professor Hopkins, the Latin teacher. Hopkins during 1882-1883 visited several Northern institutes of technology and for the Board meeting of 1883 produced a printed report which contrasted the two kinds of education: "The Utilitarian Vs. the Useless."[34] (At the same time a state committee was engaged in the same groundwork, considering the possibility of strengthening the University by the addition of a technological institute in Athens.)

Emory's "school" was blessed by the Trustees and began in October 1884, two months before the severance of Haygood's relationship with the Emory faculty—Hopkins succeeding Haygood as president. The "School of Tool-Craft" in late 1884 had as equipment two foot-operated lathes in Hopkins' yard. Before he resigned, Haygood secured contributions from Atlanta businessmen and William Slater, and a brick building was erected on the Oxford campus, between the day chapel and a classroom building adjoining Seney Hall, for the fall term of 1885. This Southern "first" in technological training attracted attention, and in 1888 a U. S. government circular issuing from the commissioner of education said: "The chief strength of Emory College, and the foundation of its claims to high repute in educational circles, centre in its Department of Technology."[35]

The enthusiasm for the teaching of manual skills on the historic campus was not universal. Alumni and some students were when not openly hostile, skeptical. In a speech in 1886 to the alumni Dr. Haygood defended the development of industrial training and ridiculed the nature of most of the critics. One boy who had barely managed to "squeeze through the regular course" had expressed his pleasure at finishing before they "introduced 'a blacksmith-shop at Emory.' "[36] (The brick shop contained several lathes run by a steam engine, and in the back a foundry and forge.) At least one of the Trustees, an old Burke County planter, disapproved of the new courses—as did Candler. The decline of the enrollment during Hopkins's regime, and the state's initiation of a technological institute in Atlanta, which they invited Hopkins to head, were used as excuses for closing up the shop on the Oxford campus. The commercial courses were also discontinued upon Candler's insistence, and McIntosh soon centered his main occupation off the campus. Carry-overs from Haygood's and Hopkins's administrations were the law school and the helping halls—reduced from their maximum of five under Haygood.[37]

Haygood's venture into technological training, which he began with some hesitation, convinced him of the value and "dignity" of such adjuncts to college education. In 1889, after he had broken his ties with Emory in order to give Candler a free hand in both curricular and financial matters, he moved to Sheffield, Alabama, specifically to organize a "university" which would teach white girls the arts of handicraft. The school was taken seriously by Haygood, although the land speculators considered it in the light of a promotion device to boost their city. Haygood wrote of his new commitment:

My friends in Sheffield give me a good home—worth $7,000 in fee simple. They believe it will be worth that to their city and school & I think so too. . . . I . . . go to the help of their enterprise—a school for white girls, with the industrial features pronounced. There is no sorer need in the South. . . . I resign all my Trusteeships in Georgia [Emory and Wesleyan] & divers other things I have been in for twenty years.[38]

Haygood's aegis of Emory, ended with the accession by his onetime protégé in 1888, was obscured because of the college's continuing financial difficulties. The bold experimentation of the

1880's and the Seney gift were thus forgotten. Haygood's administration was later totally and unfairly discredited when the death of G. W. W. Stone (treasurer and bursar) in 1889 led to an examination of accounts. A finance committee of the Trustees was baffled to learn that the true debt of the college was unknown. Until Bishop Pierce's death in 1884, Emory had suffered from having in effect three treasurers: Stone, Bishop Pierce, and Haygood. Stone's accounts were in good shape, being subject to yearly review at the Board meeting. But Bishop Pierce had built the four new buildings of the early 1870's on the strength of promises that the "notes" of alumni and friends would be honored. The money he borrowed to pay for the construction, he counted a *personal* debt. At his death Haygood took it over, and paid interest charges until the Candler regime.

Haygood's merging of personal and school accounts began naturally enough when he was financial agent from 1876 to 1878. The Trustees had allowed him to consider his collections on the notes of Pierce (and a few more that he solicited) as his "salary" as agent. The helping halls were bought with borrowed money. Since Haygood was responsible for payment until a permanent arrangement could be made, the titles were in his name. Haygood also borrowed money to plaster the wings added to the town church, to furnish Seney Hall with cabinets for the library-museum, and to make other necessary physical improvements. This confusion of personal and college accounts was confounded in the mid-1880's—probably because the optimistic Doctor felt that his connections (Seney and/or Slater) would make other major contributions to *his* school. In 1887, Haygood sold "the President's home" to Bishop Key, although Emory had helped to pay the Parks estate for the cost of it; he doubtless considered this a just settlement because of his unpaid back salary. Even worse than this action, when his brother William needed financial aid, Atticus loaned him the use of a few of Emory's railroad bonds (he kept the securities separate from the older endowment) and William transferred "Emory's endowment" to another party—this without the knowledge of the Trustees, but possibly known to the aging Stone.[39]

The reorganization of Emory's debt and its retirement was the major achievement of Candler as president. Bishop Haygood, realizing the disgrace of his mismanagement, was greatly beholden to the young man. Young L. G. Harris bought, at decreased value, the helping halls from Haygood and presented them to the school.

Candler collected $100,000 in cash *from Georgia Methodists* by the mid-1890's and doubled the endowment. The tragedy is that Haygood had had two opportunities to take care of the "old debt" (which had been added to by the refinements of Hopkins' institute). In the spring of 1881, Seney had pledged $5,000 to retire the debt, with the understanding that the Trustees would retire the rest (they did not). This would have been an appropriate occasion for Haygood to consolidate, especially his obligations on the helping halls. Seney might have given $7,000 as easily as $5,000 in the spring of 1881. The other occasion for clearing the school of debt came in the fall of 1884, when Haygood agreed to the demands of the Slater Trustees that he be a full-time agent. William Slater, and others, at this time gave Emory's retiring president a promise to pay off the debt. Once again Haygood did not include his helping-hall responsibility. Even so, the Slater Trustees did not contribute all that they pledged.[40]

Dr. Haygood's poor managerial ability, which came to light only after 1889, sadly obscured his accomplishments at Emory College, especially between 1881 and 1884. As a consequence, Emory's "modern history" is usually indicated as beginning in 1888, with Candler.

ELEVEN
◊ ◊ ◊
◊

Dr. Haygood and Negrophilia

BETWEEN 1882 AND 1891 Atticus Haygood was agent of the Slater Fund, a foundation in support of Negro higher education in the South which became almost as well known as the Peabody endowment. Haygood's own reputation as a friend of the Negro antedated the Slater association, going back to the favorable reception that Northerners, especially Northern churchmen, gave to *Our Brother in Black,* published in 1881. In the South, moreover, especially between 1881 and 1887, Haygood's writing, lecturing, and Slater work were applauded by an enthusiastic, if somewhat small, number of white Protestants who to an extent shared his idealism and sense of optimism about the solution of the "Negro question." Among Southerners generally, who were in the 1880's more tolerant of the Negro's maintaining his voting rights than they were after 1890, when disfranchisement began, the Georgia Methodist preacher's name was inextricably linked with his work in behalf of Negro education, voting, and ownership of property.

While Haygood was surely viewed as an eccentric by some, he was not—it is absolutely clear—considered by most as a "traitor" to his race. It should be remembered here that in Georgia the Colquitt-Gordon-Brown organization of the Democrats prided itself on attracting Negro votes away from the Republicans, and the cajoling of the Negro voter had become what seemed a permanent element of politicking in other Southern states, notably in South Carolina and Virginia. The Alliance threat to one-party domination of the Southern states after 1888 made the Negro voter a possible makeweight in elections, hence a menace, and led directly to the various constitutional devices which in twenty years practically ended a twenty-year acceptance of Negro voting in the South. As to Haygood's place among his fellow white Southerners in the 1880's, his desire to "integrate" the Negro into free society never contemplated disturbing the natural segregation that had grown up during the post-war years. He specifically asserted that white and Negro public schools should be separate.

Haygood's position as Slater agent made him, in the eyes of American Negroes, their friend. It was he who had the final word, more often than not, about the distribution of $40,000 annually among Negro colleges. Public adulation of him by Negroes close to higher education must have been at times unpleasantly fulsome. In 1884, for example, J. W. Hood of the A. M. E. Church in North Carolina, which maintained a small college at Salisbury, requested Dr. Haygood to do him the honor of writing an introduction to his book, calling this small gesture "another evidence of the interest which this great philanthropist feels in the advancement of the interests of the Black Brother, by which he has placed us under lasting obligations."[1]

The high regard of Southern Negroes outlasted Haygood's occupation of the Slater agency. When he died in 1896, five years after he had lost systematic contact with the Negro colleges, Negroes in Atlanta associated with the several institutions of higher education in Georgia's capital joined in what appears to have been a spontaneous memorial service for a man they loved.[2] A surer sign of his reputation among Negroes is a comment made by the outspoken New York editor, Thomas Fortune, before Haygood became agent of the Slater Fund. Writing in 1882, Fortune declared that Albion Tourgee and Atticus Haygood were the *only* American whites for whom he held esteem. Fortune's prejudice especially toward Southerners is pronounced in the statement that "The white man having asserted his superiority in the matters of assassination and robbery, has settled down upon a barrel of dynamite . . . and will await the explosion with the same fatuity and self-satisfaction . . . of . . . other days." Nevertheless, Fortune found in Haygood "a man of the largest culture, Christian intelligence and progressive ideas."[3]

Among white Northerners, especially early Protestant converts to the social gospel, Dr. Haygood by 1885 was considered to be the foremost friend of the Negroes among native Southerners. George Washington Cable of Louisiana forfeited his claim as a resident Southerner by moving to New England. The Slater Fund was therefore fortunate to have such a man as Haygood in its employ. His work was principally at institutions supported by Northern Protestant bodies, the Methodists, the Congregationalists, and the Baptists, churches which would have confidence in the Slater agent's judgment and zeal. His sincere dedication was evident in all that he wrote, and in all that he said on the platform. In reply to the Southerner who wrote the *Advocate* asking "[when can] we have some rest on the negro question?" Haygood replied, "not in your lifetime." In explaining why the conscience of the Southern white man would not let him be excused from his social obligations, Haygood continued: "It is not because they are negroes that the question will not down; it is because they are human beings, with souls in their bodies."[4]

Haygood exuded hopefulness about the solution of "the question," predicting that by 1900 the most gifted Negro men would be equally as public spirited as any ever produced by the Southern white communities. The only disturbing sign to him in the early 1880's was that the school-age population was growing faster than legislative appropriations. If the states did not rectify the imbalance there was a definite prospect for a *decrease* in literacy. The programs of the Negro colleges were crucial in the battle for increased literacy among Negroes. Not only were they the suppliers of teachers in shortened normal courses; they did their own work directly in teaching special elementary classes.[5]

In 1884 Haygood became Slater agent on a full-time basis. Two years of observation had made him as enthusiastic about teaching Negro boys and girls useful manual skills as old John Slater had been when he reached his final decision as to how his bequest could best be used. Industrial training was pioneered at Hampton Institute in Virginia, a school without need of additional finances since it was subsidized by the Federal government (it taught Indians as well as Negroes), the Commonwealth of Virginia, and the American Missionary Association. Hampton boys learned highly specialized skills, from management of a greenhouse to master masonry. The girls learned cooking and sewing. A portion of the students worked at their trades during daylight hours, attending at night academic classes of an elementary nature. The "academic" students worked an hour or two every day in the garden or a workshop. Hampton's pattern of dividing students according to their talents was a direct model for schools founded during the decade of the 1880's especially those by Philander Smith in Little Rock and Morris Brown in Atlanta.

Dr. Haygood came to prefer schools where the trades were really taught well. His favorites were Clark University in Atlanta; Spelman, for girls, in Atlanta; and Tougaloo in Mississippi. He shared in the pride of Clark students and faculty, who pointed out to the agent that the wagons made in their shops were superior to any to be bought in Atlanta stores; Haygood repeated their claim that the wagons drove the competition "off the streets." Parallel to his growing prejudice in favor of such institutions with obviously sound vocational training was a fast developing dislike for pretentious "universities" which opened shops only to get some of Slater's money. Schools like Atlanta University, Fisk in Nashville, Howard in Washington, Rust in northern Mississippi, and Leland in New Orleans were influenced by Northern white faculty and administrations to disdain industrial training. Not realizing the trend of language requirements in the best schools for Eastern whites, Atlanta University particularly valued its Latin and Greek scholars above most others. By the late 1880's Haygood used all his influence in division of the Slater fund to reward colleges like Clark and to rebuke those schools like Atlanta whose curricular emphasis he considered irrelevant to the greatest needs of Southern Negroes.[6]

Haygood was at home with the denominational cast of most of the Negro colleges. The only truly secular institution which he favored in appropriations was Lincoln Memorial, an Alabama school which moved from Marion to Montgomery during the decade. His satisfaction with Lincoln, though, was a satisfaction with the president, who "has had more experience in industrial education than most directors." Other schools (Hampton, an adjunct of Claflin in South Carolina, and Atlanta University) received state subsidies, but were primarily the creation of the philanthropies of Northern Protestants.

The morality taught Negroes by their white and colored teachers was everywhere identical with the morality Haygood sought for all Southern Negroes: industry, a respect for property, a regard for literacy, a high evaluation of religion. The Northern Protestants during the 1880's were quick to accede to the "separate but equal" pattern which Southerners began to legalize after about 1883. In fact, during the decade the Northern Methodists abandoned their plan to run Chattanooga University as a bi-racial experiment. It became a school for whites.[7]

From the standpoint of the president of the Slater board, Rutherford B. Hayes, Haygood's commitment to the cause which Slater had intended to promote made him the most appropriate man for agent. Clearly, Slater, Bacon, and Hayes contemplated a transformation of attitudes on the part of Southern whites about the Negro's potential as a major part of the accomplishments sought. Jesup, the Treasurer of the Board, however, would have preferred as agent a Northern expert on industrial training, a kind of shop foreman who would make the college shops self-sustaining by efficient production and selling. Once when he was in Atlanta, he inquired as to the "unit cost" per article in the shop at Clark— much to the disgust of Dr. Haygood and the bewilderment of the Negro supervisor.

Gilman, Secretary of the Board, and as President of Johns Hopkins very conscious of academic criteria, seems to have looked on the Slater enterprise often in terms of its possibilities for graduate research. In 1885, two years after a pattern for the distribution of the money had been established by Haygood, he suggested that further use of the income should be halted until a survey could be made, using the methods of "political economy," by which an intelligent priority list would emerge. He expressed, in lieu of this investigation, a continuing preference for the schools most academically minded—Howard, Hampton, Fisk, Atlanta. After Haygood had been eased out of office, Gilman's idea of concentrating the money in a few places was more nearly followed. Gilman considered Haygood's compassionate wide distribution of the funds a futile attempt to build up "a regional education system," and he was probably right.[8]

Gilman and Jesup by 1890 managed to alter the thrust of the Slater endowment, in a sense dishonoring the donor's obvious intentions. Dr. Haygood therefore felt on firm ground when the first arguments arose over his preferring Clark University to Howard, for instance. In the early stages of the quarrel Haygood relied on the support of Hayes, to whom he wrote letters in the confiding way a young son might write his father for justification of his actions. He did not conceal from Hayes his abomination of Jesup's incapacity to judge educational results in any terms other than yearly balances of accounts. Unhappily his peevishness toward Jesup colored his attitude toward the other Trustees. He did not respect their judgment; he felt they were thinking in terms of abstract theoretical problems. Since he traveled thousands of miles every year to see first-hand and to *sense* what was really going on, in some cases contradictory to the glowing reports of college presidents, he considered his own judgment close to infallible.

Haygood did not perceive, as the Trustees could, his increasing pettiness in school preferences. His disparagement of Negro Latinists, as an instance, grew out of his modern language plans for Emory College. Furthermore, anyone examining the appropriations carefully could see that he favored institutions supported by Northern Methodists and Congregationalists (Mrs. Hayes was a Congregationalist, as were Leonard Bacon and the Slaters) over those supported by Northern Baptists. Since Howard and Hampton were the most thriving Negro institutions in the country, his prejudice against helping them attain even greater contributions to Negro advancement appears narrow and ill-advised.

Finally, he was delinquent in the reports he made to the Trustees about the exact use of the appropriations. His reports are marvels of imprecision; often he would account for the money spent at a single school in the largest of categories—one-third for "tools," one-third for "scholarships," one-third for teachers' salary supplements. In a case like this the Trustees would have no way of knowing the basis of scholarship selection. Nevertheless, he expected the board automatically to approve his recommendations for appropriations. In 1889 he decided impulsively that a Northern Baptist school in New Orleans was half-hearted about its industrial program. He wanted to cut off the Slater subsidy, now a permanent part of the school's budget plans. The subsequent attempt by the president to address his problem to the Slater board was quite embarrassing to the Trustees since they did not know the real situation. Dr. Haygood, who obviously disliked the Negro president, seemingly was unmoved by the blow he had struck at the man's reputation. J. L. M. Curry, much more businesslike and rational in his recommendations, succeeded Haygood in 1891 as Slater agent. From the board's standpoint the change was an improvement.[9]

One of the accomplishments of Haygood, not recorded at the time of his resignation, was in moderating the antipathy Negroes had toward the Southern white man. The more sophisticated perspective of the Negro is seen in an ability in the 1880's—unknown during the Reconstruction period—to be critical of the failings of their own race, with criticisms not derived from an "Uncle Tom" docility. In 1888 a Detroit Negro, Augustus Straker, condemned those Negroes who went out of their way at the kind of institutions which Gilman favored (Atlanta, Howard, Fisk) to avoid taking a vocational course. He said they were to be classed with the poor whites of the South, who, "lacerated in feeling and debased in pride," were in danger of causing further collapse of civilization in a region which had "inherent possibilities" of being a "great section of the country."[10] In 1891 J. C. Price, head of a North

Carolina college which Haygood favored—and the Doctor's candidate as the best example of the postwar Negro—registered his opinion that the burden of improvement for his race was now on the Negro, not the Southern or Northern white. The Negro had to "prove himself 'a man and a brother,' even if 'in black,' as an eminent Southern author has put it."[11] And it should be recorded that Tuskegee Institute in Alabama, which began its operation under Booker T. Washington after 1881, virtually owed its existence and certainly its prospering to the Slater largesse—and to Haygood's policy of helping small schools in which he had faith.[12]

The need for moderation of prejudice in the South was great, and the accomplishment of some cordiality in the 1880's is remarkable. The newspapers—and the grapevines—were full of reports of violence between the races. In August 1882 a Negro in Newnan who had raped a twelve-year-old white girl was lynched after escaping from jail. In McDonough, in 1884, the most widely heralded "social event" was the hanging of Leonidas Johnson, a short bull-necked Negro rapist and burglar (a boy who had never been to school and who had been a sneak thief since he was fourteen). In 1881 a Negro boy in Atlanta in an excited try to push his way into the Opera House in order to attend a memorial service for President Garfield had forgot himself and pushed a white lady off the sidewalk outside. When the police arrested him, his mother picked up one of the stacked rifles of the military and shot the policeman. The result was the threat of a race riot. In 1884 a college-educated Negro editor of a local newspaper wrote about the "brutal murder" by the Athens police of a Negro in the streets. (The *Constitution* chided the editor: "If the negroes [such as you] are to be educated, let them be educated to know that the law is to be respected.") In 1889, east of Macon, a gang of disguised whites whipped a white man who had given permission for a rural school for Negroes to be built on his farm. The avengers then shot up the house where the college-educated Negress teacher lived.

The heightening of anxieties in the 1880's undoubtedly was based on sexual fears. Frederick Douglass candidly announced that the Negro problem in the South would be solved by colonization of the race elsewhere, the race's extinction through poverty and resulting disease, or—what seemed likeliest—"assimilation." The Negroes, such as Bishop Wesley Gaines, were no happier about "amalgamation" than Southern whites. Gaines was close to the lower economic strata and believed that "amalgamation is no longer a theory, but well nigh an accomplished fact."[13] As the Negroes knew, American mulattoes were not all produced by acts of rape nor by the casual misalliances of the slave era.[14]

It is in the context of racial antagonism that Dr. Haygood's success in altering white opinions in the South must be judged. In 1883 an Emory student wrote:

"Is Emory college sorely in favor of the education of the negro?" No, while we believe our beloved president has the cause at heart, we cannot agree with him, nor do all of the students, as might be supposed. The liveliest discussion we have ever heard was between the Few and Phi Gamma societies recently, subject: 'Resolved, that the United States should furnish sufficient means to educate the negro.'— The Fews' debated from a good standpoint, but the Phi Gammas' gained a complete victory with the negative side. We would not write this, but there are some people who think that everybody who goes to Emory college must make a Methodist preacher, or advocate Northern views, etc., which is false.[15]

During 1884 a young Florida preacher named McKibben F. McCook in letters to the *Advocate* changed his mind within a few weeks from an apathetic acceptance of the unchanging "direct relation" between the races "providentially caused," to a zeal for progressively Christianizing the Negro.[16] J. C. C. Newton, a Maryland preacher, openly registered his indebtedness to Haygood's lead, regretted the non-intellectual orientation of Southern Methodist preachers, and shared Haygood's belief in the perfectibility of the Negro. Newton ridiculed those "Southern men [who] will tell you that the Negro is getting worse . . .; that he is utterly unreliable and thriftless; that it is impossible to elevate him . . ., that his enfranchisement was a political outrage, and his education a failure."[17] In 1889 a Vanderbilt professor said that "Dr. Haygood is the one Southern man I should be willing to follow blindfold on the Negro question."[18] James H. Carlisle, president of Wofford, while sharing Haygood's progressive hope for the Negro, was more understanding of the reserve of judgment held by some of the better educated Southern whites, whose private thoughts he imaginatively recorded:

Will the representative survivor of the war times . . . easily come to the point where he will frankly say: "I see I have been mistaken in my views about this singular people. I had played with little negroes in the back yard every day in my boyhood, and I took for granted that *this* made me a philosopher."[19]

Working in favor of a spirit of helpfulness during the 1880's was the progressive bent of the "Bourbons," which was not entirely a pose for political purposes, and was not entirely dominated by commercial values. The fact that Governor (later Senator) Colquitt sat on the board of the Slater Fund certainly added to the respectability of Haygood's work, and Southern Methodism must have held a denominational pride in the choice of Haygood for the important foundation. There was restricted but genuine pride in establishing a college in Augusta, supported by the white Methodists of the South, to train Negro preachers and teachers—Paine College. Paradoxically the two greatest supporters for this effort were Holiness leaders—J. E. Evans and W. C. Dunlap. In 1881 Evans arranged, in his phrase, an "Integrated funeral" when his old cook, "Aunt Eady," died, and it was he, of course, who had organized the C. M. E. Church during the 1860's. Dunlap was solicitor in North Georgia for financial support of Paine, sharing Haygood's "conviction from God, that the . . . Church . . . was sleeping over the grandest opportunities of any church in Christendom, in failing to enter the open door of missionary work among the colored people."[20]

Under the influence of Haygood's commitment, Professor Morgan Callaway, of Emory, became the first president of Paine, unhappily struggling with meager resources during 1883-1884. Callaway analyzed his decision to leave Oxford as a response to a call "by the Holy Ghost." Since he returned to his chair of literature two years later, his motivation was likelier a commingling of the voice of conscience, the Southern aristocrat's feeling of *noblesse oblige*, and Haygood's behest.[21] Paine was voted into existence in 1882 at the General Conference, but did not flourish because, as Haygood wrote Hayes, "Our late Senior [Bishop Pierce] threw cold water on the negro education business." Pierce considered the "prompting" by Southern whites like Haygood of the Negro in his claims of equality a "violence [contrary to] the ordination of nature."[22] Candler's attitude toward the enterprise in 1882 was also negative. He rejected Haygood's request that he be Paine's president. Later, perhaps partly out of a guilty conscience, he became a principal patron of the school among white Georgia Methodists.[23]

Although the 1880's were years of optimism about many enterprises and Haygood's plea received respectful attention at the conference of the whole church, the majority of Southern Methodists had at best an equivocal attitude toward extensive efforts in behalf of the Negro. A writer in the *New Orleans Advocate*—probably the editor Linus Parker with the sanction of the negrophobe Bishop Keener—wrote a severe criticism of Haygood's efforts:

> Dr. Haygood, in quiet Oxford, has found a bonanza, which, under his skillful and enterprising management, has turned out a handsome yield. . . . The . . . negro . . . who has been the disturbing cause of the conscience of Christendom, is now . . . the means of appeasement, and by getting right with these just discovered brothers the new light and a better civilization breaks upon the South. Well, we are glad that relief is coming, but we . . . do not see exactly where the relief is. . . . The true difference between the Caucasian and the African is not in mere color of garb . . ., but lies in the very natures.[24]

Criticisms of Haygood's "bonanza" were apt to be more severe when they come from laymen. A Georgia Methodist wrote the *Macon Telegraph* thus: "I said to myself, 'What a lucky thing he is not our bishop.' . . . I hope some of the Northern churches will 'call' him soon." Lay resentment reached a peak in the summer of 1883, after the Emory president made speeches at the chautauquas in Monteagle, Tennessee, and in New York. In alleged asides, not found in printed versions of these speeches, the new Slater agent expressed a radical belief in the unity of mankind, an idea offensive to many white Southerners. A paper in Sparta—Bishop Pierce's town—totally rejected Haygood's continuing argument that the Negro churches were civilizing forces. "If this be true we want a new religion. A church member that will steal a watermelon on his way to church and a hog on his return home, will . . . never . . . enter the pearly gate. It may be [though] that Dr. H. can see farther than we can."

Similar ideas when expressed by Methodist college faculty members were more indirect but frequently no less critical. W. W. Bennett, a professor at Randolph-Macon, observed that "The attempt to arraign the Southern Methodist Church for neglect of the religious interests of the negroes . . . is one of the strange things of the present day." While not an enthusiast for Haygood's cause, Bennett was willing for "The negro . . . to remain free, and to reach the highest degree of culture his nature is capable of."[25] F. C. Woodward shared some of Haygood's enthusiasm. As a professor at Wofford he felt that "Everybody" wanted to help the ex-slave become an intelligent citizen. He could not share Haygood's prediction, however, that a reform of opinion could be effected by 1900—it would, he said, take that long to eliminate the absolute distrust which many white men held for the former slave.[26]

Among Southern Methodists the hopeful progressive tone of utterances of the 1880's about many social problems changed rather quickly into a "realism" that was often cynical. Typically the realists of the 1890's thought that the "Negro problem" was insoluble in any immediate terms. An early statement, in 1885, made by a Southern Methodist preacher to the Louisiana Educational Association is in sharp contrast to the tone of Haygood's exhortations and of others (like George W. Cable) whom the Louisiana preacher sought to disparage:

> There is . . . another class of writers . . . who might justly claim all sympathy . . . because they write and speak for the elevation of the negro with enthusiasm . . . and who also have all the fitness . . . because they have had their birth and rearing and life among the negroes, who yet proclaim themselves to be unfit . . . by the blind and not sufficiently discriminating zeal which they manifest. The consciousness that they are subjecting themselves to adverse criticism on account of the recent, and perhaps, too sudden conversion of their sentiments influences them to attempt to make too strong a case of the capacities of the negro on the one hand, and of his illtreatment on the other. . . .[27]

By 1889 disparaging voices were heard everywhere. Professor Scomp of Emory College wrote an article for *The Forum*, titled "Can the Race Problem Be Solved?", a question which he answered in the negative.[28] Two years later a Methodist lady wrote in the denomination's *Quarterly Review* of her unhappiness with the disappearance of faithful and skilled Negro help. She blamed the unsteadiness of young Negro women on their being subject to the "capriciousness and selfishness" of their men.[29] A Tennessee preacher objected to the propagation of "The heresy that 'all men are born free and equal,'" a teaching which promised fulfillment at the price of a political crisis in the South.[30]

The decline of both enthusiasm and respect among white Southerners toward reform efforts having as their object immediate elevation of the Negro's status was so obvious as to be recognized in the North—an area where among Protestants social concerns had directed their primary focus away from the Southern dilemma. A Northern Methodist writer in 1890 recorded that the "respectable" secular press in Nashville, Atlanta, New Orleans, Mobile, Macon, and Savannah counted as a failure the experiments with the Negro as a voter.[31] In 1888 Dr. Haygood and Senator James Biddle Eustis had a journalistic tilt over Eustis's attack on Cable. Haygood's article represents his sole reply made personally to the growing band of critics in the "Populist era" of the negrophile platform of what may be called the "Bourbon progressivism" of the early 1880's. Eustis hit hard at Cable's lack of realism, of his glossing over the problem of the races in the South as no more than a misunderstanding which education and refined thoughts could eliminate. Eustis argued that no amount of literacy and civilization could eliminate the instinctive hostility between the races. The only solution for the hostility was the unthinkable complete amalgamation of the two peoples. Haygood's rebuttal was out of character and weak; indeed it came near to admitting that the arguments of Eustis would eventually triumph in the South.[32]

The diminution of hopefulness among Southern whites about the improvement of race relations tended to embitter leaders of the Negro community. At the turn of the century Bishop Lucius Holsey, a former slave ordained to preach by Bishop Pierce, lamented that "The great majority of the Southern white people hold that education ruins the negro."[33] In 1899 a young Kentucky Negro at a student conference in Nashville condemned the whites of the South for withholding from the Negro all the rights of citizenship until the inferior race attained a "spotless purity." The principal Negro problem, he felt, was to teach the black man to "think highly of himself."[34]

Young Negroes would not accept Booker T. Washington's "Atlanta Compromise," whereby Negroes acquiesced in their disfranchisement in return for a white promise to help in the race's educational and economic advancement. The spokesman for the young Negroes was W. E. B. DuBois of Atlanta University. In perhaps his most dramatic challenge of Booker Washington, whose rise to prominence the Slater contributions had helped to make possible, DuBois in 1907, in a debate with Washington, said that the whites had ignored their part of the bargain. Indeed, he maintained, the loss of the Negroes' voting rights "has stripped them naked to their enemies; discriminating laws of all sorts have followed."[35]

There was among some young Negroes, nevertheless, a residue of good feeling fostered by the Slater fund. In 1904 a Negress in a thesis written for the University of Paris named Atticus Haygood as originator among Southern whites of an active desire to help the Negro attain his rights.[36] The kindly feeling toward Haygood expressed nearly ten years after his death by a young woman who had never known him is significant evidence that the Slater agent was accepted by the Negroes as a devoted friend. On Haygood's part, of course, the friendliness began with his boyhood association with the admiration for Uncle Jim. The "New South" sermon and *Our Brother in Black* were vehicles whereby Haygood understood how deeply his attachments were to the former slaves. It pleased him, in 1881, when he attended an integrated preachers' meeting in New York City that "one very dark colored brother . . . came straight to our seat and sat down by us. It was pure instinct. . . . We have often observed this . . . instinct; the Negroes know who their best friends are."[37]

When Dr. Haygood became agent for the Slater foundation, he became a favorite among audiences at the Negro colleges. A Nashville newspapermen wrote of such a function in 1887, "The day was inclement, but Dr. Haygood can command an audience here of any color at any time."[38] When Haygood spoke at the commencement of Claflin College in Orangeburg, South Carolina, 10,000 people, mostly Negro, came to hear him. His eloquence was well suited to the Negro audiences, and he prided himself on avoiding a patronizing tone. He knew that Negroes did not like to be addressed as "colored people," just as he knew in writing to capitalize the "N" of Negro. He adopted these habits of respect even before some Negroes did, their use apparently having been emphasized at a national meeting of the race's leaders in St. Louis in 1885.[39]

Knowing of the Negroes' confidence in his speeches and sermons, Haygood did not hesitate when he felt the need for sharpness. He condemned as unforgivable the Kentucky Negress who slapped a train conductor's face when he asked her to change her seat. He defended segregation and defended Southern Protestant whites. He said that the Negroes should be grateful for the Christianity given them, but grateful also to the whites of slavery times, whose civilization had been the agency of Christianization.[40]

It was inevitable that Haygood's close association with Negroes and the good opinion they held of him should lead to stories of unseemly intimacy between the Slater agent and the "black brother." Some of the stories appeared in print, for the titillation of Southern whites. In 1883 "Si" Hawkins, editor of a newspaper in Covington which denounced Haygood's chautauqua addresses of that year, reported that

Sometime, within the past two or three years, the amiable and accomplished wife of Mr. Warren Hill, of Oxford, gave birth to twins—a lovely girl and boy. Forthwith Mr. Hill called his little darlings after that great and perfect man, Dr. Haygood. Recently the kind and generous Doctor, to manifest his high appreciation of the distinguished honor conferred upon himself, presented Mrs. Hill with an elegant twin baby carriage. It is hardly necessary to add that Mr. Hill is a dearly beloved "Brother in Black."[41]

The veiled hint of miscegenation in this story led Haygood's friend, Dr. Henry Gaither, to write in defense of the Emory president's disinterested charity toward the family. He twitted Hawkins for hinting that Haygood was the true father of the twins; Gaither said Haygood was not responsible "any more than Gen. Washington."[42]

The cause of the breakdown of efforts in behalf of the Negro may be attributed principally either to an increasing advertisement of the menace of the Negro rapist or to the political upheavals of the Populist era. A factor seldom noted, however, and perhaps the most important factor, is the coming to leadership in the South of whites of a generation which had no experience with ownership of the Negro as property. As early as the 1890's slaveholding was thought of as an institution of the distant past, and the zealous devotion to elevation of the Negro remembered often as a youthful missionary excess.[43] Bishop Charles B. Galloway, though an ardent prohibitionist, shortly after 1900 denied that Christian gospel should be "interpreted . . . as a social passport," that is, as argument for social change.[44] In 1904 Charles E. Dowman, Candler's successor as president of Emory, and as a young man in the 1880's subject to Haygood's eloquence, said: "The Southern white man has . . . lost confidence in the negro." The reasons: "The increase of crime, the comparative failure of education, the frequent divorce of religion from morality, the menace of the rapist." The result: a "sympathetic helpfulness" had become a "strained toleration."[45]

At Emory's commencement, 1904, H. M. Hamill of Atlanta agreed that "The negro of post-bellum birth and education is usually a thorn in the flesh to one who seeks or uses his services." The old-time darky, he remembered fondly, had "integrity, pride, . . . industry."[46] Bishop Candler in 1902 refused to attend a Negro meeting in Atlanta organized by Bishop Wesley Gaines of the A. M. E. Church. His conception of the "Negro problem" was hardly sympathetic: "For one, I am not nearly so afraid of the race question as I am of the race of 'chautauqua platformers and performers!' I know how to get on with the negroes, for I was brought up with them.' "[47]

The new generation of whites found the new generation of Negroes unpromising to a degree that would have horrified Dr. Haygood and would have seemed immoderate even to Bishop Pierce. In 1906 a well-bred Augustan, William H. Fleming, speaking at the commencement of the University of Georgia, said flatly that "It is true that the right of suffrage is not one of those inalienable rights of man."[48] In 1907 a recent graduate of Vanderbilt wrote a book with the thesis that race prejudice ought to be *encouraged* since prejudice would slow down amalgamation. He felt, moreover, that mulattoes could never be trusted.[49] In 1911 the Southern Methodist Publishing House printed the first of several books by E. H. Randle, who ridiculed those "Christians who are leaving no stone unturned to find evidence of the unity of the human race."[50]

Before he died in 1896, Bishop Haygood was aware of his failure to convert the majority of Southerners to acceptance of the possibility of a society in which Negroes would attain a level of civilization equal to that of the "Anglo-Saxons." As his strength and hope failed, memory of past triumphs became prominent. He could remember enlisting white leadership in Memphis and Little Rock, sites of LeMoyne Institute and Philander Smith College. In the 1890's his writings on the subject were undistinguished, and indistinguishable from comments of younger men who had never experienced his idealism. "The white men in the South," he wrote, "who are fighting all manifestations of lawlessness, ought not to be handicapped by the indifference of colored bishops, editors and teachers to the monstrous assaults so frequently committed."[51]

His long residence in California and his sickness upon returning to Georgia broke his ties with any Negro community except that of Oxford. It is unlikely that he knew of the successes of young Georgia Negroes, since their names did not reach the pages of Atlanta papers read by whites. The attainments of educated Georgia Negroes are nevertheless indicative of the soundness of the hopeful zeal Haygood had held as Slater agent. Dr. W. F. Penn of Atlanta was a graduate of Yale's medical school. Allen Griggs, a Negro born in Hancock County, became a leading preacher in Texas and president of the National Baptist Convention. W. S. Scarborough of Macon attended Atlanta University in the 1870's, went on to Oberlin, and was by the 1890's the classics professor at Wilberforce University in Ohio. Another Georgia Negro was prominent as a classicist. John Wesley Gilbert was a product of

Paine College, and Haygood probably knew of his promise there during the presidency of G. W. Walker. Paine's continuing pride in Gilbert, who eventually taught as a Greek scholar in the American School in Athens, was such that the ailing bishop may have continued to be informed about *this* example of the product of Negro higher education.[52]

Such evidences of reward for his labors in the 1880's were few. Even the *Wesleyan Christian Advocate,* his own creation, participated in the common derogation by Southern whites of Negro churches and Negro preachers. The *Advocate* reported with obvious mirth the tale of a Negro preacher who tried to keep his flock in line by whipping offenders after acts of sexual immorality.[53] Haygood was still alive in 1895 when Booker T. Washington made his famous speech at the Atlanta Exposition, expressing gratitude to the white man for his willingness to allow the Southern Negro all the comforts possible, consistent with second-class citizenship. Tragically the good Doctor's once lively mentality had so declined that it is doubtful that he could enjoy the irony of such an expression of thanks.

TWELVE

Act of Faith: The Abdication of Will

ATTICUS HAYGOOD was taught that "Every exertion of the human will is a miracle."[1] This aphorism, which he repeated for the benefit of his readers of the *Wesleyan Advocate,* neatly characterized his own understanding, at the age of forty, of both Methodist theology and Methodist psychology. The Arminian argument behind Wesleyan thought, reinforced by the Enlightenment, maintained above all that each man had, through the exercise of his will, the key to his spiritual destiny. At the same time Methodism no less than Calvinism affirmed that God controlled the history which swept up man in *its* momentum. The maintenance of the Methodist faith therefore required in each believer a non-rational balancing of the two ideas. Haygood's own solution, as the aphorism indicates, accomplished the balance by a de-emphasis of conscious control as the *cause* of any act.

In the years of Haygood's prime, between 1876 and 1885, the Holiness overemphasis on the sovereignty of the conscious will over behavior moved him farther from the root Arminian position. But de-emphasis of the control of the individual over both his behavior and his fate put Dr. Haygood in the situation of being an ally of materialistic nineteenth-century science. Science's gospel was that man was a natural creature moved by powerful physical and biological determinants in the direction of his "natural" development and destiny. Haygood was aware of the similarity of his faith in Providence to science's faith in Natural Law. He wrestled against succumbing to what seemed to be an impersonal and non-theistic view of life—but in his forties he did succumb. He ceased to be a "believer" because he ceased to be a Wesleyan Methodist.

Loss of belief in the Wesleyan gospel of Southern Methodists occurred because of approximately two years of self-examination,

1878 to 1880. Haygood was approaching forty at the beginning of the period; a re-examination of his life in accordance with beliefs he had held up until then was in order. He felt that he had been promised as a young boy that the mastery of life would follow upon the mastery of behavior through the use of will. But in retrospect it seemed clear that the quest for "holiness" through self-discipline had contributed only fitfully to well-being, and that the richness of his inner life had been brought about to no considerable degree by his totally correct behavior, by a career which met all standards of judgment of the "success" of a Methodist preacher.

His career, and his acts of will, had pleased others, but were no source of self-satisfaction. He had "willed" to be converted, at the impressionable age of fifteen, in order to please his grandmother and the pastor of Trinity Church; the tangible result was formal acceptance by adults of his membership in the church society. In no sense was it the beginning of a new kind of existential experience. When he was eighteen he decided to become a preacher—with as little seriousness as the decision he made to grow a beard—in order to please Young Allen, who had preceded him in both decisions and who was his idol and "father substitute." When he was twenty, he resolved to please Lovick Pierce by studying Richard Watson's *Institutes* in order to become a credit to the Georgia Conference, as a doctrinally literate preacher. And after he became twenty-one, he pleased Bishop George Pierce by being a good presiding elder, a satisfactory Sunday school secretary, and an able president of Emory College. By 1879—when he reached forty—Atticus Haygood saw that the choices to please others had left his life devoid of real self-fulfillment.

On the other hand, there seemed to be a leaven, a force—daemonic rather than divine—which had already enriched his life without any conscious direction on his part, and which promised the fulfillment that adherence to what Methodists considered the correct choices had somehow thwarted. It was not through an act of conscious will that he had been saved from epilepsy, that the boy had become a man, that his acts of pleasure had produced four living children. His wartime choice of the Confederacy as the civilization which *must* survive seemed ironical: he had chosen wrong. Morality and decency in the South had been strengthened by an act of history, the disappearance of slavery, and by the necessity for hard labor on the part of former slaveholders.

Haygood's partial fulfillment in the various assignments of a Methodist preacher was transformed in his becoming editor of the new *Wesleyan Christian Advocate*. The creation of this journal, with the moving of the *Southern Christian Advocate* from Georgia back to South Carolina in 1878, was another "accident" of history. The will did not create the opportunity, at long last, to play the role of the "great editor." Writing for the *Advocate* led him into the writing of *Our Brother in Black* and into all that followed the notice given it. In those marvelous years for him, 1880 and 1881, history gave a special role to Governor Colquitt and Gustavus Orr, whose reputations extended Northward, just as Haygood's own name was becoming known.

It is likely that Haygood experienced in a dramatic way his rejection of the Methodist frame of reference. The freedom he felt in 1880 in following Governor Colquitt's "wave of the future" rather than the backward-looking plans of the aging Bishop Pierce must have precipitated a psychic revolution. This biographer conjectures that Haygood was most conscious of giving himself over to destiny, to his "daemon," when writing on a chilly November night the "New South" sermon which voiced sentiments that must have been unsettling to him as he reread them in preparation for delivery. It was as though the writing had been produced—had been "controlled"—by some inner being beyond his ken.

Haygood believed in a "spirit world," was taught as a child to be afraid of ghosts, and always lived in the expectation of reunion with those now dead, like his grandmother and deceased children. His awareness of *consciously* delivering himself over to what he considered Providence in some new and possible dangerous guise required great courage. The experience was not to be described in theological language as a conversion. It required, nevertheless, as much "faith" to embrace an unknown quotient in the depths of his being as any historic reconciliation with a seemingly unfriendly Creator, such as Luther's or Wesley's. The liberation of Atticus Haygood enhanced his secularist tendencies in speech, dress, manners, and preferred friendships.

For seven years, from approximately June of 1880 to October of 1887, Dr. Haygood's star rose. The rate of his achieving prominence must have startled even those who thought most highly of his talents. During the first year he was brought into the orbit of George I. Seney's ambition, and during the second into the philanthropic scheme of John Slater. Events from May 1882 to November 1884 speeded up the pace and complexity of his life. He rejected the opportunity to be a bishop; he became the agent of the Slater Fund; he decided to resign from Emory College; and with Bishop Pierce's death he took the first steps against the "Pelagianism" of the Holiness preachers. However, these months in retrospect would serve as a harbinger of future difficulties. In 1883 his mother died; his son Wilbur disturbed him by insisting on studying music in Boston; he was embarrassed because of the collapse of the Seney empire and the decline of Emory's income from endowment; and he was alarmed at the unfriendly response to his chautauqua statements by much of the Georgia press.

During 1885 and 1886, however, his happiness in his destiny was unmarred. The "Growth in Grace" sermon led to a successful undermining of the Holiness preachers' political influence. Emory's technical education experiment was at the peak of its reputation. The state legislature passed an act making local option votes on prohibition easier. Paine College became a going concern. Haygood was called upon to speak on a variety of subjects—in favor of the elimination of the state convict lease system, in Atlanta, and in favor of Federal aid to education, in Washington. He enlisted Rutherford B. Hayes's sympathy in a temporarily successful deflection of the criticisms of Gilman and Jesup of the Slater board. At the Southern Methodist General Conference in 1886 his poised assurance impressed the delegates so much that all bitterness aroused by his refusal to accept the episcopacy in 1882 was erased.

The summer of 1887 was the seventh anniversary of his surrendering to the Providence which promised worldly renown and inward serenity, which had filled his cup more than amply. By late summer, after the grueling prohibition campaign in Texas, Haygood felt that his suddenly experienced tiredness, following years of seemingly limitless vitality, was coupled with a premonition of a tragic destiny in the years that remained to him. In August 1887 he advertised his house in Oxford as follows:

I am now too much from home to look after boarders or a large place, and my wife is no longer strong enough to do it. Therefore my home-place in Oxford is for sale. Six acres—rich garden and patches —pretty fish pond—bearing fruit trees—two good wells. . . . Possession given any time.[2]

After sale of the house to Bishop Key, the Haygoods moved to Decatur, in October 1887, to what he called a "modest pleasant place" of nine rooms and eleven acres. The new surroundings were nevertheless depressing to him. From the radical change in his writing style, between August and November, it is reasonable to infer that Haygood's mental depression had at its base a physical fatigue and at its roots relapse in the direction of the childhood epilepsy.[3]

The Haygoods lived two years in Decatur, a time of increasing troubles and world-weariness. All four of their children lived with the aging couple during at least part of this unhappy period. Mamie finished her musical study at Wesleyan, and Atticus, who had completed his college course at Emory, did not proceed immediately to furtherance of his medical career. Wilbur married a Covington belle in December 1887, and brought his bride to Decatur, where their son Paul was born, a child who would be brought up by his grandparents. Mollie was unhappy away from Oxford, as always, and the move did not ease her burdens as hostess. Nearly every day, it seemed, they shared their dinner either with Haygood's Atlanta relatives or other guests. The house in Decatur was near the railroad station there, and Decatur was only six miles by rail from the Atlanta terminal, where Haygood's acquaintances from all over the country were frequently stranded for hours in stopovers. In order to give his wife some solace from his guests, Dr. Haygood built a fish-pond behind the house. Mrs. Haygood was forty-eight when they moved to Decatur, fast becoming a nervous old lady.

During 1888 at Decatur, Haygood's financial situation deteriorated. He had a large salary for the time, $5,000, and some income from his writing. His personal debt was large, although not so high as in 1882 when he owed approximately $15,000, having just borrowed $2,000 from an Atlanta bank to buy a new "helping hall" for Emory College. He was somewhat relieved by selling the "President's house" in 1887 to Bishop Key, and the helping halls, at a loss, along with some other property in Oxford. However, he apparently contracted to buy the house in Decatur, and interest payments on other debts caused him occasionally to be short.

In the fall of 1888 he wrote an embarrassed note to Rutherford Hayes, requesting Hayes to borrow $600 for him from the bank in Fredonia, Ohio. (Hayes complied, perhaps understanding the small likelihood that Haygood would repay. Eventually he had to pay the debt himself.)[4] A similar embarrassment occurred in 1889 when the former president of Emory College, lionized at the previous commencement, was unable to fulfill his alumni pledge. He offered Candler a young Jersey cow and the oval desk he had

had built for his Seney Hall office as payment.[5] The same year the college Trustees discovered that the accounts were in disarray. It must have been difficult for any Trustee, or Candler, to sympathize with Haygood. His salary was considerably larger than that of the bishops, and during 1889 alone he produced four books and many articles, all of which brought in some income. *Our Brother in Black* was reissued. He and McIntosh collaborated once again on a songbook. He edited his speeches as Slater agent, under the title of *Pleas for Progress*. And he attracted attention within Southern Methodism with *The Man of Galilee*.[6]

The Man of Galilee was an appropriate expression of Haygood's continued intellectual growth. Having ceased to be an Arminian, but still formally a Methodist preacher, he was faced with the problem of a proper use of the symbols of his former faith. Admiration for the humanitarian qualities of Jesus was never lost. In 1881 Haygood was distressed by a book entitled *The Manliness of Christ* by Thomas Hughes, the author of *Tom Brown's School Days*. He feared that especially young preachers would so revel in the conception of Christ as a virile extravert that they would forget "the toiling, suffering, dying Humanity."[7] But Hughes provoked him into an attempt to visualize the Christ about whom he still preached when occasion allowed. The imaginative effort occupied his time in his many hours of railroad travel and in hotel rooms during the 1880's. Whereas he could easily visualize the faces of dead loved ones, the Christ of his book is an intellectual abstraction. The main argument of the book is that the accomplishments of Jesus are so enormous that a simple Aramean boy could not unaided have had the wisdom to rise above his culture. The final paragraph is therefore of enormous significance. Haygood leaves unsettled for the reader and himself the question of the divinity of Christ. Rather limply he suggests that even if Jesus was "only a man" his ideals are "a thousand times worth dying for."[8]

The years in Decatur, 1888 and 1889, although worrisome with money and family problems, provided continued triumphs. Emory College recognized Haygood at the commencement of 1889 as its most beloved living alumnus, unveiling a crayon portrait of him. In the fall of 1888, on the platform in Ohio from which Haygood lionized the modest political accomplishments of Rutherford B. Hayes, the former President emotionally pronounced the complimentary remarks by the Georgian as a " '*final verdict of history on my* Administration.' "[9] Haygood shared vicariously in the plaudits given Henry W. Grady, especially in the famous "New South" speech in New York. (Haygood spoke in like vein. In 1888, at the Emory commencement he echoed Grady's phrases: "Coming to commencement, I saw at Lithonia, over a shop door, in huge letters, 'Chicago Beef'. . . .")[10]

There were lesser triumphs, all rewarding. The Claflin College commencement of 1888 demonstrated the respect held for him by Negroes. His debate with Senator Eustis sparked interested support for his position on the possibility of erasing prejudice. His sermon in Atlanta on the educational needs of Georgia children "raised a breeze." And in 1889 his article on Southern education was accepted by *Harper's* magazine.

In December 1889 the Haygoods moved from Decatur to Sheffield, Alabama, a month after Dr. Haygood's fiftieth birthday. The Sheffield Land, Iron, and Coal Company offered the Slater agent the deed to a house and promised a substantial income in the future if Haygood would organize a "University" designed to teach poor white girls of northern Alabama, and from the whole Southeast, the kind of vocational skills which Negro girls learned at colleges supported by the Slater foundation. The vice president of the company, W. L. Chambers, a former Georgian and "old friend," said that the company would put up $50,000 to erect a college building and set up the initial endowment. The land company was interested in boosting the town in any way it could. Sheffield was located on the Tennessee River and had some promise of competition with Birmingham in the production of pig iron, since Birmingham's products had to pay the freight charges of the monopolized rail system of the South.

The collapse of the competition which had existed in the days of the Seney syndicate had proceeded apace since 1884. Chambers probably thought that Northern entrepreneurs like Jesup, who was on the Slater board, would be influenced by Haygood to add to the proposed school's endowment, and just possibly to buy into Sheffield's industrial future. Unfortunately for the Haygoods, Sheffield's bubble burst in early 1890. The family had just become settled in their gingerbread home, secured a job at the bank for Wilbur, and spent $2,000 in improvements on the house. It was not in the interest of Eastern capitalists to encourage the use of the Tennessee River for barge traffic. The word was passed not to buy Sheffield pig iron, and Sheffield's economy was immediately ruined.

In September 1890 Haygood, now a bishop of the Methodist Church, South, told Chambers that he would not be able to continue as agent of the Slater fund. Chambers made it clear that, since this was so, Haygood's presence would not be helpful to Sheffield. In February 1891, the bishop being sick with bronchitis, the Haygoods made the decision to move to an episcopal parsonage in Los Angeles, California. He gave the deed to the Sheffield house back to the land company, and agreed to pay $100 a month in *rent* so that Wilbur's family could continue to live there while Wilbur was out West looking for work as an Indian agent. The whole experience was mortifying to Haygood, and convinced him that his destiny was no longer one for joyful expectation. Perhaps most irritating to him was the rumor that he was moving to California as a health cure.[11]

Had Mrs. Haygood anticipated with pleasure living so far from Georgia, the California episcopate might have revived Haygood's hopeful nature and given him time to reorder his finances. W. B. Stradley, the Southern Methodist preacher at a large church in Los Angeles, provided an episcopal parsonage for the Haygoods— the only episcopal parsonage then in existence. The episcopal family moved in during May 1891. Bishop Haygood announced that "they" had set "our hearts on ending our days" in a missionary work, for two California and two Mexican conferences. By August all their belongings had arrived from Georgia. The house was in a suburban area of the little metropolis, having a gorgeous view of Mount Wilson to the northeast. Haygood liked the view but was not impressed by the "cheap redwood" bookcases in his diminutive study. He wrote Candler about the sound financial support given the public schools of California and said, referring to his study, "Y'r picture is over my desk—*Mc*'s [R. M. McIntosh's] close by & tell Lundy [Harris] I must have his. Laura's to my left. My wife's father & mother near—Bishop Pierce & his father watching me from another side."[12]

Mrs. Haygood's unhappiness in the new, dry environment was constant. The move had not allowed escape from the heavy obligations of the Southern hostess. Young J. Allen and George I. Seney visited with them, and McIntosh overstayed his invitation, spending four months during late 1892. Mamie and her new husband, Jule Ardis, a preacher, lived with the Haygoods until after their first baby came. Attie arrived after completing his medical course at Vanderbilt. The senior Haygoods continued to bring up Wilbur's son Paul as their own child. Young Atticus, Jule Ardis, and Claude Dimon, Mrs. Haygood's brother-in-law, liked California life, especially the beach trips to Redondo Beach, easily reached by train from the city. The bishop liked the climate, but never took to playing in the surf. Dimon joked about the fact that "He takes his bath in his own quiet tub."[13] The bishop did enjoy surf fishing, though.

Mollie's ill humor compounded her physical frailties. She had to cook for a large number of people, with no Negro help. She tried, unsuccessfully, to use a young German girl. She agreed to make a tour of the Mexican conferences in the fall of 1891, but on their return to California her health failed considerably. However, she gladly returned to Georgia in the late fall with Bishop Haygood, who wanted to persuade young Georgia preachers to transfer to the California conferences. A car full of these preachers and their families, and the Haygoods, traveled across the continent during January 1891, filling the desert places in the western half of the nation with much praying and hymn-singing, the devotions being frequently interrupted by necessary attentions to the babies.

Mollie's health, which had improved almost miraculously during their stay in Georgia, declined almost immediately after the train's arrival at the Los Angeles terminal. Her rheumatism got steadily worse, and by February's end she could hardly bend over to tie her shoes. That spring she almost died. By summertime she could sit up in a wheel chair. Bishop Haygood, still plagued with bronchitis, pushed her around the house, took her to the beach once, and supervised Paul, whom they considered their adopted child. When he went to Mexico in the fall of 1892 he took Paul with him. The third and final episcopal visitation to Mexico proved physically disastrous to him. In Mexico City he contracted the Caribbean fever known as dengue; from 1892 until his death he would never be free of infection and pain, either in the throat or chest.

On his return to Los Angeles, in 1892, he learned the dreadful news that he was blacklisted by a credit agency in Atlanta. This event undermined what remained of his will. The Haygoods made plans to return to Oxford, ostensibly for the purpose of improving their health. They were offered homes in Texas, North Carolina, and the Bay area of California. They left for Oxford in March 1893. The despondent bishop was depressed further by having to live with his wife's in-laws, the Evanses, in the old Yarbrough house he had moved into as a college sophomore thirty-six years before.[14]

The Providence in which Haygood had trusted had picked an exotic locale for the crushing of the man's vitality and spirit. In

1891 California had only six thousand Southern Methodists in two skeleton conferences. Mexico, where American Protestants had flourished, particularly in the mining cities like Zacatecas, had about four thousand members in Southern Methodist churches, all enlisted since 1873. Mexico under Porfirio Diaz guaranteed as much religious freedom as was possible. In secular states like Chihuahua, Protestants were not molested, but elsewhere the Roman hierarchy did what it could to hinder Protestants in the buying of property for churches and schools, in the holding of public meetings, and in the publishing of evangelical periodicals and tracts. Proselyting among nominal Catholics was therefore not particularly promising.

There were only ten "Americans" in the Mexican conferences, most of the preachers being natives. One Southern Methodist preacher was killed by a mob, and a presiding elder was knocked unconscious by a stone thrown at him during a public meeting in Durango, a town in northwestern Mexico in that area which had been Christianized by Father Kino and other Jesuits two hundred years before Haygood's missionary episcopacy. The major organizational accomplishment in Mexico was the establishment of a third mission conference. Some progress was also made in the primitive chapels of Lower California. The main strength of Southern Methodism, and other Protestant churches, was in the cities where the churches maintained English schools, patronized by what there was of a middle class.[15]

Southern Methodism was as exotic a plant in California as in Mexico, especially in Los Angeles. Bishop Haygood felt more hopeful about the churches in the mushrooming towns along the railroad in the San Joaquin Valley, where there had been congregations since the 1850's. But even in this valley the population reached by his pastors was heterogeneous, and the regular worship services, revivals, and quarterly and district conferences seemed on the whole to lack even a formal piety. In Los Angeles, a city of 70,000 hedonists, Stradley's church especially disturbed him. The "prominent families—that is, prominent in society and in wealth—fell into the habit of dancing, theater going, card playing and the rest of it." When, on Bishop Haygood's urging, Stradley called the families to account for their irreligiousness, "a very considerable number of the very foremost ones withdrew" their membership.[16] "Prominent families" would not have dared voluntarily to withdraw from the church in Georgia. Even with such disadvantages, Bishop Haygood urged his church to increase support, through the missions and church extension boards, of the California bridgehead. His last, futile plea came in May 1893, barely a month after he moved back to Georgia.[17]

The main business in Oxford was, if possible, to restore Haygood's good name by paying off some of his debts. Candler, aided by Haygood's old classmate, R. U. Hardeman, Georgia state treasurer (who lived in Oxford), made a list of all the debts which Haygood owed. Many of the bishop's creditors had given up long since, and Haygood's memorandums were in chaos, so the list was not complete. The known debt added up to about $10,000. Candler and Hardeman "funded" $7,500 of the most pressing obligations, borrowing on Haygood's life insurance policy. They arranged with the church for his salary as bishop, after September 1894, to be applied as they saw fit, since they had the power of attorney. For a few months Candler even required that the bishop send him the receipts for groceries charged at Branham's store, across the street from the Yarbrough home. The bishop had borrowed money extensively ever since his presidency of Emory; he was in obligation to Southern Methodists throughout the "connection," and in many cases to the friends of other Methodist bishops and preachers. In California a layman mortgaged his home in order to borrow some cash which the newly arrived bishop needed, a debt not repaid on time. Stradley paid the expenses of moving. Turning from the debt problem, Candler in 1894 won his old protégé's speechless gratitude by spreading the word of the bishop's need to the former students. Enough money was collected in the summer of 1894 to build the Haygoods a home of their own. They moved into it in September. Not built with the best lumber, it was nevertheless graced by columns across the porch and a fishing lake behind.[18]

To his credit, the sick bishop determined to do what he could to help pay off his debts. He wrote. He wrote articles for the *Nashville Advocate* for a stipend, and a book called *Jack-Knife and Brambles* while still at the Yarbrough house. In his new home he finished *The Monk and the Prince* and edited a new edition of his *Sermons*, first printed in 1883.[19] The two newly written books, *Jack-Knife*, and *The Monk and the Prince*, are both weak. *Jack-Knife* was advertised as an arsenal of arguments against the very kind of questioning which Bishop Haygood had engaged in during the 1880's, before his episcopal ordination. It sold well among the Southern Methodists of the 1890's. Its thesis today would be indefensible. Bishop Haygood agreed that the Bible could no longer be read literally, but his selection of the "right people" who could intuit the right meaning was quite arbitrary. He denied to the "philologists," experts in the Semitic and Greek languages, the right to say what the Holy Scriptures really mean.[20] *The Monk and the Prince*, with a heavy humor, told in moralistic fashion the story of the relationship of the Florentine prince, Lorenzo de' Medici, and the monk Savonarola. Haygood tried to point out that the immoral prince was a more honorable man than the "congenitally sensitive" Dominican who posed as a messiah. The point of the book, the unnaturalness of Holiness piety, was obvious enough, and Southern Methodists of the late 1890's did not like it.[21]

Haygood's articles for the *Nashville Advocate* were written with a kind of cathedral tone. The subjects were chosen, as in the old days, from random reading in the public press, but the commentary upon events was often irrelevant when not irrational. A typical article was one entitled "The Negro's 'Rain God,'" begun after his reading of religious practices in Africa:

There seems to be a very general impatience of authority and a disposition to smash the established order of things. As one expressed it, "speakers and writers are on the hunt for something to attack."

For a generation we have been consumed with desire to be rich. We have not been content with wealth as the natural fruitage of growth or as the accumulation of a life of patient toil and frugality. . . .

Men jump to the conclusion that the prevailing order is responsible for all their troubles. . . .[22]

These articles were written for a public which no longer existed. A layman wrote:

the Methodists do not need bishops to stand as moral mediators between the world and the Church, men who use their dignity and position to conciliate . . . the world. . . . Instances are not wanting. . . . May their generation soon and forever end.[23]

The writer doubtless was angered by the bishops' stand against the Holiness movement. But Haygood's once creative role in his church, fruitful especially in the 1880's when his formal relationship was peripheral, was nearing its end. The prayer with which the above article closed would soon be granted. The bishop hastened the end, in the summer of 1894, by over-indulging his taste for alcohol, which he had always thought was acceptable as medicine. His cough required more than medicine, but liquor did fairly well to obliterate part of the pain he felt in the dusty still heat of an Oxford summer.

The church press was discreet about the failing, although Oxford's residents, whose one open impiety was gossiping, were scandalized. The bishop tried to conceal his condition from the outside world in September 1894, when he failed to show up at a preaching appointment. He wrote the *Wesleyan Advocate* that he "lost my memorandum book, had a week's sharp attack. . . . Let it be attributed to coming age, or what not."[24] In the fall he became very ill, and in response to a pathetic request from Dr. Candler that he quit using liquor he did so. He improved slowly, and in April 1895 preached at the traditional Oxford spring revival. He also drew a churchful of people for an Easter sermon in Thomson and even attended the bishops' meeting in Nashville in May. His spirits were greatly aided by the return to Georgia of his sister Laura, from her ten years' mission as a teacher in China.[25]

The quiet days of his third Oxford summer since returning from California, however, got the best of him. He was seen to "stagger on the sidewalk, and support himself by catching at a garden fence." His explanation was that "overcome by heat, [he] had an attack of vertigo."[26] This was at least partially true. There was some improvement in the fall. He was happy that Dr. Candler sent some students to board with the Haygoods. He recuperated sufficiently to preside over the Kentucky conferences, making a fine impression. By October, though, after some sort of circulatory failing, he was back in bed, partially paralyzed. Against the doctor's orders, he got out of bed without Mollie's knowledge, hailed a farmer passing down the road in a wagon, and made his way by train to Atlanta, determined to hold upcoming conferences. He collapsed in Atlanta, and stayed there until he was "in his right mind."

In November the doctor allowed him to go to the Arkansas conferences, with Laura accompanying him. He began to drink again, and his manner in the chair was so disorganized as to leave a bad impression in a state which had respected him since 1873. As rumors about this performance spread, the distraught Candler considered resigning from the presidency of Emory College in order to be freed from association in the public mind with his impious episcopal ward. But Atticus would soon be no more an embarrassment. After preaching in the Oxford church on Sunday, January 5, 1896, he complained of a numbness and by Tuesday was almost totally paralyzed. On Wednesday he became unconscious, and died early on Sunday morning, January 19. His last exertion of *will* had been an effort to write an article which might be sold.

The eulogists were puzzled as to what they could say about Bishop Haygood's life, which was obviously weighty but seemed, in 1896, already anachronistic. Within two years Dr. Candler became Bishop Candler, and Atticus Haygood's long career of service to Georgia Methodism, Emory College, public education, and racial relations was obscured when not forgotten. Perhaps the Providence in which he trusted understood him and gave him his just reward.

Notes

Numbers in brackets at the top of the following pages indicate the pages in the text to which these notes refer.

CHAPTER ONE
[1-5]

1. Haygood Papers, Emory University Library; Clarke County Deed Record Book Q, p. 430; Greene Haygood's tombstone, Oakland Cemetery, Atlanta.

2. Atticus G. Haygood, "Our Methodist Parents," *Wesleyan Christian Advocate*, LVII (Jan. 11, 1893), 3, the periodical hereafter referred to as *WCA*; John W. Burke, *Autobiography: Chapters from the Life of a Preacher* (Macon, 1884), p. 199; William J. Cotter, *My Autobiography* (Nashville et al., 1917), p. 82.

3. George White, *Statistics of the State of Georgia; including an Account of its Natural, Civil, and Ecclesiastic History; Together With a Particular Description of Each County* . . . (Savannah, 1849), pp. 87, 179-80.

4. Richard H. Shryock, *Georgia and the Union in 1850* (Philadelphia, 1926), p. 23; Ralph B. Flanders, *Plantation Slavery in Georgia* (Chapel Hill, 1933), pp. 76, 86; and the works of Ulrich B. Phillips, particularly *Georgia and State Rights. A Study of Georgia From the Revolution to the Civil War, with Particular Regard to Federal Relations* (Washington, 1902), maps opposite pp. 140, 206; and "The Economic Cost of Slave-holding in the Cotton Belt," *Political Science Quarterly*, XX (1905), pp. 268-75.

5. "Oconee County," W.P.A. paper in Oconee County Folder, University of Georgia Library; Hugh J. Rowe, ed., *History of Athens and Clarke County* (Athens, 1923), pp. 108-11.

6. *The* (Athens) *Southern Banner*, Feb. 20, 1845, p. 3; *The* (Athens) *Southern Whig*, July 18, 1850, p. 3; George White, *Historical Collections of Georgia* (New York, 1854), p. 393; White, *Statistics*, pp. 98-100, 393.

7. White, *Statistics*, pp. 98-100; Walter B. Posey, *The Development of Methodism in the Old Southwest, 1783-1824* (Tuscaloosa, 1933), pp. 35-47, 123-29.

8. Atticus G. Haygood, "Camp-meeting Salmagundi," *WCA*, II (Sept. 27, 1879), 4; Cotter, *Autobiography*, pp. 125-27; J. D. Anthony, *Life and Times. . . . An Autobiography With a Few Original Sermons* (Atlanta, 1896), pp. v-vi, 42, 87.

9. Rowe, *History of Athens and Clarke County*, pp. 9-10, 111; Charles M. Strahan, *Clarke County, Georgia, and the City of Athens* (Athens, 1893), *passim*.

10. Horace Montgomery, *Cracker Parties* (Baton Rouge, 1950), pp. 2, 4-5; Athens *Southern Banner*, Oct. 10, Nov. 14, 1844; Oct. 9, 1845; Athens *Southern Herald*, Nov. 14, Dec. 5, 1850.

11. Burke, *Autobiography*, p. 199.

12. Testimony (by George W. Yarbrough?) in the Haygood Papers, hereafter called Yarbrough testimony; Clarke County Ordinary Records; Clarke County Deed Record Book Q, p. 430; *The* (Covington) *Georgia Enterprise*, Aug. 31, 1883, p. 2; Haygood, "Our Methodist Parents," *WCA* (Jan. 11, 1893), p. 3; Cotter, *Autobiography*, pp. 168-69.

13. Haygood, "Our Methodist Parents"; Haygood, "Thanks and Goodnight," *WCA*, LIX (Jan. 30, 1895), 4; Clarke County Deed Record Book S, p. 150; Burke, *Autobiography*, p. 199; Oswald E. and Anna M. Brown, *Life and Letters of Laura Askew Haygood* (Nashville, 1904), pp. 1, 6, 15.

14. Haygood, "Winding and Unwinding," *Southern Christian Advocate*, XXXIV (Oct. 18, 1871), the periodical hereafter referred to as *SCA;* Group for the Advancement of Psychiatry, *The Person With Epilepsy at Work* (New York, 1957), pp. 136-40.

15. "Our Methodist Parents," *WCA* (Jan. 11, 1893), p. 3.

16. Haygood, *Jack-Knife and Brambles* (Nashville, 1893), pp. 3-6; "Thanks and Goodnight," *WCA* (Jan. 30, 1895), p. 4.

17. Haygood, "Concerning Skeletons," *SCA*, XXXVIII (Dec. 3, 1875), 174; "Our Methodist Parents," *loc. cit.*

18. Haygood, "The Session of 1837," *SCA*, XL (Sept. 4, 1877, 142.

19. Cotter, *Autobiography*, pp. 168-69.

20. "Our Methodist Parents," *loc. cit.*

21. Haygood, "Death of Carlyle," *WCA*, III (Feb. 12, 1881), 4.

22. Haygood, "Winding and Unwinding," *SCA*, XXXIV, 166; Brown and Brown, *Life of Laura Haygood*, p. 7 and *passim*.

23. Haygood, *Jack-Knife and Brambles*, p. 4; Clarke County Deed Record Book T, pp. 90-91; Haygood, "Winding and Unwinding," *SCA*, XXXIV, 166.

24. Cotter, *Autobiography*, p. 169; Yarbrough testimony, Haygood Papers.

25. Greene B. Haygood, "Sketch of Atlanta," in *Williams' Atlanta Directory, City Guide, and Business Mirror*, I (Atlanta, 1859), 14.

26. De Kalb County Deed Record Book N, pp. 373-76, 400A-400B; Clarke County Deed Record Book V, p. 219; G. M. Hopkins, *City Atlas of Atlanta, Georgia* (Baltimore, 1878), p. 8; Reilly and Thomas, *Atlanta, Past Present & Future, Embracing Historical Sketches of Its Growth and Progress . . .* (Atlanta?, 1883), pp. 14, 136, 153; *Pioneer Citizens' History of Atlanta* (Atlanta, 1902), p. 41; Wilbur G. Kurtz, "Map of Atlanta, 1864," *Atlanta Historical Bulletin*, VIII (Oct. 1945), 32, the periodical hereafter cited as *Atl. Hist. Bull.;* Franklin M. Garrett, *Atlanta and Environs, A Chronicle of Its People and Events*, three vols. (Atlanta, 1954), I, 329; *Williams' Directory*, p. 11.

27. Haygood, "Our Old Friend Seems 'Rattled,'" *WCA*, XII (Apr. 2, 1890), 4; George W. Yarbrough, *Boyhood and Other Days in Georgia* (Nashville, 1917), p. 153; Elizabeth H. McCallie, "Atlanta in the 1850's," *Atl. Hist. Bull.*, VIII (n. d., no. 32), 95-102, 105.

28. Garrett, *Atlanta and Environs*, I, 328-55, 357, 369, 379; *Pioneer Citizens' History*, p. 36; McCallie, "Atlanta in the 1850's," *loc. cit.*, pp. 97, 104.

29. "Names from the Fulton County Tax Digest of 1854," *Atl. Hist. Bull.*, I (May 1930), 60, 78; John D. Humphries, "A Sketch of the Atlanta Bench and Bar Prior to 1890," *Atl. Hist. Bull.*, X (Nov. 1936), 34-36; *Williams' Directory*, p. 101; *The (Atlanta) Daily Intelligencer*, Oct. 7, 1858, p. 1.

30. J. S. Peterson, "Memoir of Greene B. Haygood, Esq.," *SCA*, XXVI (Jan. 1863), 1; *Atlanta Daily Examiner*, July 28, 1857, p. 2; Allen P. Tankersley, "Basil Hallam Overby, Champion of Prohibition in Ante Bellum Georgia," *The Georgia Historical Quarterly*, XXXI (March 1947), 9-16; Garrett, *Atlanta and Environs*, I, 356-409, *passim;* "Memoir of Colonel C. R. Hanleiter," *Atl. Hist. Bull.*, IX (Nov. 1936), 49-55.

31. *The Atlanta Daily Intelligencer and Examiner*, Oct. 7, 1857; Jan. 10, 17, 20, 1858; Peterson, "Memoir," *SCA*, XXVI, 1; Humphries, "Sketch of Atlanta Bench and Bar," *Atl. Hist. Bull.*, IX, 33-35; Avery O. Craven, *The Growth of Southern Nationalism, 1848-1861* (Baton Rouge, 1953), pp. 238-78, *passim;* Montgomery, *Cracker Parties*, pp. 77, 86, 99.

32. (Atlanta) *Daily Intelligencer*, Oct. 27, Dec. 21, 1858; Dorothy Orr, *A History of Education in Georgia* (Chapel Hill, 1933), pp. 171-73; Elbert W. G. Boogher,

Secondary Education in Georgia, 1732-1858 (Philadelphia, 1933), pp. 71, 79, 95; Herbert Fielder, *A Sketch of the Life and Times and Speeches of Joseph E. Brown* (Springfield, Mass., 1883), *passim*.

33. *Centennial Program, Trinity Methodist Church* (Atlanta, 1954), p. 7; *Minutes of the Georgia Annual Conference of the Methodist Episcopal Church, South, Held At Atlanta, Georgia, Dec. 13th-20th, 1854* (Macon, 1855), p. 31 and *passim*, titles of conference minutes, in similar form, hereafter abbreviated; Peterson, "Memoir," *SCA*, XXVI, 1.

34. *Minutes of the Ga. Conf. . . . 1856* (Atlanta, 1857), pp. 6-9, 34; family records in the Haygood Papers; Yarbrough, *Boyhood and Other Days*, p. 154; Reilly and Thomas, *Atlanta*, pp. 25-26.

35. McCallie, "Atlanta in the 1850's," *Atl. Hist. Bull.*, VIII, 102; Garrett, *Atlanta and Environs*, I, 375.

36. James Dixon, *Methodism in America* . . . (2nd ed.; London, 1859), pp. 222-35, 420; Posey, *Development of Methodism*, pp. 35-47; Edmund J. Hammond, *The Methodist Episcopal Church in Georgia* (Atlanta, 1935), pp. 71-92.

37. Alfred M. Pierce, *A History of Methodism in Georgia* . . . (Atlanta, 1956), pp. 129-40; Josephus Anderson, *Our Church: A Manual for Members and Probationers of the Methodist Episcopal Church, South* (Nashville, 1860), pp. 169, 180, 195-96.

38. *The Doctrine and Discipline of the Methodist Episcopal Church, South* (Nashville, 1859), pp. 13-16, 33-41, 47-66, 113-14.

39. Dixon, *Methodism in America, passim*.

40. George P. Cuttino, "Methodism in History," *The Emory University Quarterly*, XIII (Dec. 1957), 218-28; *Discipline*, pp. 17-41.

41. Anderson, *Our Church, passim*.

42. *Discipline*, pp. 17-41.

43. *Ibid.*

44. *Ibid.*; Haygood, "Our Methodist Parents," *WCA*, LII (Jan. 11, 1893), 3.

CHAPTER TWO

1. John D. Wade, *Augustus Baldwin Longstreet, A Study of the Development of Culture in the South* (New York, 1924), pp. 257-67; Allen P. Tankersley, *College Life at Old Oglethorpe* (Athens, 1951), p. 67; Anne Lide, "Five Georgia Colleges From 1850 to 1875," M. A. Thesis, Emory University, 1957, p. 13; George G. Smith, *The History of Georgia Methodism from 1786-1866* (Atlanta, 1913), p. 312 and *passim*.

2. Nathaniel J. Hammond, *The University of Georgia. A Short History* . . . (Atlanta, 1893), *passim*; Augustus L. Hull, *A Historical Sketch of the University of Georgia* (Athens and Atlanta, 1894), pp. 61-62; E. Merton Coulter, *College Life in the Old South* (New York, 1928), pp. 248-53, 258.

3. Yarbrough testimony.

4. *Minutes of the Ga. Annual Conference . . . 1858* (Charleston, 1859), p. 30.

5. Henry M. Bullock, *A History of Emory University* (Nashville, 1936), pp. 97, 110, 116-24, 139, and photos; *Catalogue of the Officers and Students of Emory College . . . 1856 & 1857* (Augusta, 1857), p. 10; Emory College. Minutes of the Board of Trustees, 1837-1871, p. 280—hereafter referred to as Minutes of the Board.

6. White, *Statistics*, pp. 78-79, 449-52.

7. The best sources for catching the flavor of Oxford in the 1850's are the annual *Catalogues*.

8. Emory College. Matriculation Book, 1836-1865, p. 1.

9. *Ibid.*, pp. 73-75.

10. Yarbrough testimony.

11. "Expenses at Emory College from Sept 5th/56," Haygood Papers.

12. *Catalogue*, 1856-57, p. 10; *Annual Catalogue of the Officers, Alumni & Students of Emory College, . . . 1876-77* (Macon, 1877), pp. 28-29.

13. *Person With Epilepsy At Work*, pp. 138-39; Yarbrough testimony.

14. John W. Heidt, "Memoir," *The Atlanta Constitution*, Jan. 27, 1896, reprinted in *Year Book and Minutes of the North Georgia Conference* . . . (Atlanta, 1896); Elam F. Dempsey, editor, *Atticus Greene Haygood* (Nashville, 1940), p. 497.

15. Warren A. Candler, *Young J. Allen, "The Man Who Seeded China"* (Nashville, 1931), pp. 1-25, 34-35.

16. *Ibid.*, pp. 24-34; Mrs. F. A. Butler, *History of the Woman's Foreign Missionary Society, M. E. Church, South* (Nashville and Dallas, 1904), p. 20; *Emory College Commencement Day, July 22, 1857* (Covington, 1857).

17. Haygood, *Sermons and Speeches* (Nashville, 1883), pp. 215-20; letter to Warren A. Candler, Sheffield, Ala., Feb. 28, 1891, Candler Letters; also see Marion L. Smith, "Atticus Greene Haygood; Christian Educator," Ph.D. Dissertation, Yale University, 1929, pp. 16-18.

18. Heidt, *loc. cit.*; Bullock, *Hist. of Emory*, pp. 89-90, 98, 133-35; *Catalogue of Emory College*, 1858-59 (Charleston, 1859), p. 11; Emory College Faculty Minutes; *Minutes of the Ga. Annual Conf.*, 1858 (Charleston, 1859), pp. 29-30.

19. Emory Faculty Minutes, *passim*.

20. Yarbrough testimony; see Bullock, pp. 121, 134, 137-38.

21. Yarbrough testimony; James W. Hinton, "My First Circuit," *WCA*, LV (March 4, 1891), 2; Quimby F. Melton, "When Bishop Haygood 'Toted Bricks,'" *The Atlanta Journal*, magazine section, June 13, 1926, p. 11; Walter A. Clark, *A Lost Arcadia, Or the Story of My Old Community* (Augusta, 1909), p. 7.

22. *The Foot-Prints of the Creator: Or, The Asterolepsis of Stromness* (Boston, 1857), pp. 278, 328; *The Two Records* . . . (Boston, 1854).

23. Thomas A. Davies, *Answer to Hugh Miller and Theoretic Geologists* (New York, 1860), p. 18. Emory University Library copies of these three books bear the Phi Gamma and Few Society bookmarks.

24. Joseph W. Krutch, "Lost Certainties," review of Gertrude Himmelfarb's *Darwin and the Darwinian Revolution*, in *The Reporter*, XX (May 28, 1959), 41; also see Richard Hofstadter, *Social Darwinism in American Thought, 1860-1915* (Philadelphia, 1945), pp. 11-17.

25. Bullock, *Hist. of Emory*, pp. 103-24; Faculty Minutes; Yarbrough testimony; Heidt, "Memoir," *loc. cit.*, pp. 52-59; *Emory College Junior Exhibition, July 21, 1857* (Covington, 1857), pp. 1-4.

26. The address by Thomas on this subject is found in *The Educational Repository and Family Monthly*, I (Jan. 1860), 4-9; also see pp. 10-17.

27. *Ibid.*; Yarbrough testimony.

28. Bullock, *Hist. of Emory*, pp. 93-115, 142-43; Yarbrough, *Boyhood and Other Days*, p. 151; Richard Hoftstadter and C. DeWitt Hardy, *The Development and Scope of Higher Education in the United States* (New York, 1952), pp. 23-25.

29. W. J. Sasnett, *Progress: Considered With Particular Reference to the Methodist Episcopal Church, South* (Nashville, 1855), pp. 5-8, 16, 40, 121-23, 142; George G. Smith, *The Life and Times of George Foster Pierce, D.D., LL.D.* . . . (Sparta, 1888), pp. 160-61; *Atlanta Daily Intelligencer*, Oct. 19, 1858; Haygood to Candler, Sheffield, Feb. 28, 1891, Candler Letters; *In Memoriam. Geo. W. W. Stone, D.D., 1818-1889* (Atlanta, 1889), pp. 9-26.

30. Gustavus J. Orr, Jr., "Hon. Gustavus J. Orr, LL.D., State School Commissioner," Orr Papers.

31. Orr (Sr.), *The Choice of a Profession* . . . (Atlanta, 1859), pp. 3-4, 9; Candler, *Allen*, pp. 34-35; *Minutes of the Ga. Annual Conf.*, 1858, pp. 3, 29-30.

32. Heidt, "Memoir," *loc. cit.*; Haygood Papers.

33. Bullock, *Hist. of Emory*, pp. 92-97, 145.

34. Haygood Papers; "Our Methodist Parents," *WCA* (Jan. 11, 1893); Haygood, "A Notable Woman," *WCA*, LVI (Dec. 17, 1891), 4-5.

35. *Commencement Day, Emory College, Senior Exhibition* . . . , *July 20, 1859* (Atlanta, 1859), 4 pp.; Melton, "When Bishop Haygood 'Toted Bricks,'" *Atl. Journal*, June 13, 1926, mag. section.

36. Haygood, "Plan of my First Circuit," Haygood Papers; Haygood, "A Notable Woman," *WCA*, LVI (Dec. 17, 1891), 4-5; James I. Robertson, Jr., ed., *The Diary of Dolly Lunt Burge* (Athens, 1962), p. 64.
37. Quoted in Smith, *Life of Pierce*, pp. 75-76.
38. *Diary of Dolly Lunt Burge*, pp. 64-65; Haygood, "Camp-meeting Salmagundi," *WCA*, XLII (Sept. 27, 1879), 4; *Minutes of the Ga. Annual Conf.*, 1858, pp. 3, 24, 36-37.
39. Typed copy of "Autobiography of George Gilman Smith of Georgia," original in the University of North Carolina Library, p. 59.
40. Smith, *Hist. of Georgia Methodism*, p. 309.
41. *Minutes of the Ga. Annual Conf.*, 1859 (Macon, 1860), *passim; Discipline*, 1859, pp. 57-58, 73; Burke, *Autobiography*, pp. 52-53.
42. *Minutes*, 1859, pp. 12-13; Burke, *Autobiography*, pp. 91-92.
43. Yarbrough, *Boyhood and Other Days*, p. 90; Haygood, "The Gospel Among the Slaves," *Nashville Christian Advocate*, LV (July 12, 1894), 3—hereafter the organ will be cited as *NCA*; Haygood, ed., *Bishop Pierce's Sermons and Addresses, With a Few Special Discourses by Dr. Pierce* (Nashville, 1886), pp. 4, 18.
44. Lovick Pierce, "A Semi-Centennial Discourse . . . , 1856," in Thomas O. Summers, editor, *Sermons and Essays by Ministers of the Methodist Episcopal Church, South* (Nashville, 1857), pp. 7-9; Oscar P. Fitzgerald and Charles B. Galloway, *Eminent Methodists. Twelve Booklets in One Book* (Nashville, 1897), pp. 1-5, 28.
45. Haygood, preface to *Bishop Pierce's Sermons*, op. cit.; Burke, *Autobiography*, p. 80.
46. Smith, *Life of Pierce*, pp. 188-89.
47. *Theological Institutes: or, a View of the Evidences . . . of Christianity* (Nashville, 1857), *passim; A Biblical and Theological Dictionary* (Nashville, 1857); Thomas Jackson, *Memoir of the Life and Writings of The Rev. Richard Watson* (New York, 1834), pp. 255-56; Oscar P. Fitzgerald, *Dr. Summers, A Life-Study* (Nashville, 1885), pp. 183-86.
48. *Theological Institutes*, see especially pp. 410-14; James Nichols, *Calvinism and Arminianism Compared in Their Principles and Tendency . . .* , 2 vols. (London, 1824), I, i; W. H. Browning, *An Examination of the Doctrine of the Unconditioned Final Perseverance of the Saints, As Taught by Calvinists* (Nashville, 1860), pp. 11, 42-43; William R. Cannon, *The Theology of John Wesley With Special Reference to the Doctrine of Justification* (New York and Nashville, 1946), pp. 81-106, 193-95, 225, 239.
49. Haygood's intro. to Smith, *Life of Pierce*, pp. ix-x.
50. *Discipline*, 1859, pp. 67-89, 101, 118-21.
51. "Autobiography of George Gilman Smith," p. 64.
52. *Minutes of the Annual Conferences of the Methodist Episcopal Church, South, for Year[s] 1858-1865* (Nashville, 1859-70—eight vols. bound as one), pp. 259-62—hereafter referred to as *Minutes, M. E. Ch., S., 1858-1865*.

CHAPTER THREE

1. Smith, *Hist. of Ga. Methodism*, p. 317.
2. *Memoirs of Georgia, Containing Historical Accounts of the State's Civil, Military, Industrial and Professional Interests, and Personal Sketches of Many of Its People* (2 vols.; Atlanta, 1895), I, 1032-35; Smith, *Life of Pierce*, pp. 143-49; Dempsey, *Haygood*, p. 76.
3. Smith, *Life of Pierce*, pp. 143-49.
4. *Ibid*.
5. *Ibid.*, pp. 55, 436-37, 445-49, 465-77.
6. Robert D. Clark, *The Life of Matthew Simpson* (New York, 1956), pp. 246-62.
7. Smith, *Life of Pierce*, pp. 465-77.
8. I (Jan. 1860), 1-33.

9. I (Aug.), 490; II (Jan. 1861), 59-60; Richard B. Harwell, "Atlanta Publications of the Civil War," *Atl. Hist. Bull.* VI (July 1941), 173, 192.
10. *Educational Repository and Family Monthly*, II, 59-60.
11. *Ibid.*, II, 31-35.
12. *Ibid.*, II (Feb. 1861), 69-77; Harwell, *Atl. Hist. Bull.*, VI, 192; *WCA*, LXII (Feb. 9-16, 1898), reprints.
13. "Autobiography of Geo. G. Smith," pp. 65-66.
14. James W. Folsom, *Heroes and Martyrs of Georgia. Georgia's Record in the Revolution of 1861* (Macon, 1864), Clement A. Evans, *Confederate Military History, A Library of Confederate States History in Twelve Volumes* . . . (Atlanta, 1899), VI, 20-35; Charles E. Jones, *Georgia in the War, 1861-1865* (Augusta, 1909), pp. 40, 77, and *passim*; Allen D. Candler, ed., *The Confederate Records of Georgia* (Atlanta, 1910), III, 57-58, 91-92, 98-99, 114; T. Conn Bryan, *Confederate Georgia* (Athens, 1953), p. 25.
15. Lillian Henderson, comp., *Roster of the Confederate Soldiers of Georgia, 1861-1865* (Hapeville, Ga., 1955-1958), II, 408-73; General Order 89, Yorktown, Virginia, Oct. 3, 1861, *Official Records*, I, 4, 668-70; *The* (Athens) *Southern Banner*, July 17, Aug. 7, 21, 1861; *The* (Atlanta) *Daily Intelligencer*, July 21, Aug. 9, 1861.
16. W. Harrison Daniel, "The Protestant Church in the Confederate States of America," Ph.D. Thesis, Duke University, 1957, pp. 63-68; W. J. Scott, *Biographic Etchings of Ministers and Laymen of the Georgia Conference* (Atlanta, 1895), pp. 20-21; T. Conn Bryan, "The Churches in Georgia During the Civil War," *Ga. Hist. Q.*, XXXIII (Dec. 1949), 288.
17. Smith, *Life of Pierce*, pp. 438-49.
18. Dempsey, *Haygood*, pp. 90-99.
19. *Ibid.*
20. Yarbrough testimony.
21. James D. Waddell, ed., *Biographical Sketch of Linton Stephens, Containing a Selection of His Letters, Speeches, State Papers, etc.* (Atlanta, 1877), pp. 132-33, 242-45.
22. Henderson, *Roster of the Confed. Soldiers of Ga.*, II, 408-10, 442.
23. *The Southern Banner*, Sept. 4, 1861.
24. *Ibid.*
25. E. Merton Coulter, *The Confederate States of America, 1861-1865* (Baton Rouge, 1950), p. 351.
26. *The Southern Banner*, Oct. 30, 1861.
27. Henderson, *Roster*, II, 408-17; Dempsey, *Haygood*, pp. 76-77; copy of poem in Haygood Papers; gravestone, Oakland cemetery, Atlanta; *The* (Atlanta) *Daily Intelligencer*, Sept. 1, Oct. 3, 4, 9, 1861.
28. *Daily Intelligencer*, Nov. 27-Dec. 5, 1861.
29. *Ibid.*; Bryan, "Churches in Ga. During the Civil War," *Ga. Hist. Q.*, XXXIII, 285; Burke, *Autobiography*, pp. 101-02.
30. *Minutes of the Annual Conferences*, 1858-1865, pp. 339-44; copy of license as deacon, Dec. 1, 1861, Haygood Papers; *Cat. of Emory, 1870-71*, p. 11.
31. Hinton, "My First Circuit," *WCA*, LV (March 4, 1891), 2.
32. Haygood, "Bishop Key Making Glad the Parsonage," *WCA*, LVI (Dec. 14, 1892), 4.
33. *Ibid.*
34. Dempsey, *Haygood*, pp. 114-17.
35. Haygood, "Revivals on the Watkinsville Circuit," *SCA*, XXV (Oct. 16, 1862), 159; . . . "The Gospel Among the Slaves," *NCA*, LV (July 12, 1894), 5; *The Southern Banner*, March 12, 19, 1862; *WCA*, VIII (April 6, 1886), 5, and (April 21), 2; Yarbrough testimony.
36. "Revivals on the Watkinsville Circuit," *SCA*, XXV, 159.
37. Scott, *Biographic Etchings*, pp. 153-54; Eugene P. Southall, "The Attitude of the Methodist Episcopal Church, South, Toward the Negro . . . to 1870," *Journal of Negro History*, XVI (Oct. 1931), 368 and *passim*.

38. "Making Glad the Parsonage," *WCA*, LVI (Dec. 14), 4.
39. *The Southern Banner*, March 12, 19, 1862.
40. *Ibid.*
41. Copy in Haygood Papers.
42. Dempsey, *Haygood*, pp. 114-17.
43. Smith, *Hist. of Ga. Methodism*, pp. 325, 401; Bryan, *Ga. Hist. Q.*, XXXIII, 285-86; Burke, *Autobiography*, p. 105.
44. "Memoir," *SCA*, XXVI (Jan. 4, 1863), 1; *The Daily Intelligencer*, Dec. 28, 1862; gravestone in Oakland Cemetery; Haygood Scrapbook, property of Mary Louise Haygood Trotti, Decatur, Ga.
45. *SCA*, XXV (Dec. 11, 1862), 190; Mary G. Jones and Lily Reynolds, *Coweta County Chronicles for One Hundred Years* . . . (Atlanta, 1928), pp. 120, 149, and *passim*.
46. Gravestone, Oakland Cemetery.
47. *The* (Atlanta) *Southern Confederacy*, Jan. 30, 1863; Daniel, "Prot. Church in the C. S. A.," pp. 72-74, 91-97, 108; Gross Alexander, "History of the Methodist Episcopal Church, South," in Vol. XI, The American Church History Series (New York, 1894), 71.
48. *SCA*, Feb. 6, 1896, clipping in Haygood Papers.
49. Joseph M. Brown, *The Mountain Campaigns in Georgia, Or War Scenes on the W. & A.* (Buffalo, 1896), pp. 11-17; Daniel, *op. cit.*, pp. 104-08, 219; Alexander, *op. cit.*, XI, 71-72; R. F. Bunting, *The Mysteries of Providence: A Fast-Day Discourse Delivered August 21st, 1863* . . . *Near Rome* (Atlanta, 1864), p. 9 and *passim*; "An Army Scene at Dalton, Ga.," *WCA*, LVII (Feb. 1, 1893), 2.
50. Sermon MS, Haygood Papers.
51. Smith, *Hist. of Ga. Methodism*, pp. 326-27; Haygood, *Life of Pierce*, p. 482.
52. *SCA*, XXVI (Nov. 19, Dec. 10, 17, 1863), *passim*; *Daily Columbus Enquirer*, Nov. 26, 1863.
53. *Minutes of the Annual Conferences*, 1858-1865, pp. 452-57; Bryan, "The Church in Ga. During the Civil War," *Ga. Hist. Q.*, XXXIII, 289.
54. *Daily Columbus Enquirer*, Nov. 28-Dec. 3, 1863.
55. Haygood, "From Gen. Longstreet's Army," *SCA*, XXVII (March 24, 1864), also (March 10); Wilbur Fletcher Haygood's tombstone in Oxford, Ga.
56. "Missionary Report," *SCA*, XXVIII (Jan. 26, 1865), and XXVII (March 24, 1864).
57. Walter A. Clark, *Under the Stars and Bars, Or, Memories of Four Years Service* . . . (Augusta, 1900), pp. 97-102; Luther B. Bridgers, *Trinity Methodist Episcopal Church, South* . . . (mimeographed; Atlanta, 1935), p. 5; *Daily Intelligencer*, July-Aug., 1864; A. A. Hoehling, *Last Train from Atlanta* (New York and London, 1958), pp. 164, 295, and *passim*.
58. Wilbur G. Kurtz, ed., "Persons Sent From Atlanta By Gen. Sherman," *Atl. Hist. Bull.*, I (Feb. 1932), 29.
59. Haygood, "Atlanta, the 'Gate City' Again," *SCA*, XXVII (Dec. 15, 1864); also see (Nov. 3, Nov. 24); Meta Barker, ed., "Atlanta As Sherman Left It . . . ," *Atl. Hist. Bull.*, I (May 1930), 15-20; Brown and Brown, *Life of Laura Haygood*, p. 5.
60. *The* (Athens) *Southern Banner*, Jan. 11, 18, 1865; *SCA*, XXVIII (Jan. 19, 1865).
61. Bridgers, *Trinity Church*, p. 5; "Atlanta, the 'Gate City' Again," *SCA*, XXVIII (Dec. 15).
62. *The Southern Banner*, Feb. 15, March 8, 1865; *Weekly Intelligencer*, April 19, May 24, 1865; May 9, 1866; "Col. C. R. Hanleiter, Reminiscences . . . ," *Atl. Hist. Bull.*, II, 52; *SCA*, XXVIII (April 13, 1865).
63. Haygood, "Atlanta Redivious [sic]," *Army and Navy Herald*, II (April 13, 1865); see also Feb. 9.
64. Dempsey, *Haygood*, pp. 102-03.

CHAPTER FOUR

1. (Atlanta) *Weekly Intelligencer*, June 7-Oct. 18, 1865; V. T. Barnwell, comp., . . . *Atlanta City Directory and Stranger's Guide* . . . (Atlanta, 1867), pp. 27-35; John S. Wilson, "Atlanta As It Is" (published originally 1871), *Atl. Hist. Bull.*, VI (Jan.-April 1941), 17; Kate Massey, "A Picture of Atlanta in the Late Sixties," *Atl. Hist. Bull.*, V (Jan. 1940), 32-36.

2. Scott, *Biographic Etchings*, pp. 20-21.

3. *Ibid.*, pp. 287-89; Eugene M. Mitchell, "Atlanta During the 'Reconstruction Period,'" *Atl. Hist. Bull.*, II (Nov. 1936), 18-24.

4. *Weekly Intelligencer*, Jan. 10-July 4, 1866; Barnwell, *Atlanta City Directory*, *passim*.

5. Mary V. Womble, "Condensed History of the First Methodist Episcopal Church, South, Atlanta, Georgia," *Atl. Hist. Bull.*, I (Jan. 1928), 23-32; Smith, *Life of Pierce*, p. 494; Bridgers, *Trinity Church*, pp. 1, 5; *Southern Methodist Review*, III (Nov. 1887), 247-55; (Jan. 1888), 401-08; *WCA*, LIX (Feb. 27, 1895), 3.

6. Oliver S. Heckman, "Northern Church Penetration of the South, 1860 to 1880," Ph.D. Thesis, Duke University, 1939, especially pp. 184, 190; Ralph E. Morrow, "Northern Methodism in the South During Reconstruction," *Mississippi Valley Historical Review*, XLI (Sept. 1854), 202; Matthew Simpson, *A Hundred Years of Methodism* (New York and Cincinnati, 1879), p. 179; W. M. Leftwich, *Martyrdom in Missouri, A History of Religious Proscription, The Seizure of Churches, and the Persecution of Ministers* . . . (St. Louis, 1870), I, 278-95, 432; II, 126, 423; *Portrait and Biography of Parson Brownlow, The Tennessee Patriot* . . . (Indianapolis, 1862), p. 44.

7. Wesley J. Gaines, *African Methodism in the South; or Twenty-five Years of Freedom* (Atlanta, 1890), pp. 8-14; Smith, *Hist. of Ga. Methodism to 1866*, p. 397.

8. Smith, *Life of Pierce*, pp. 490-95.

9. Caldwell, *Slavery and Southern Methodism: Two Sermons Preached* . . . *in Newnan, Georgia* (n. p., 1865), pp. iii-xi, 47.

10. *The Macon Daily Telegraph*, Nov. 17, 21, 22, 1865.

11. *Ibid.*

12. Gaines, *African Methodism*, pp. 6-10; Benjamin T. Tanner, *An Apology for African Methodism* (Baltimore, 1867), pp. 413-16; also see J. W. Hood, *The Negro in the Christian Pulpit* . . . (Raleigh, 1884), pp. 3-6; Joseph B. Earnest, *The Religious Development of the Negro in Virginia* (Charlottesville, 1914), pp. 105-06; Beverly F. Shaw, *The Negro in the History of Methodism* (Nashville, 1954), p. 145; Carter G. Woodson, *The History of the Negro Church* (Washington, 1921), pp. 191-97; Hunter D. Farish, *The Circuit Rider Dismounts, A Social History of Southern Methodism, 1865-1900* (Richmond, 1938), pp. 27, 69; Willard Range, *The Rise and Progress of Negro Colleges in Georgia, 1865-1949* (Athens, 1951), pp. 12-20.

13. *SCA*, XXVIII (Aug. 31, 1865).

14. Gaines, *African Methodism*, pp. 10, 18-19; *Journal of the General Conference* . . . *Held in New Orleans, 1866* (Nashville, 1866), p. 39; Holland N. McTyeire, *A History of Methodism* . . . *Down to* . . . *1884* (Nashville, 1895), pp. 671-73 and *passim*.

15. Theodore L. Flood and John W. Hamilton, editors, *Lives of Methodist Bishops* (New York and Cincinnati, 1882), pp. 791-92; *SCA*, XXIX (May 18, 1866), 4; Southall, "Attitude of the M. E. Church, South, Toward the Negro," *J. of Negro Hist.*, XVI, 368.

16. Smith, *Life of Pierce*, p. 492.

17. Jesse H. Barton, "The Definition of the Episcopal Office in American Methodism," Ph.D. Thesis, Drew University, 1960, *passim*; Thomas M. Finney, *The Life and Labors of Enoch Mather Marvin, Late Bishop* . . . (St. Louis, 1886), p. 423.

18. *Macon Daily Telegraph*, Nov. 15, 18, 22, 1865; also see Smith, *Hist. of Ga. Methodism to 1866*, p. 334.

19. Finney, *Life of Marvin*, pp. 432-39; McTyeire, *Hist. of Methodism*, p. 667; Alexander, "Hist. of the M. E. Church, South," *loc. cit.*, XI, 79-82; *SCA*, XXIX (May 18, 1866), 4; (June 22), 3.

20. Haygood, "High Steeple and . . . Its Official Staff," *Quarterly Review of the Methodist Episcopal Church, South*, XV (July 1893), 62-63.

21. *SCA*, XXIX (May 18, 1866), *passim*.

22. See James M. Buckley, *A History of Methodists in the United States* (New York, 1896), *passim*.

23. Smith, *Hist. of Ga. Methodism to 1866*, pp. 334, 398-400.

24. Eugene M. Mitchell, "H. I. Kimball; His Career and Defense," *Atl. Hist. Bull.*, III (Oct. 1938), 249-83; C. Mildred Thompson, *Reconstruction in Georgia, Economic, Social, Political, 1865-1872* (New York, 1915), pp. 175-269.

25. Edmund J. Hammond, *The Methodist Episcopal Church in Georgia* . . . (n. p., 1935), pp. 105-09, 119-25; *The* (Atlanta) *Methodist Advocate*, I (June 16, 30, 1869).

26. Buckley, *Hist. of Methodists*, p. 517; Morrow, "Northern Methodism in the South," *MVHR*, XXXXI, 206, 209; Henry L. Swint, *The Northern Teacher in the South, 1862-1870* (Nashville, 1941), p. 118.

27. *The* (Atlanta) *Daily Constitution*, Sept. 5, 1880, gives information about a Rev. Caldwell; Atticus G. Haygood, *Our Brother in Black, His Freedom and His Future* (New York and Cincinnati, 1881), p. 229; Hammond, *M. E. Church in Ga.*, pp. 119-25.

28. Brown, *Mountain Campaigns in Ga.*, map, p. 17; J. D. Walsh, "The Methodist Episcopal Church in the South," *Methodist Review*, LXX (March 1888), 245-52; Anthony, *Autobiography*, p. 157; *Minutes of the Annual Conferences, 1866-1873*, pp. 23-28.

29. Haygood, "Twenty-six Years Ago," *WCA*, LVI (Dec. 21, 1892), copy in Haygood Papers; W. C. Dunlap, "Bishop Haygood, 'Twenty-six Years Ago,'" *WCA*, LVII (Jan. 4, 1893), 4; for corroboration see Elisha Lowery to J. S. Dobbins, April 17, 1866, and J. O. Dobbins to J. S., Aug. 12, 1866, Dobbins Correspondence, Emory University Library.

30. Dunlap, *WCA*, LVII (Jan. 4), 4.

31. John T. Norris, "From Dalton, Georgia," *SCA*, XXX (May 8, 1867), 60.

32. "Autobiog. of George G. Smith," p. 113.

33. *Rome Weekly Courier*, April 24, 30, 1868; *Minutes of the Conf., 1866-73*, pp. 27, 117, 221.

34. William J. Northen, ed., *Men of Mark in Georgia* . . . (Atlanta, 1910), III, 442-44; William B. Hesseltine, *Confederate Leaders in the New South* (Baton Rouge, 1950), pp. 51-52.

35. *Min. of the Conf.*, pp. 119, 122-23.

36. John E. Talmadge, *Rebecca Latimer Felton, Nine Stormy Decades* (Athens, 1960), *passim;* Thompson, *Reconstruction in Ga.*, pp. 210, 255, 269; John W. Heidt, "The Rome District Convention," *SCA*, XXX (May 31, 1867), 85.

37. *SCA*, XXX, 85; (Aug. 16), 130.

38. *Catalogue of the Officers, Alumni and Students of Emory College, 1870-71*, pp. 41-42, and *passim*.

39. *SCA*, XXX, 85, 130.

40. Gravestones, Oakland Cemetery, Atlanta; testimony of Laura Haygood Watts, given to Lon H. Eakes of Downey, California, Feb. 1960, cited in letter to author, Feb. 28, 1960; *SCA*, XXXI (Apr. 3, 10, 17, 24, May 4, 1868).

41. *SCA*. XXX (Jan. 11, Apr.-May, Oct. 18).

42. *Ibid.;* also see XXXI (June 26, 1868), 102; (July 31), 123; (Oct. 2), 158.

CHAPTER FIVE

1. Thompson, *Reconstruction in Ga.*, pp. 190-260.
2. *The* (Atlanta) *Constitution*, Feb. 10, 1869.

3. DeKalb County Deed Record Book N, pp. 373-76, 400A-400B; Fulton County Deed Record Book B, p. 212; Book L, p. 183; Book M, pp. 499, 511; Newton County Deed Record Book O, pp. 292-93; *City Atlas of Atlanta, Georgia* . . . (Baltimore, 1878), Plate A.

4. John Tryon, "Letter," XXXII (Oct. 1, 1869); W. J. Parks, "From Georgia," *Baltimore Episcopal Methodist*, IV (Oct. 9, 1869), 2; Anthony, *Autobiography*, pp. 162-66.

5. *The Constitution*, see Feb. 23, May 1, 2, 5, 6, 15, 20, July 25, 1869.

6. *The Weekly Atlanta Intelligencer*, Aug. 22, 1866, and 1869 issues.

7. *The* (Atlanta) *Methodist Advocate*, I (June 16, 1869), 2; Scott, *Biographic Etchings*, pp. 31-33.

8. *The Constitution*, May 2, 7, June 2, 6, July 24, Aug. 12, 13, 1869.

9. Douglas G. MacRae, "The Georgia Education Association," M. A. Thesis, Emory University, 1940, p. 1.

10. C. J. Sheehan, "Atlanta Public Schools, 1873-1883," *Atl. Hist. Bull.*, II (Nov.) 1936), 5; *The Constitution*, Oct. 6, 8, Nov. 20, 1869; March 8, 17, 1870.

11. Haygood, "Atlanta City Mission," *NCA*, XXX (Dec. 3, 1870), 2; Laura Haygood, "The History of a Mission Sunday-school," *The Sunday-School Magazine*, II (Feb. 1872), 33-35.

12. *Min. of the Annual Conf.*, 1866-1873, pp. 221-23, 322-23, 428.

13. Sermon, Haygood Papers.

14. Myers, "Presiding Elders and More Bishops," *SCA*, XXXII (Feb. 12, 1869), 26.

15. *Sunday-school Visitor*, I (1855); VI (1860); H. B. Browne, *Methodist Sunday Schools After a Hundred Years* (Camden, S. C., 1911), pp. 7-11.

16. Addie G. Wardle, *History of the Sunday School Movement in the Methodist Episcopal Church* (New York and Cincinnati, 1918), pp. 82, 90, 100, 121-51.

17. John Tryon, *SCA*, XXXII, 46, 54.

18. *SCA*, XXXII (Aug. 20, 1869), 134; (Oct. 29), 173; *The Constitution*, May 2, 7, 1869.

19. *Journal of the General Conference* . . . , *1870* (Nashville, 1870), pp. 220, 232, 264-65, 327, 333-34.

20. Elijah E. Hoss, *David Morton, A Biography* (2nd ed.; Louisville, 1916), pp. 91-98; *SCA*, XXXIII (May 20, 1870), 77.

21. *The Constitution*, May 28, 1870; *The* (Covington) *Georgia Enterprise*, July 15, 1870; (Nashville) *Republican Banner*, July 10, 1870; *Nashville Union and American*, Aug. 13, 1870; *SCA*, XXXIII, 118, 130; *NCA*, XXX (July 16), 1; (July 30), 2; (Aug. 6), 2; (Aug. 20), 1.

22. W. W. Clayton, *History of Davidson County* . . . (Phila., 1880), *passim;* J. Wooldridge, editor, *History of Nashville, Tenn.* . . . (Nashville, 1890), pp. 360, 369.

23. C. Vann Woodward, *Origins of the New South, 1877-1913* (Baton Rouge, 1951), pp. 107, 162.

24. Francis A. Walker, editor, *Ninth Census* (Washington, 1872), I, 102, 262; Charles E. Robert, *Nashville and Her Trade for 1870* . . . (Nashville, 1870), pp. 43-45, 59, 173 ff.

25. Robert, *Nashville and Her Trade*, pp. 307-434, *passim*.

26. Wooldridge, *Hist. of Nashville*, pp. 456, 603-04, *passim*.

27. Edwin H. Ewing, *An Address . . . at the Celebration of the Centennial Anniversary of the University of Nashville* . . . (Nashville, 1885), pp. 16-17.

28. *Nashville City and Business Directory for 1860-61* (Nashville, 1860), pp. 88, 99-101, frontispiece map; Charles C. Jarrell, editor, *Methodism on the March, A Study of Methodism Mobilized* (Nashville, 1924), pp. 160, 171-74.

29. Oscar P. Fitzgerald, *Dr. Summers: A Life-Study* (Nashville, 1885), pp. 219, 473-77; Charles H. Poole, "Thomas O. Summers, A Biographical Study," M. A. Thesis, Vanderbilt University, 1957, p. 64.

30. Redford, *Exhibit of the Publishing House . . . for the Four Years Ending April 30th, 1870* (Nashville, 1870), pp. 3-6, 8, 18-19.

31. R. M. Heriges, compiler, "Complete List of Members of the Book Committee," typewritten, property of the Methodist Publishing House, Nashville, pp. 23, 37-38; William M. Green, *Life and Papers of A. L. P. Green, D.D.* (Nashville, 1877), pp. 219, 473-77.

32. Attested to by both Fitzgerald and Poole; see Fitzgerald, p. 248.

33. *SCA*, XXXIII (July 28, 1870), 118; (Aug. 19), 130; (Sept. 23), 150; (Dec. 9), 192; also see XXIX (June 22, 1866), 3.

34. Haygood, "Supplement," *WCA*, XLI (Dec. 14, 1878), 1; *NCA*, XXX (Aug. 20, 1870), 1; (Sept. 3), 5; (Sept. 17), 4; (Oct. 1), 4.

35. Dempsey, *Haygood*, pp. 136-37.

36. *NCA*, XXX (Nov. 26, 1870), 4; (Dec. 17), 1; (Dec. 24), *passim*; *SCA*, XXXIII, 195-96, 202; XXXIV (Nov. 1, 1871), 173.

37. *Sunday-School Visitor*, VI (Aug. 1, 1860); cf. with IX (1875).

38. Edwin W. Rice, *The Sunday-School Movement . . . and the . . . Sunday-School Union . . .* (Phila., 1917), pp. 105, 112, 121, 158, 160, 163-69, 296.

39. Summers, *Outlines of Sunday-School Lectures . . .* (Nashville, 1855), pp. 34-123; Jarrell, *Methodism on the March*, pp. 205-08.

40. *Our Little People for 1872*, II; cf. Vincent's *Our Little People's Picture Annual for 1872* (New York, et al., 1872).

41. *Sunday-School Magazine*, I (July 1871), 197-201; (Nov.), 330-31; V (April 1875), 107-08; Jarrell, *op. cit.*, pp. 205-09.

42. T. J. Magruder, "Uniform Lessons," *NCA*, XXXI (Jan. 7, 1871), 1.

43. *SCA*, XXXIV (Dec. 27, 1871), 205; Haygood, *Jesus the Christ, Lessons from the Evangelists* (Macon, 1871), pp. 5 ff.

44. See Donald Sheehan, *This Was Publishing, A Chronicle of the BOOK TRADE in the Gilded Age* (Bloomington, Ind., 1952), pp. 13, 206.

45. *The Methodist Harmonist . . .* (New York, 1833), pp. iii-vii.

46. Arthur L. Stevenson, *The Story of Southern Hymnology* (Roanoke, 1931), pp. 30-31.

47. Everett, *The Wesleyan Hymn and Tune Book . . .* (Nashville, 1859), pp. ii, v, 273.

48. Lafferty, *Sketches and Portraits of the Gen. Conf., 1886*, p. 97; *The Sunday-School Magazine*, I (June 1871), 172; *Tabor: or, the Richmond Collection of Sacred Music . . .* (3rd ed.; Columbia and Nashville, 1867), *passim*.

49. Haygood's "Preface" to *The Amaranth . . .* (Nashville, 1877 [first in 1871]); *NCA*, XXI (May 13, 1871), 4.

50. *Ibid.*; *A Collection of Hymns and Tunes . . .* (Nashville, 1885), pp. iii-v.

51. *A collection of Hymns for Public Social and Domestic Worship* (Nashville, 1874), pp. 3-5; *NCA*, XXI (April 22, 1871), 5; XXXIV (May 2, 1874), 5; (July 18), 13; (Dec. 12), 12.

52. *The Gem: A Book of Songs and Tunes . . .* (Nashville, 1878).

53. Haygood, "The Singing Question," *NCA*, XXXIV (Sept. 12, 1874), 7; *SCA*, XXXVII (June 24, 1874), 7; *The Sunday-School Magazine*, I (Sept. 1871), 270-71; also see Summers on the Episcopalians, *NCA*, XXXI (April 15, 1871), 5.

54. *NCA*, XXXIV (Sept. 12), 7.

55. *SCA*, XXXIV (Dec. 27, 1871), 205; XXXV (May 1, 1872), *passim*.

56. Haygood, "Supplement," *WCA*, XLI (Dec. 14, 1878), 2.

57. Samuel Smiles, *Self-Help . . .* (Nashville, 1873), *passim*.

58. *SCA*, XXXVI (July 16, 1873), 110.

59. *Go or Send: A Plea for Missions* (Nashville, 1874), pp. 7-8; Kelley, *Go or Die* (Nashville, 1899), pp. 7-8.

60. Oscar P. Fitzgerald, "The Missionary Side of Bishop Haygood's Life and Work," *The Methodist Review of Missions*, XVI (March 1896), 499-500.

61. *Op. cit.*, Part II.

62. Butler, *Hist. of the Woman's Foreign Missionary Society, passim; SCA,* XXXVII (June 17, 1874), 94; (July 8), 106; XXXVIII (Jan. 6, 1875), 2; (Jan. 20), 9; (Jan. 27), 13; *NCA,* XXV (May 29, 1875), 2.
63. *NCA,* XXXI (July 8, 1871), 6; (July 15), 4.
64. *SCA,* XXXIV (Oct. 18, 1871), 166; (Nov. 22), 186; XXXV (Dec. 11, 1872), 194.
65. R. Hiner, compiler, *Kentucky Pulpit* . . . (Nashville, 1874), pp. 265-85, also 23-59, 97-118.
66. *SCA,* XXXVI (Dec. 10, 1873), 191; XXXVII (Feb. 11, 1874), 22; Smith, *Life of Pierce,* pp. 541-84.

CHAPTER SIX

1. Robertson, ed., *Diary of Dolly Lunt Burge,* pp. 131-32.
2. "The Christian Church and the Education of the People," *SCA,* XXXVII (Aug. 5, 1874), 121.
3. Bard Thompson, *Vanderbilt Divinity School, A History* (Nashville, 1958), pp. 1-5; *Central University Chapter, Proceedings of the Board of Trust* . . . (Nashville, 1873), p. 15; Charles F. Deems, *Autobiography* . . . (New York, 1897), pp. 197, 253-57.
4. *SCA,* XXV (April 3, 1872), 49; (May 1), 65.
5. "Wesleyan and Emory," *NCA,* XXXIV (Aug. 22, 1874), 7; Emory College, Minutes, Board of Trustees, July 20-21, 1874.
6. Smith, *Life of Pierce,* pp. 590-607; *SCA,* XXXVIII (Jan. 20, 1875), 9; (Jan. 27), 13-14; (Feb. 10), 22; (Feb. 24), 29; (March 10), 37-38.
7. Emory College, Minutes, Board of Trustees, 1874 and 1875; *SCA,* XXXVI, 194, 198; XXXVII, 72, 77, 81-82, 85, 90, 170; XXXVIII, 66, 91, 94, 110, 122, 127, 154, 158, 172.
8. Gravestone, Oakland Cemetery, Atlanta; testimony of Laura Haygood Watts to Lon H. Eakes, 1960; *Diary of Dolly Lunt Burge,* p. 133.
9. "Supplement," *WCA,* XLI (Dec. 14, 1878), 2.
10. *Ibid.*
11. Newton County Deed Record Book O, p. 489; Book U, pp. 581-82; *Diary of Dolly Lunt Burge,* p. 134.
12. Emory Minutes, Board of Trustees, p. 89-97.
13. *Ibid.; SCA,* XXXVIII, 146, 150, 170, 197-98, 201; *The Sunday-School Magazine,* V (Dec. 1875), 365-66.
14. Thomas P. Janes, *Hand-Book of the State of Georgia, Accompanied by a Geological Map of the State* (Atlanta, 1876), pp. 169-75, 182-90; *Catalogues of Emory College,* 1870-1871, 1878-1879, 1879-1880.
15. Emory Record Book of Treasurer, *passim.*
16. Emory Minutes, Board of Trustees, 1875-1800.
17. See Holland N. McTyeire to wife, Atlanta, May 7, 1878, McTyeire Correspondence, Joint University Library, Nashville.
18. Harry H. Stone, compiler, *A History of the Class of Eighty. Emory College, 1876-1925* (Atlanta, 1925), pp. 15-16, 20-23, 29.
19. *In Memoriam. Geo. W. W. Stone,* pp. 16-26; "A New Thing in Oxford," *SCA,* XL (Jan. 9, 1877), 6.
20. *Emory College, The Late Commencement* (n. p., 1876), p. 2; Stone, *Hist., Class of '80,* pp. 15-16.
21. Stone, *op. cit.,* pp. 20-23, 29.
22. *Ibid.*
23. Haygood, "Professor Lundy H. Harris," *WCA,* XLII (July 19, 1879), 4.
24. Haygood, "The Vanderbilt and Dr. Winchell," *WCA,* XLI (Aug. 17, 1878), 4.
25. Mentioned in Stone, *op. cit.;* Thomas H. Huxley, Darwin's "bulldog," lectured in Nashville in September 1876, being introduced by the son of Thomas O. Sum-

mers, Southern Methodism's prominent theologian. See *New York Tribune Extra,* Sept. 23, 1876, p. 3.

26. *Musical Notation, A Course of Study* . . . (Macon, 1887); *McIntosh's Class and Chorus* . . . (Macon, 1893); *Annual Catalogue,* 1877, pp. 3, 26.

27. Oral testimony, Lon H. Eakes to author.

28. Stone, *Class of '80,* pp. 23-24.

29. "Lectures for Boys," MS, 1883-1884, Haygood Papers.

30. "Report of Visiting Committee to Emory College," *WCA,* XLIII (July 17, 1880), 5; also see Emory Minutes, Board of Trustees (1876), pp. 98-137; Emory College, Miscellaneous Records and Accounts, provides the basis for the inference that Haygood steered B. S. students into regular classes.

31. Emory College Matriculation Book, pp. 179-98; Emory College, Miscellaneous Records and Accounts, *passim;* Thomas W. Connally, compiler and editor, *Occupation and Address Register of the Graduates of Emory College* . . . (Atlanta, 1910), pp. 77-80 ff.; James A. Dombrowski, editor, *Alumni History and Directory of Emory University* (Atlanta, 1926), pp. 8-10 ff.

32. "Record of Faculty Meetings, beginning with Spring Term, 1872," Miscellaneous Records and Accounts; Minutes, Board of Trustees, pp. 87-89, 129-43, 151-67, 170, 185-90, 202-05, 224-30.

33. Melton, "When Bishop Haygood 'Toted' Bricks," *The Atlanta Journal,* magazine section, June 13, 1926, p. 11.

34. See J. E. Evans, "Oxford," *SCA,* XXXVIII (Sept. 17, 1875), 154; and Bullock, *op. cit.,* for an account of the return of fraternities.

35. *The* (Covington) *Georgia Enterprise,* Sept. 11, 1868; Nov. 13, 1868; May 21, 1869; May 12, Nov. 4, 1870; April 21, May 26, Sept. 29, Oct. 20, 1871; May 31, 1872.

36. Henry D. Howren, *'Georgia,' Anniversary Address . . . of the Few Society* . . . (Atlanta, 1879), p. 12.

37. Dempsey, *Haygood,* pp. 255-56; Emory Minutes, Board of Trustees, pp. 49-243; *NCA,* XXXIX (July 26, 1879), 4.

38. *Annual Catalogues,* 1876-1882, *passim;* Minutes, Board of Trustees, same years.

39. *SCA,* XXXVII, 202; XXXVII, 142, 154; XXXIX 150; XL, 150, 205; Minutes, Board of Trustees, 1879.

40. C. W. Norwood, compiler, *Georgia State Gazetteer and Business Directory, 1879-80* (Atlanta, 1879), pp. 233, 308, 336, 366, 461; *Memoirs of Georgia,* I, 240, 683-84; II, 369-70, 782-84; *Memorial Addresses on the Life and Character of Alfred Hoyt Colquitt* . . . (Washington, 1895) pp. 46-54; "Gov. Colquitt's Vindication," *WCA,* XLII (Aug. 9, 1879), 4.

41. *WCA,* XLII (July 19), 8.

42. Raymond B. Nixon, *Henry W. Grady, Spokesman of the New South* (New York, 1943), pp. 154-55.

43. *The Late Commencement* (1876), p. 1; *SCA,* XXXIX, 70; Carlton D. Harris, *Alpheus W. Wilson, A Prince in Israel* (Louisville, 1918), pp. 67-73.

44. *WCA,* XLI (Aug. 3, 1878), 5.

45. *WCA,* XLII (June 28, 1879), 4; (July 19), 8.

46. Haygood, *Sermons and Speeches* (Nashville, 1883), pp. 71-83, 81-102.

47. *Commencement Day, 1880* . . . , annotated program, Haygood Papers.

48. *Sermons and Speeches,* pp. 81-102; also see *WCA,* XLIII (July 3, 1880), 4; (July 10), 4, 8; Dempsey, *Haygood,* pp. 100-10.

CHAPTER SEVEN

1. Norwood, *Ga. State Gazetteer,* pp. 318, 629.

2. McTyeire to wife, May 7, 1878, McTyeire Correspondence.

3. "Mrs. Haygood Gone Home," *Pacific Methodist Advocate,* April 24, 1913, clipping in Haygood Papers; Haygood Scrapbook, property of Mary Louise Haygood Trotti; Dempsey, *Haygood,* pp. 5, 22-28, 51-55, 129.

4. Dempsey, *op. cit.*; Emory Miscellaneous Records; *Catalogues*, 1876-1881; Haygood Scrapbook, and oral testimony by Mrs. Trotti.
5. Dempsey, *Haygood;* see especially photographs of the sisters.
6. Sermon, Haygood Papers.
7. *SCA*, XXXVIII, 154, 158, 174; XLI (Aug. 6, 1878), 2; *WCA*, XLI (June 25, 1878), 98.
8. *SCA*, XL (Feb. 6, 1877), 22.
9. *WCA*, XLI (June 4, 1878), 66.
10. *WCA*, XLI (Sept. 21, 1878), 4.
11. "Of One I Love," *WCA*, LIV (Nov. 11, 1891), 1.
12. "Camp-meeting Salmagundi," *WCA*, XLII (Sept. 27, 1879), 4.
13. "The General Conference of 1878," *WCA*, XLI (July 6, 1878), 4.
14. "We Offer An Amendment," *SCA*, XL (Oct. 16, 1877), 166.
15. "The Fathers—the Brethren," XXXIX (Oct. 3, 1876), 158 (numbered as p. 159).
16. *SCA*, XXXIX, 86; XL, 134; XXXVIII, 158.
17. *SCA*, XL, 58.
18. "Unbrotherly Sneers," *SCA*, XL, 154.
19. *SCA*, XXXIX, 86; see also, 102.
20. *SCA*, XXXVIII, 158 178.
21. *SCA*, XXXVIII, 174.
22. *SCA*, XXXIX, 182.
23. *Our Children* (New York, 1876), see especially pp. 212-354.
24. *WCA*, XLII (Oct. 4, 11), 4.
25. *SCA*, XXXIX, 146.
26. *WCA*, XLII (Oct. 4), 4.
27. *WCA*, XLI (Nov. 23), 4.
28. *WCA*, XLII (Sept. 27), 4.
29. *SCA*, XXXIX, 162.
30. *Ibid.*
31. *Our Children, passim.*
32. Emory Minutes, Board of Trustees, pp. 63-87.
33. Boland, "A Psychological View of Sin and Holiness," *Quarterly R. of the M. E. Church, S.,* XVI (July 1892), 342-54.
34. *NCA*, XXXIV (June 27, 1874), 5, 14; Summers, ed., *Journal of the Gen. Conf.,* 1874, pp. 359-63, 440, 536.
35. *SCA*, XXXIX, 118; XL, 110; *WCA*, XLI (Sept. 28), 4; (Nov. 29), 4; *Sermons and Speeches*, pp. 71-73.
36. *WCA*, XLIII (Oct. 30, 1880), 4.
37. *SCA*, XL, 150; *WCA*, XLI (July 20, Oct. 5), 4.
38. *WCA*, XLII (Dec. 20), 4.
39. *WCA*, XLI (Feb. 22, 1879), 4; also Feb. 8), 4; *SCA*, XL, 94, 106.
40. *SCA*, XL, 82, 86; XLI, 54, 102.
41. *SCA*, XL, 22.
42. Candler's biographer, Alfred M. Pierce, is quite frank about his subject's egoism, but apparently ignorant of Haygood's influence on Candler: *Giant Against the Sky, the Life of Bishop Warren Akin Candler* (N. Y. and Nashville, 1948); *The Daily Constitution*, 1879-1880, especially July 11, 1880, p. 1; *Memoirs of Ga.,* II, 643-44; Candler, *The History of Sunday-Schools . . .* (N. Y., 1880).
43. *SCA*, XL, 122; XLI, 34.
44. Indispensable is Judson C. Ward's dissertation, "Georgia Under the Bourbon Democrats, 1872-1890," the University of North Carolina, 1947.
45. See *SCA*, XXXIX, 130.
46. *SCA*, XL, 6.
47. *WCA*, XLII (Aug. 2), 4.
48. *WCA*, IV (March 4, 1882), 4.
49. *SCA*, XXXVIII, 186.

50. *SCA*, XXXIX, 92.
51. *SCA*, XXXIX, 130.
52. *WCA*, XLI (July 27, Aug. 31), 4.
53. *WCA*, IV (Sept. 17, 1881), 4.
54. *WCA*, IV (June 11), 4.
55. *The Daily Constitution*, Feb. 25, July 27, Sept. 23, Oct. 3, 1879; Jan. 2, April 3, 1880.
56. *WCA*, XLI (Sept. 7), 4.
57. *WCA*, XLI (Sept. 21), 4.
58. *WCA*, XLII (May 31, 1879), 4; (Oct. 4), 4.
59. *The Daily Constitution*, Jan. 14, 29, 30, Feb. 26, May 25, June 12, 25, 26, July 20, Sept. 6, Nov. 9, 28, 1879; Jan. 17, Feb. 10, 19, 20, 28, March 2, 7, 12, April 9, 30, May 30, Aug. 3, 4, 5, 19, 20, 24, Sept. 18, Oct. 15, 17, 1880.
60. *Ibid.*, July 3, 7, 22, 28.
61. *SCA*, XL, 18.
62. *WCA*, XLII (Nov. 22), 5.
63. *WCA*, XLII (May 3, 10, 1879), 4.
64. *SCA*, XLI (Feb. 22, 1879), 4.
65. *The Daily Constitution*, 1879-1881, *passim*.
66. *WCA*, XLIII (May 10, 1879), 4.
67. *Close the Saloons* . . . (Macon, 1880).
68. *WCA*, XLIII (1880), *passim*.
69. *The Daily Constitution*, July, 1881, *passim*.
70. See *WCA*, III-IV.
71. C. Vann Woodward, *Reunion and Reaction, The Compromise of 1877 and the End of Reconstruction* (Garden City, N. Y., 1956), *passim*.
72. *WCA*, XLII (May 31, 1879), 4; Paxton Hibben, *Henry Ward Beecher: An American Portrait* (N. Y., 1927), pp. 286, 295.
73. *SCA*, XL, 102.
74. *The Daily Constitution*, May 9, 1880; *WCA*, XLIII (May 29), 5.

CHAPTER EIGHT

1. J. C. C. Newton, *The New South and the Methodist Episcopal Church, South* (Baltimore, 1887), v.
2. Nixon, *Grady*, pp. 178, 240-41.
3. *The Daily Constitution*, Feb. 11, 1879, and *passim* 1879-80.
4. Cf. *The New South: Gratitude, Amendment, Hope* (Oxford, 1880) with *Our Brother in Black, His Freedom and His Future* (New York, 1881).
5. Yarbrough testimony.
6. *The New South*, pp. 1-16.
7. *The Daily Constitution*, Feb. 1, 1881.
8. *The Christian Citizen: A Sermon* (Nashville, 1881), 3; *Sermons and Speeches*, pp. 4, 147-81; *The Daily Constitution*, Jan. 30, 1881.
9. Abel Stevens, *History of the Methodist Episcopal Church* . . . (N. Y., 1867), I, 3.
10. William B. Shaw, "George Ingraham Seney," *Dictionary of American Biography*, XVI, 583-84.
11. Henry V. Poor, *Manual of the Railroads of the United States* . . . (N. Y., 1881), pp. 460-66, 531-32; Stuart Daggett, *Railroad Reorganization* (Cambridge, Mass., 1924), pp. 48, 146, 151; Woodward, *Reunion and Reaction*, pp. 20-24, 73-75, 87-90, 120-24, 138-42.
12. Joseph M. Brown, *A Commercial Revolution Which the Opening of Muscle Shoals Will Bring About for the People of Georgia and the Southeast* . . . (Atlanta, 1889), pp. 12-18; H. I. Kimball, "The Cotton Exposition and Education," *WCA*, IV (Aug. 6, 1881), 5.
13. *WCA*, III (June 4, 1881), 4; also see Poor's *Manuals* (1877), pp. 36-38, 227-30, 368-72, 944; (1881), pp. 407-08, 446-47, 451-52, 456; B. W. Wrenn, *A Guide Book to*

Health and Pleasure Resorts on The Great Kennesaw Route . . . (Atlanta, 1879), pp. 37-38, 45, 48; J. H. Hollander, *The Cincinnati Southern Railway* . . . (Baltimore, 1894), pp. 30, 43, 49; Jefferson M. Dixon, "Georgia Railroad Growth and Consolidation, 1860-1917," M. A. Thesis, Emory University, 1949, pp. 44-45, 50, 72; Harry DeButts, *Men of Vision "Who Served the South"* (N. Y. 1955), pp. 9-10.

14. Poor's *Manuals* (1881), pp. 449-50; (1882), 438, 480-81; (1885), 437, 479, 561-64; Allen P. Tankersley, *John B. Gordon: A Study in Gallantry* (Atlanta, 1955), pp. 322-45; *The Daily Constitution*, Aug. 10, 1881.

15. *WCA*, III (Feb. 26, March 5, 12, April 16, 23, 1881), 4; Haygood, *"Seney Hall." An Address* . . . (Macon, 1881), *passim;* for the extent of contemporary knowledge about Seney's motives see Nathaniel J. Hammond, *The University of Georgia* . . . (Atlanta, 1893), pp. 102-03.

16. Emory Minutes, Board of Trustees, June meetings, 1881, 1882.

17. *WCA*, III (May 7), 4; IV (June 4, July 9, Aug. 6), 4; copy of Seney's August telegram, Haygood Papers; *The Daily Constitution*, Aug. 12, 27, Sept. 1, 1881); *Minutes, North Ga. Conf.*, 1881, p. 48.

18. Cf. *WCA*, IV (June 11), 2, 8, with *Quarterly Review of the M. E. Church, S.*, III (July 1881), 516-17.

19. *SCA*, XLIV (Sept. 10, Oct. 8, Dec. 3, 1881), 4.

20. *The Daily Constitution*, May 14, 1881, p. 2.

21. Candler, "A Means of Grace to the South," *WCA*, IV (June 11), 2.

22. Roy F. Dibble, *Albion W. Tourgee* (N. Y., 1921), pp. 21-108.

23. *Our Brother in Black* anecdotes on pp. 11, 13, 14, 15, 16, 37, 40, 43, 44, 49, 82-83, 85, 89, 90, 91, 93, 95, 98, 99, 120n, 123, 139, 140n, 146, 153, 154-55, 157, 178-79, 185, 190, 202, 207, 220, 222, 222-23, 225, 228-31, 235.

24. *Ibid., passim.*

25. *Middletown* (Conn.) *Sentinel & Witness*, Nov. 26, 1881, copy in Haygood Papers; also Haygood to Candler, Oxford, Dec. 26, 1881, Candler Letters; *Documents Relating to the Origin and Work of the Slater Trustees* . . . (Baltimore, 1894), p. 19; Charles R. Williams, ed., *Diary and Letters of Rutherford Birchard Hayes* . . . (Columbus, 1925), IV, 42; Curtis W. Garrison, ed., "Slater Fund Beginnings . . . ," *Journal of Southern History*, V (May 1939), 226; John E. Fisher, "Atticus Greene Haygood and Negro Education in the South," M. A. Thesis, Vanderbilt University, 1951, pp. 4-5; Larry D. Rubin, ed., *Teach the Freeman*, 2 vols. (Baton Rouge, 1959), I, xii-xxi, 3-4, 23-65.

26. Rubin, *op. cit.*, I, 67-69.

27. Joseph E. Roy, "Our Brother in Black," *WCA*, IV (June 25, 1881), 2.

28. Rubin, *op. cit.*, I, 22-42; *Organization of the John F. Slater Fund* . . . (Baltimore, 1882) 13, 19.

29. Rubin, *op. cit.*, I, 35-75; *WCA*, IV (Nov. 11, 18, 1882), 4-5.

30. Emory Minutes, Board of Trustees, June meetings, 1882-1887; Central Trust Co. to G. W. W. Stone, New York, April 2, 1886; Poor's *Manual* (1885), pp. 389, 395, 415, 476, 561-64.

31. Emory Minutes, 1882-1887; "Geo. I. Seney, Esq.," *WCA*, VI (May 28, 1884), 8; "Visit of Geo. I. Seney," VII (Nov. 19), 8; "Mr. Seney's Money," IX (June 2, 1886), 1; Daggett, *Railroad Reorganization*, pp. 149-67.

CHAPTER NINE

1. P. A. Peterson, comp., *Hand-Book of Southern Methodism* . . . (Nashville, 1883), pp. 17, 83-90; (1891), 61-63.

2. *WCA*, IV (Aug. 27, Dec. 14, 1881), 4.

3. D. C. Kelley to Candler, Bell Buckle, Tenn., Jan. 31, 1896, Candler Letters.

4. James L. Chapman, *Defence of the Government of the Methodist Episcopal Church . . . at Canton, Miss., May, 1885* (Nashville, 1885), pp. 1-20; W. P. Harrison, *The High-Churchman Disarmed; A Defense of Our Methodist Fathers* (Nashville,

1886), p. 26; J. Hamby Barton, Jr., "The Definition of the Episcopal Office in American Methodism," Ph. D. thesis, Drew University, 1960, *passim; NCA,* XLVI (May 8, 1886), 6.

5. *NCA,* XLII (Feb. 25, 1882), 8; (April 22), 6; (May 13), 1; (May 27) 1; (June 17), 9; XLIV (March 29, 1884), 1; (Oct. 25), 9.

6. *WCA,* XLI (Sept. 14, Nov. 2, Dec. 14, 1878), 4; supplement, (Dec. 14), 1-2.

7. S. A. Weber, "Nolo Episcopari," *SCA,* XLV (June 10, 1882), 4; J. S. Boswell, "Our Bishop—The Sources of Supply," *NCA,* XLVI (April 3, 1886), 13.

8. R. M. McIntosh to Candler, Atlanta, Feb. 5, 1896, Candler Letters.

9. *The Man of Galilee* (N. Y. and Cincinnati, 1889); *WCA,* XII (June 12, 1889), 4, 8; (Aug. 14), 4; (Nov. 13), 5; *NCA,* XLIX (Aug. 22, 1889), 9; XL (June 28, 1890), 2-3, 5, 12.

10. Peterson, *Hand-Book* (1891), p. 148.

11. *NCA,* XLIII (Oct. 13, 1883), copy in Haygood Papers.

12. Haygood to Candler, Aug. 15, 1891, July 5, 1892, Jan. 25, 1893, Candler Letters; *Annual Reports, Board of Missions* (Nashville), especially (1893), pp. 84-104; James Cannon, *History of Southern Methodist Missions* (Nashville, 1926), pp. 55-61, 209.

13. Pierce, *Giant Against the Sky,* pp. 28-40, 63-68; Emory Minutes, Board of Trustees, pp. 392-423.

14. John E. Talmadge, *Rebecca Latimer Felton, Nine Stormy Decades* (Athens, 1960), pp. 102-11; Hammond, *The University of Georgia, passim.*

15. See Candler-Haygood correspondence, 1882-1895.

16. D. Leigh Colvin, *Prohibition in the United States, A History* . . . (N. Y. 1926), pp. 283-89.

17. Small, *Pleas for Prohibition* (Atlanta, 1890), p. 129.

18. McKibben F. McCook, *Preaching and Its Application to Our Times* . . . (Nashville, 1889), pp. 12-14; Theo. M. Smith, ed., *Sermons By Rev. Sam P. Jones* . . . (Phila. and St. Louis, 1887), pp. 244-62, 550.

19. Leon C. Field, "Was Jesus a Wine-Bibber?" *Methodist Q. R.,* LXIV (Jan.-Oct. 1882), 117-682, *passim.*

20. T. A. Kerley, *The Methodist Episcopal Church, South, A Prohibition Church* . . . (Nashville, 1894), pp. 21-27.

21. *WCA,* VIII (April 28, 1886), 5.

22. *The Doctrines and Discipline* . . . (Nashville, 1894), pp. 97-98, 125-30.

23. Scomp, *King Alcohol* . . . (n. p., 1888), pp. 31-33, 656-69, 682-84.

24. *The Atlanta Constitution,* April 21, 1883; April 11, 29, May 21, 1884.

25. Nixon, *Grady,* pp. 281-96; Dewey W. Grantham, *Hoke Smith and the Politics of the New South* (Baton Rouge, 1958), p. 31.

26. Sermon, April 5, 1884, Haygood Papers; "Neglected and Neglecting," in *Pleas for Progress* (Nashville, 1889), pp. 235-49.

27. Candler, "A Part of the Subject Omitted by Dr. Haygood," *WCA,* VII (Sept. 10, 1884), 5; also VI (July 25, 1883), 8; (March 12, 1884), 5; (March 19), 2.

28. *The Atlanta Constitution,* Dec. 3, 1884, p. 7.

29. Haygood to Candler, March 27, July 10, 1882; R. F. Burden to Candler, Macon, April 21, 1882; Harris to Candler, especially "sealed items," 1882-1898, all in Candler Letters; Haygood, "Thanks and Good Night," *WCA,* LIX (Jan. 30, 1895), 4.

30. *Open Letters on Prohibition: A Controversy Between Hon. Jefferson Davis, and Bishop Chas. B. Galloway* . . . (Nashville, 1893), pp. 7-12; *National Perils and Opportunities* . . . (N. Y., 1887), pp. vii, 1, 155-65; Haygood, *The Good and the Bad. A Thanksgiving Sermon* . . . (Macon, 1886); cf. with *Save Our Homes. A Prohibition Sermon* (Macon, 1884), pp. 2-36; *WCA,* X (June 1, 1887), 5; (June 8, June 22, Aug. 10, Dec. 14), 4; (Dec. 28), 5; *The Atlanta Constitution,* Oct. 22, 1886, p. 4.

31. *Growth in Grace* . . . (Macon, 1885), pp. 3-23.

32. Tillett-Miller controversy in *NCA,* XLIV (Jan.-Oct. 1884).

33. Smith, *Life of Pierce,* pp. 188-89, 578; "Autobiography of Geo. G. Smith," p. 60, indicates existence of second blessing theory in Georgia as early as 1860.

34. Haygood, sermon, "A True Ground for Rejoicing," undated, Haygood Papers; O. P. Fitzgerald, "The Cant of Heterodoxy," *NCA,* XLVI (April 17, 1886), 8; *WCA* and *NCA,* 1881-1886.

35. "Autobiography of Smith," p. 129; W. C. Dunlap, "My Tobacco Experience," *NCA,* XLIV (Aug. 23, 1884), 6; "The Holiness Matter," *The Atlanta Constitution,* Jan. 9, 1883, p. 4, also Feb. 3, 1884, p. 1.

36. Lee, *The Making of a Man* (N. Y., 1892), pp. 203-52; "Autobiography of Smith," p. 125.

37. *Minutes of the North Ga. Conf.,* 1880-1884; Candler, "The Meeting in Augusta," *WCA,* VII (Nov. 5, 1884), 5, and "J. B. R.'s Tactics," (Jan. 28, 1885), 4.

38. Ralston, "Holiness and Sin—New Theory Noticed," *Q. R. of the M. E. Ch., S.,* III (July 1881), 441-51; Tillett, "Albert Taylor Bledsoe," *Southern Meth. R.,* XIV (July 1893), 219-42; *The Theologians of Methodism, Theses by Senior Class of Biblical Dept. of Vanderbilt University* (Nashville, 1895), p. 125.

39. Boland, *Problem of Methodism,* p. 23; *Q. R. of the M. E. Ch., S.,* IX (Jan. 1886), 132-36; Leo Rosser, "Sanctification," *Southern Meth. R.,* III (Nov. 1887), 23-46; also V (Jan. 1889), 373-93, and VI (April 1889), 97-107.

40. A. C. Thomas, *WCA,* VIII (Sept. 23), (Sept. 30, 1885), 5.

41. Bell, *WCA,* VIII (Sept. 23), 2-3, 5; (Nov. 18), 2.

42. Haygood sermons, Feb. 7 and June 6, 1886, and one undated, Haygood Papers; *WCA,* IV (Oct. 8, 1881), 8.

43. Haygood to McTyeire, Decatur, Oct. 25, 1887, McTyeire Correspondence; Pierce, *Giant Against the Sky,* pp. 45-48; *The Atlanta Constitution,* Oct. 24, 1887.

44. *WCA,* LVII (Oct. 11, 18, 1893), 4.

45. *WCA,* LVIII (April 18, 1894), 4; also see Haygood's funeral sermon on the death of Bishop Pierce, *NCA,* XLIV (Sept. 13, 1884), 4-5.

46. Haygood, "Two Tramps," *WCA,* LVII (May 17, 1893), 1; "Methodists Are Liberal," *WCA,* LVIII (July 11, 1894), 1; *The Monk and The Prince* (Atlanta, 1895), especially pp. 41-55; also *WCA,* LVIII (May 2, 1894), 3; (May 9), 1; (May 16), 2; (Sept. 5), 1; (Oct. 3), 5; (Dec. 12), 4; LIX (Aug. 14, 1895), 4; (Sept. 18), 1-2; O. P. Fitzgerald, *Christian Growth* (Nashville, 1889), p. 31.

47. *William F. Quillian, M. D., His Life and Sermons . . .* (Atlanta, 1907), pp. 2, 15-18, 48-59.

48. "Georgia Letter," *NCA,* LIV (Sept. 7, 1893), 3.

49. Best history of the ethos of the 1890's is Harold U. Faulkner, *Politics, Reform and Expansion, 1890-1900* (N. Y., 1959), pp. 163-86.

CHAPTER TEN

1. *The* (Covington) *Georgia Enterprise,* Feb. 26, 1869; also Nov. 21; and March 24, 1870.

2. *SCA,* XXXVII, 202.

3. *WCA,* III (July 31, Aug. 21, 1880), 2.

4. *WCA,* III (Aug. 7), 2; (Oct. 9), 4.

5. *WCA,* XLII (Aug. 2, 1879), 4; also III (Sept. 11, 25, 1880), 4.

6. *WCA,* III (Jan. 8, 1881), 4.

7. *The Daily Constitution,* Feb. 4, 16, 20, 26, May 27, June 26, Oct. 1, 1879; Jan. 9, Feb. 8 supplement, Feb. 27, 1880; April 16, 1881; *WCA,* III (May 21), 4; IV (July 2, 1881), 4.

8. *The Daily Constitution,* July 20-23, 1881; *WCA,* IV (April 22), 5; V (June 3, 1882), 5; (June 10), 4.

9. Gordon C. L. Lee, *The Struggle for Federal Aid, First Phase* . . . (N. Y., 1949), pp. 23-91, 148-55; Mayo, *Southern Women in the Recent Educational Movement in the South*, pp. 54-87.
10. Haygood, *Pleas for Progress*, pp. 98-117, 157-74.
11. Haygood, "The South and the School Problem," (*Harper's New Monthly Magazine*, LXXIX (July, 1889), 225-31.
12. Lee, *Struggle for Federal Aid*, pp. 148-55.
13. *WCA*, XI (Feb. 13, 1889), 4.
14. *The Cry of Half a Million of Georgia's Children* . . . (Atlanta, 1888), p. 3.
15. *WCA*, XII (Oct. 31, 1888), 4-5; (Nov. 19), 5; (Nov. 28), 1; (Dec. 5), 4; (Jan. 2, 1889), 2, 4.
16. *WCA*, XII (Dec. 12), 4-5; (Dec. 19), 4.
17. *Speech of the Rev. . . . Candler . . . on Higher Education . . . in the House of Representatives* . . . (Atlanta, 1889), p. 3; *Georgia's Educational Work. What It Has Been—What It Should Be* (Oxford, 1889), p. 5.
18. *Acts and Resolutions of the General Assembly of the State of Georgia,* (1888), p. 11; (1888-1889), p. 33.
19. *WCA*, XI (April 17, 1889), 5.
20. Charles H. Curd, "Preparatory Education from a Southern Standpoint," *Quarterly R.*, IX (Oct. 1890), 17-31.
21. *WCA*, VII (Aug. 6, 1884), 4; also see Haygood's sermon preached in Oxford, Oct. 5, 1884, Haygood Papers.
22. Hammond, *Univ. of Ga.*, pp. 108-09.
23. Candler, *Not Less Education, But More of the Right Sort* (Nashville, 1897), pp. 12-16.
24. *The Atlanta Constitution,* July 17, Oct. 25, 31, Nov. 2, 1884; Stacy, *Hist. of the Presby. Church in Ga.*, p. 217.
25. "The New South," *The Atlanta Constitution,* July 22, 1883.
26. Corra Harris, *As a Woman Thinks* (Boston and N. Y., 1925), pp. 110-15. Mrs. Harris also authored a "classic" caricature of Candler; see *A Circuit Rider's Wife* (Boston and N. Y., 1933), pp. 174-89. An example: "He talked too much about sacrifice and was entirely too fortunate himself."
27. O. P. Fitzgerald, "The General Conference and Education," *NCA*, XLVI (April 17, 1886), 1.
28. Haygood, "Broaden the College. Better the School," speech at Emory commencement, 1886, in *Pleas for Progress*, pp. 157-74.
29. Emory Minutes, Board of Trustees, pp. 220-327; W. B. Short and W. S. Branham, compos., *Emory College Class of 1885 . . . (Oxford, 1926)*, pp. 22-24 ff.
30. Bullock, *Hist. of Emory*, pp. 184-259; Dempsey, *Life of Bishop Dickey*, pp. 34-40.
31. Bullock, op. cit., pp. 184-85, 191-92, 221-23, 246-49, 256-59; Connally, *Occupation Register of Graduates*, pp. 81-95 ff.
32. *WCA*, IV (July 9, 1881), 4; Emory Minutes, Board of *Trustees*, pp. 270-327; *Emroy College Commercial Department* . . . (n. p., 1883?), pp. 1-5.
33. *The Atlanta Constitution,* July 23, Aug. 9, 1881; Dec. 14, 1882; Feb. 1, 4, March 24, June 16, 19, 28, July 13, 15, 1883; Feb. 22, April 13, Oct. 8, 1884; Oct. 2, 21, 1886.
34. Isaac H. Hopkins, *Industrial Education: A Statement and a Plea* . . . (Macon, 1883), pp. 1-13.
35. Charles E. Jones, *Education in Georgia* (Washington, 1889), p. 88.
36. *WCA*, IX (July 7, 1886), 2; (Nov. 10), 8; *Pleas for Progress*, pp. 157-74.
37. *The Covington Star*, Sept. 8, 1890, March 3, 1891; *WCA*, XII (Aug. 28, 1889), 4; (Oct. 2), 4; (Jan. 8, 1890), 5; (March 5), 4; XIII (Sept. 17, 1890), Haygood Papers.
38. Rubin, *Teach the Freeman*, II, 74-75; *NCA*, XLIX (Aug. 22, 1889), 9; *WCA*, XII (June 19, July 10), 5.

39. Haygood to Candler, Sept. 16, 26, 1883; May 31, Dec. 30, 1889; Haygood to Stone, Sheffield, March 10, June 11, Nov. 12, Nov. 17, 1890, all in Candler Letters; copy of contract with plasterer, April 29, 1880, Haygood Papers; Emory Record Book of Treasurer, 1851-1863 and 1866-1892.

40. Bullock, *Hist. of Emory*, pp. 226-28; copy of resignation, Haygood Papers; Smith, "Atticus Greene Haygood," pp. 205-07; Emory Minutes, Board of Trustees, *passim*; Newton County Deed Books O, U, V, W, X.

CHAPTER ELEVEN

1. Hood, *The Negro in the Christian Pulpit* (Raleigh, 1884), pp. 3, 150.
2. *In Memoriam. Bishop Atticus G. Haygood . . . Services at Bethel A. M. E. Church . . .* (Atlanta, 1896), pp. 1-4.
3. T. Thomas Fortune, *Black and White: Land, Labor, and Politics in the South* (N. Y., 1882), pp. 40-42, 56, 70, 83, 189, 240; Dibble, *Tourgee*, pp. 84-89.
4. *WCA*, IV (July 23, 1881), 4; also (Jan. 2, March 11, 18, 1882), 4.
5. Haygood, *The Case of the Negro, As to Education in the Southern States . . .* (Atlanta, 1885), pp. 18-36; Myron W. Adams, *A History of Atlanta University* (Atlanta, 1930), pp. 1-37; Alrutheus A. Taylor, *The Negro in Tennessee, 1865-1880* (Washington, 1941), pp. 189-204.
6. Samuel C. Armstrong, *Normal School Work Among the Freedmen* (Boston?, 1872), pp. 3-10; Francis G. Peabody, *Education for Life, The Story of Hampton Institute . . .* (Garden City, N. Y., 1919), pp. 93, 101.
7. Jay S. Stowell, *Methodist Adventures in Negro Education* (N. Y. and Cincinnati, 1922), pp. 31-39, 68-69, 74, 77, 83, 94-95, 111, 134-36; Mason Crum, *The Negro in the Methodist Church* (N. Y., 1951), pp. 58, 65.
8. *Proceedings of the Trustees of the John F. Slater Fund for the Education of Freedmen*, 1883-1885, 1887-1890 (Baltimore and Hampton, Va.), *passim*; John H. Burrus, *Educational Progress of the Colored People in the South* (Nashville, 1889), p. 3; Rubin, *Teach the Freeman*, I and II, *passim*.
9. J. L. M. Curry, *Difficulties, Complications, and Limitations Connected with the Education of the Negro* (Baltimore, 1895), *passim*.
10. *The New South Investigated* (Detroit, 1888), pp. v-vi, 16, 24-150.
11. "The Negro in the Last Decade of the Century," *The Independent*, XLIII (Jan. 1, 1891), 5.
12. *Proceedings of the Trustees of the Slater Fund*, 1883-1890.
13. Wesley J. Gaines, *The Negro and the White Man* (Phila., 1897); *The (Daily) Atlanta Constitution*, Oct. 2, 1881; Sept. 28, Aug. 1, 11, 15, 19, 1882; July 17, 19, 20, 21, Dec. 18-19, 1883; March 15, 22, April 1, 10, May 24, 1884; *WCA*, IV (July 16, 1881), 8; VII (June 25, 1884), 4; XI (March 6, 1889), 2; XII (Sept. 11, Nov. 13), 4; *The Covington Star*, June 25, 1889.
14. *The Atlanta Constitution*, June 19, July 1, 24, 27, 1884.
15. (Covington) *Georgia Enterprise*, Feb. 9, 1883.
16. McKibben F. McCook, *WCA*, VII (Aug. 13, 1884), 2; *NCA*, XLIV (Aug. 30, 1884), 4.
17. Newton, *New South and the M. E. Ch., S.*, pp. 31-45, 51-64.
18. *A Symposium on Dr. Haygood's Reply to Senator Eustis's Paper on Race Antagonism* (N. Y. and Nashville, 1889), pp. 2-12.
19. Carlisle, "To Dr. A. G. Haygood," *WCA*, VII (Feb. 4, 1885), 1.
20. *WCA*, IV (July 16, 1881), 8; LIX (Jan. 16, 1895), 3.
21. Callaway, *Our 'Man of Macedonia:' His Needs and Our Duties . . .* (Nashville, 1883), pp. 5, 7-8, 10-11; ———— "Every Seventh Soul," *Q. R. of the M. E. Ch., S.*, VI (July 1884), 513-24; *WCA*, V (Feb. 14, 1883), 1.
22. *WCA*, VI (June 20, 1883), 1; Rubin, *Teach the Freeman*, II, 6.
23. Haygood to Candler, Aug. 30, 1882, Candler Letters.
24. *WCA*, IV (March 11, 1882), 4.

25. *The Georgia Enterprise,* Aug. 18, 31, 1883; Bennett, "Southern Methodism and Six Million of Negroes," *NCA,* XLII (Feb. 18, 1882), 4-5.

26. Woodward, "The Freedman's Case in Reality," *Q. R. of the M. E. Ch., S.,* VII (Jan. 1885), 1-12.

27. C. G. Andrews, "Education of the Colored Race," *ibid.,* IX (April 1886), 88-89.

28. Scomp, *The Forum,* VIII (Dec. 1889), 356-76.

29. Mary V. Woodward, "The Negro and Domestic Service in the South," *Q. R., M. E. Ch., S.,* XI (Oct. 1891), 58-74.

30. W. M. Leftwich, *ibid.,* VI (April 1889), 86-89.

31. *The Methodist R.,* see LXXII (Jan.-Oct. 1890), 35-52, 90-305.

32. Eustis, *The Forum,* VI (Oct. 1888), 144-54; G. W. Cable, *ibid.,* (Dec.), 392-403; *Symposium on Dr. Haygood's Reply,* pp. 2-12.

33. Wesley J. Gaines, comp., *The United Negro: His Problems and His Progress* . . . (Atlanta, 1902), pp. ix, 6, 8-11, 20, 33-40, 90-100, 600.

34. Charles S. Smith, *'A Hot Time in the Old Town To-night; or, the Conflict Between John and Tom.'* . . . (Nashville, 1899), pp. 3-16.

35. Washington and DuBois, *The Negro in the South, His Economic Progress in Relation to His Moral and Religious Development* (Phila., 1907), pp. 23-62, 102-12.

36. Kate Brousseau, *L'education des nègres aux états-unis* (Paris, 1904), pp. 25, 231.

37. *WCA,* III (Feb. 12, 26, 1881), 4.

38. *NCA,* XLVII (Dec. 3, 1887), 9.

39. Haygood, *Pleas for Progress,* pp. 118-46, 175-234, 297-320; Rubin, *Teach the Freeman,* II, 20, 35.

40. *WCA,* VI (Nov. 21, 1883), 5.

41. *The Georgia Enterprise,* Aug. 31, Sept. 7, 1883.

42. *Ibid.,* Nov. 1, 1883.

43. Morgan, *The Negro in America and The Ideal American Republic* (Philadelphia, 1898), pp. 5-6, 37, 79, 82, 88-90, 136, 162, 170.

44. William L. Duren, *Charles Betts Galloway, Orator, Preacher, and "Prince of Christian Chivalry"* (Emory Univ., 1932), pp. 265, 267.

45. Willis B. Parks, ed., *The Possibilities of the Negro in Symposium. A Solution of the Negro Problem Psychologically Considered. The Negro 'Not a Beast'* (Atlanta, 1904), pp. 1-127.

46. Hamill, *The Old South, a Monograph* (Nashville and Dallas, 1904?), pp. 3, 33-36.

47. Parks, *Possibilities of the Negro.*

48. Fleming, *Slavery and the Race Problem in the South* . . . (Boston, 1906), pp. 2-62; cf. Thomas N. Page, *The Negro: The Southerner's Problem* (N. Y., 1904), pp. 78, 306.

49. A. H. Shannon, *Racial Integrity and Other Features of the Negro Problem* (Nashville and Dallas, 1907), pp. 20, 34, 52, 101, 224-27, 305.

50. Randle, *Plurality of the Human Race. According to the Teachings Both of the Bible and of Science* (Nashville and Dallas, 1911), pp. 7, 10-11, 81.

51. Haygood, "The Negro Problem: God Takes Time—Man Must," *Meth. Review* (Nashville), XL (Sept.-Oct. 1895), 40-53; *NCA,* LIV (Oct. 12, 1893), 1. During the 1890's Bishop Haygood took vigorous issues with those who wanted to exile all the Negroes from the South; one of those advocating this "solution" was John Temple Graves, related to a Newton County family, who spoke at the University of Chicago on this theme in 1899: Parks, *Possibilities of the Negro in Symposium.*

52. Edward A. Johnson, *A School History of the Negro Race in America* . . . *to 1890* . . . (Raleigh, 1891), pp. 148-82; J. J. Pipkin, *The Story of a Rising Race* . . . (Atlanta?, 1902), pp. vii-xiii, 84, 113-14, 228-40; J. W. Gibson and William H. Crogman, *The Colored American From Slavery to Honorable Citizenship* (Atlanta and Nashville, 1901), pp. 189, 299-301, 310-11, 577-82.

53. *WCA,* LIX (Oct. 16, 1895), 1.

CHAPTER TWELVE

1. "Miracles Round About Us," *WCA*, XLII (Sept. 27, 1879), 4.
2. *NCA*, X (Aug. 31, 1887), 8.
3. This inference is based on a radical change in his writing style. See Haygood to McTyeire, Oct. 25, 1887, McTyeire Correspondence; *NCA*, X (Oct. 5, 1887), 4; (Oct. 26), 8; *WCA*, XI (May 15, 1889), 2; Haygood to Candler, Oct. 26, 1887, Candler Letters.
4. Rubin, *op. cit.*, II, 38-39, 54-57, 74, 100, 123, 176-77, 206-07, 265.
5. Haygood to Candler, May 31, Dec. 30, 1889, Candler Letters.
6. *Pleas for Progress* (Nashville, 1889); *The Man of Galilee* (N. Y. and Cincinnati, 1889), with subsequent editions in Spanish (Nashville) and Japanese (Tokyo); Haygood and McIntosh, *Pure Songs for Sunday-Schools* (Macon, Nashville, and St. Louis, 1890).
7. See for verification of mood: *WCA*, III (Feb. 5, 1881), 4; XII (June 12, 1889), 4; Rubin, II, 54, 56.
8. This quotation is from the final paragraph.
9. Williams, *Diary and Letters of Hayes*, IV, 430.
10. *WCA*, XI (July 4, 1888), 5; *Pleas for Progress*, pp. 212-34, 297-320.
11. *The Atlanta Constitution*, Feb. 22, April 13, Oct. 8, 1884; July 1, 1888; Rubin, II, 74-75, 100-01, 145-46, 206; *The Covington Star*, Feb. 4, 1896; *NCA*, XLIX (Sept. 12, 1889), 7; L (April 26, 1890), 2; LI (March 27, 1891), 12; *WCA*, XII (June 18, July 10, 1889), 5; (Aug. 28), 4.
12. Haygood to Candler, Aug. 15, 1891, Candler Letters.
13. *WCA*, LV (Dec. 16, 1891), 2.
14. Haygood to Candler, July 5, 1892; Feb. 6, 1893; *NCA*, LIV (March 9, 1893), 10; (May 11, 18), 10.
15. Haygood, "The Republic of Mexico," *The Musical Advocate and Family Journal*, I (Jan., 1892), 171-72; *The Missionary Reporter*, X-XII (1890-1891); David W. Carter, "Mexico as a Mission Field," *Q. R. of the M. E. Ch., S.*, IX (Jan. 1891), 319-34; I. G. John, *Hand Book of Methodist Missions* (Nashville, 1893), pp. 235-69, 379.
16. Haygood, "High Steeple and . . . Its Official Staff," pp. 73-74.
17. John C. Simmons, *The History of Southern Methodism on the Pacific Coast* (Nashville, 1886), pp. 14, 21, 452-53; Charles Nordhoff, *California: For Health, Pleasure, and Residence* . . . (N. Y., 1872), pp. 69, 106-07, 120-21, 129, 136-44; *Annual Reports of the Board of Missions*, 1890-1893 (Nashville).
18. Candler Letters, 1892-1896, *passim;* Newton County Deed Book Z, pp. 235-36.
19. *Jack-Knife and Brambles* (Nashville, 1894); *The Monk and the Prince* (Atlanta, 1895); *Sermons*, I (Nashville, 1895).
20. See especially the introductory chapters.
21. *NCA*, LVI (April 25, June 6, 1895), 5; (July 4), 1, 3.
22. *NCA*, LV (Dec. 27, 1894), 9.
23. "The Model Bishop," *NCA*, LV (April 5, 1894), 8.
24. Candler Letters, 1894-1896, *passim;* also see *WCA*, LVIII (Sept. 12, 1894).
25. *NCA*, LV-LVI; *WCA*, LVIII-LIX.
26. *NCA*, LVI (Aug. 1, 1895), 5.

Selected Bibliography

MANUSCRIPTS

Personal Papers and Records

Candler Letters. This collection of Warren A. Candler's papers, found in the Emory University Library, has been the most helpful source in the delineation of Haygood's adult personality. I have been privileged to read restricted items on the conditions that I would not cite them or quote from them. The relationship between Haygood and Candler was in a paradoxical sense both intimate and strained. Haygood's behavior in his declining years was a severe trial to his "guardian," while on the other hand Candler's egoism and unlimited self-confidence must have been distasteful to the older man, with his complicated value system. The letters date back, unfortunately, only to the 1880's, and are not full except for the last four years of Haygood's life. Tragically the correspondence between Haygood and Bishop Pierce, which would have provided the same sort of insight into a younger Haygood, is non-existent. In lieu of such a manuscript collection I have had to use the many personal references from Haygood's voluminous "public" articles for church periodicals, articles which are in effect epistles and are in many cases certainly unedited by him before the press preserved them.

Samuel B. Clark Papers. This collection, found in the Duke University Library, contains several letters from two sons who attended Emory College in the 1850's. The author is the great-grandson of Samuel B. Clark.

J. B. Dobbins Correspondence. Emory University Library. The Dobbins family lived in Cherokee, Georgia. Their letters during the late 1860's testify to the destruction and disorder of the area at the time that Haygood was presiding elder of the Rome District.

Haygood Papers. Emory University Library. These papers are a jumble of materials collected by the family and made available for latterday research by the efforts of two men. Elam F. Dempsey began

.. Selected Bibliography 235

to write a biography of Haygood in 1916, according to all evidence. He knew the Bishop personally when he was a young man, but regretfully had little understanding of historiography. His memorial volume, published in 1939, drawn from his collection, contains a few valuable items not now found in the Haygood Papers, notably during the Civil War period. His volume is of course a "Haygood Handbook," rather than a biography. It is filled with redundant eulogies and some excerpts from the subject's writings. Marion L. Smith, a more adept historian, received his doctoral degree from Yale in 1929 with a dissertation concentrating on Haygood's philosophy of Christian education. Smith created some order in the Haygood Papers, and secured sympathetic cooperation from the family. About two fifths of the dissertation is a biographical sketch; Smith, however, since a minister himself, was understandably timid in how much he said both about the declining years and about the Holiness controversy. His dissertation contains quotations from a few items not found in the Haygood Papers. The papers gathered by the family were largely newspaper and magazine clippings. The single most useful manuscript—most are copies of manuscripts once presumably in the family's attics and closets—is a deposition made in 1916 or 1917 to Dempsey. I have felt secure in calling this the testimony of George W. Yarbrough, since the style and range of memory is quite similar to that found in Yarbrough's book, *Boyhood and Other Days*.

Haygood Scrapbook. The property of Mary Louise Haygood (Mrs. H. H.) Trotti, of Decatur, Georgia, the daughter of Wilbur. It contains valuable photographs and photostats of documents. Its greatest value is in establishing birth dates and clearing up genealogical questions.

McTyeire Correspondence. Joint University Library, Nashville, Tennessee. Part of this burned in a fire. Most but not all is available on microfilm in the Vanderbilt vaults as well as in manuscript.

Gustavus J. Orr Papers. Emory University Library. Most useful was a biographical sketch of Orr by his son and a manuscript by the father on his religious life. The latter was published in the *Wesleyan Christian Advocate* in 1887 after his death; X (Dec. 28, 1887), 5.

"Autobiography of George Gilman Smith of Georgia." Typed copy of MS. bound with Diary. Original in University of North Carolina Library.

Ella Gertrude (C.) Thomas Diary-Journal. Duke University Library. This lady apparently inserted items at the time the events happened, even if she learned of them later. This is the case for the first Seney gift to Emory College, February, 1881.

Miscellaneous Manuscripts. Emory at Oxford Library. A deed of land in Oxford, belonging to Greene Haygood's estate, sold by Atticus in 1868, and a letter from the Central Trust Company of New York to Emory's Treasurer, George W. W. Stone, 1886.

Records of Emory College, Emory University Library:
   Faculty Minutes, 1858-1859.
   Matriculation Book, 1838-1865.
   Minutes of the Board of Trustees, 1837-1871.
   Minutes of the Board of Trustees, 1871-1887.
   Record Book of Treasurer, 1851-1863 and 1866-1892.
   Records of Emory Alumni Association, 1880-1924.

County Records

State of Georgia. Clarke County. Roster, 1861.
   University of Georgia Library.
———. Clarke County. Deed records and ordinary records, 1838-1854.
———. DeKalb County. Deed records, 1850-1890.
———. Fulton County. Deed records, 1854-1890.
———. Newton County. Deed records, 1865-1902.
———. Oconee County. Folder, in University of Georgia Library containing four manuscript articles produced by the Works Progress Administration, 1938-1940.

Theses

Barton, Jesse H., Junior. "The Definition of the Episcopal Office in American Methodism." Ph.D. thesis, Drew University, 1960.
Daniel, W. Harrison. "The Protestant Church in the Confederate States of America." Ph.D. thesis, Duke University, 1957.
Fisher, John E. "Atticus Greene Haygood and Negro Education in the South." M.A. thesis, Vanderbilt University, 1951.
Heckman, Oliver S. "Northern Church Penetration of the South, 1860 to 1880." Ph. D. thesis, Duke University, 1939.
Mann, Harold W. "Qualifications of Electors in Georgia As Related to Social Trends and Compared With Changing Electorates in Other States." M.A. thesis, Emory University, 1950.
Smith, Marion L. "Atticus Greene Haygood: Christian Educator." Ph. D. dissertation, Yale University, 1929.
Ward, Judson C., Junior. "Georgia Under the Bourbon Democrats, 1872-1890." Ph.D. dissertation, the University of North Carolina, 1947.

WORKS BY HAYGOOD

This section excludes songbooks and includes only a few periodical articles.

Haygood, Atticus G., reviser. *'Above Rubies;' or, Memorials of Christian Gentlewomen.* Nashville, 1874.
———. *Annual Report of the General Agent of the "John F. Slater Fund," 1886.* Atlanta, 1886.
Haygood, Atticus G., editor. *Bishop Pierce's Sermons with a Few Special Discourses by Dr. Pierce.* Nashville, 1886.

Selected Bibliography

Haygood, Atticus G., *The Case of the Negro, As to Education in the Southern States: A Report to the Board of Trustees.* Atlanta, 1885.

———. *The Church and the Education of the People. An Address Delivered Before the Alumni Association of Emory College.* Nashville, 1874.

———. *The Christian Citizen: A Sermon.* Nashville, 1881.

———. *Close the Saloons. A Plea for Prohibition.* 11th edition. Macon, 1884. (First edition in 1880).

———. *The Cry of Half a Million of Georgia's Children. A Plea for Six Months Schools.* Atlanta, 1888.

———. *The Clouded Intellect, and Other Stories. By the Author of Studies for Stories,"* etc. Nashville, 1872. (Also 1887).

———. *Go or Send: A Plea for Missions. Published by order of the Board of Missions of the M. E. Church, South.* Nashville, 1874.

———. *The Good and the Bad. A Thanksgiving Sermon Preached Before the Students of Emory College, and the Citizens of Oxford, Georgia, By Atticus G. Haygood, D. D., LL. D. November 26th, 1886.* Macon, 1886.

———. *Growth in Grace. A Sermon By Atticus G. Haygood, D. D., LL. D., Preached Before the District Conference of the Oxford District, North Georgia Conference, M. E. Church, South, Held at Covington, Ga., July 18th, 1885, and Published By Formal Request of the Conference.* Macon, 1885.

———. "High Steeple and . . . Its Official Staff." Reprint from *Quarterly Review of the Methodist Episcopal Church, South.* Nashville, 1893.

———. "Industrial Education for the Negro," in *Twenty-first Annual Report of the Freedmen's Aid and Southern Education Society.* N. p., 1888.

———. *Jack-Knife and Brambles.* Nashville, 1894.

———. *Jesus, the Christ. Lessons for Intermediate Classes, from the Evangelists.* 2 vols. St. Louis, 1878.

———. *Lessons from the Evangelists.* No. 2. Macon, 1877.

———. *The Man of Galilee.* New York and Cincinnati, 1889. (Spanish edition: Nashville, 1894 and 1901; Japanese: Tokyo, 1894).

———. *The Monk and The Prince.* Atlanta, 1895.

———. "The Negro in the South," in *Quarterly Review of the M. E. Church, S.,* X (July, 1891), 300-15.

———. "The Negro Problem: God Takes Time—Man Must," *Methodist Review,* XL (Sept.-Oct., 1895), 40-53.

———. *The New South: Gratitude, Amendment, Hope.* Oxford, 1880.

———. *Our Brother in Black, His Freedom and His Future,* New York, 1881 (Also, 1889)

———. *Our Children.* New York, 1876.

———. *Pleas for Progress.* Nashville, 1889.

——. *Report of the General Agent of the "John F. Slater Fund." 1891.* Sheffield, 1891.

——. "The Republic of Mexico," in *The Musical Advocate and Family Journal,* I (January, 1892), 171-72.

——. *Save Our Homes. A Prohibition Sermon.* Macon, 1884.

——. "Seney Hall." *An Address . . . on the Occasion of Laying the Corner Stone By Bishop G. F. Pierce, D.D., LL.D., June 8th, 1881.* Macon, 1881.

——. *Sermons and Speeches.* Nashville, 1883. (Also, 1885). Reissued as *Sermons,* I. Nashville, 1895.

——. "The South and the School Problem," in *Harper's New Monthly Magazine,* LXXIX (1889), 225-31.

——. *The State and Its Prisoners. A Sermon Preached November 8th, 1886, By Atticus G. Haygood, D.D., L.L.D. of Oxford Georgia.* Macon, 1887

Hodder, Edwin. Revised by Atticus G. Haygood. *Tossed on the Waves. A Story of Young Life.* Nashville, 1884.

Hughes, Thomas. Revised by Atticus G. Haygood. *Life and Times of Alfred the Great.* Nashville, 1873.

Overend, Mrs. Campbell, translator and compiler. Revised by Atticus G. Haygood. *The Resieged City, and the Heroes of Sweden.* Nashville, 1880. (This and Hodder's book of course published between 1872 and 1874.

Smiles, Samuel. Revised by Atticus G. Haygood. *Self-Help: with Illustrations of Character, Conduct and Perseverence.* Nashville, 1873.

Trimmer, Timothy. Revised by Atticus G. Haygood. *Fred Brenning: A True Story for Boys.* Nashville, 1872.

WORKS RELATING TO EMORY COLLEGE

Connally, Thomas W., compiler and editor. *Occupation and Address Register of the Graduates of Emory College, Oxford, Ga.* Atlanta, 1910.

Dombrowski, James A., editor. *Alumni History and Directory of Emory University.* Atlanta, 1926.

Emory College. *Annual Catalogue[s] of the Officers, Alumni and Students of Emory College, Oxford, Georgia. 1875-76 to 1889-90.* Macon, Atlanta, and Nashville, 1876-1890.

——. *Catalogue [s] of Emory College. . . . 1893-1894, and 1894-1895* Atlanta, 1894, 1895.

——. *Catalogue of the Officers, Alumni and Students of Emory College, Oxford, Ga. 1870, '71.* Atlanta, 1871.

——. *Catalogue[s] of the Officers and Students of Emory College, Oxford, Georgia. 1856-57, to 1858-59.* Augusta, Atlanta, and Charleston, 1857-1859.

——. *Commencement Day. Emory College. Senior Exhibition, Wednesday Morning, July 20, 1859.* Atlanta, 1859.

.. *Selected Bibliography*

———. *Commencement Day, 1880. Emory College, Oxford, Georgia 'They crowd upon us in this shade—The youth who own the coming years: Be never land or God betrayed By any youth our Oxford rears!' Wednesday, June 30th at 9:00 o'clock, A.M.* N. p., 1880.

———. *Emory College Commencement Day, July 22, 1857.* Covington, 1857.

———. *Emory College Commercial Department.* Oxford, Ga. N. p., n. d. (1883?)

———. *Emory College Junior Exhibition, July 21, 1857.* Covington, 1857.

———. *Emory College. Junior Exhibition. Tuesday Morning, July 19, 1859* Atlanta, 1859.

———. *Emory College. Sophomore Declamation. Monday Evening, July 18, 1859.* Atlanta, 1859.

———. *Emory College. The Late Commencement.* N. p., 1876.

———. *Junior Day. Emory College. Oxford, Georgia 'Palmam Qui Meruit Ferat.' Tuesday, June 29th, 1880, 9:30 o'clock, A.M.* N. p., 1880.

Hopkins, Isaac S. *Industrial Education: A Statement and a Plea. An Alumni Address, Emory College, 1883.* Macon, 1883.

Howren, Henry D. *'Georgia.' Anniversary Address . . . Delivered on the Occasion of the Anniversary of the Few Society of Emory College, October 29th, 1879.* Atlanta, 1879.

In Memoriam. Geo. W. W. Stone, D. D. 1818-1889. Atlanta, 1889.

Orr, Gustavus J. *The Choice of a Profession. A Lecture Delivered Before the Senior Class of 1858-59, in Emory College.* Atlanta, 1859.

Short, W. W., compiler, and W. B. Branham, compiler and editor. *Emory College Class of 1885. Historical and Biographical Notes 1882-1926.* Oxford, 1926.

Stone, Harry H., compiler and editor. *A History of the Class of Eighty. Emory College, 1876-1925.* Atlanta, 1925.

BOOKS

Works containing letters and other original material; books by Haygood's contemporaries; and other volumes having source material for intellectual and social history of the period.

Boland, J. M. *The Problem of Methodism: Being a Review of the Residue Theory of Sanctification and the Philosophy of Christian Perfection.* Nashville, 1888.

Brousseau, Kate. *L'education des nègres aux etats-unis.* Paris, 1904.

Burke, John W. *Autobiography: Chapters from the Life of a Preacher.* Macon, 1884.

Cable, George W. *The Silent South, Together With the Freedmen's Case in Equity and the Convict Lease System.* New York, 1885.

Dempsey, Elem F. *Atticus Green Haygood, He Took the Kingdom by Violence, Matthew 11:12.* Nashville, 1939.

Finney, Thomas M. *The Life and Labors of Enoch Mather Marvin, Late Bishop of the Methodist Episcopal Church, South.* St. Louis, 1880.

Fitzgerald, Oscar P. *Dr. Summers: A Life Study.* Nashville, 1885.

Fitzgerald, Oscar P. and Charles B. Galloway. *Eminent Methodists. Twelve Booklets in One Book.* Nashville, 1897.

Hammond, Nathaniel J. *The University of Georgia. A Short History of Its Endowment and Legal Status, As a Defense of Its Administration, Together With a Defense of the Constitutions of the United States and of Georgia Against the Charge of Hostility to the Christian Religion.* Atlanta, 1893.

Howe, (no initials). *The Bishop's Council: With Reminiscences of an Annual Conference of the Methodist Episcopal Church. By An Ex-Presiding Elder.* St. Louis, 1867.

Janes, Thomas P. *Hand-Book of the State of Georgia Accompanied By a Geological Map of the State.* Second Edition; Atlanta, 1876.

Kerley, T. A. Edited by John J. Tigert. *The Methodist Episcopal Church, South, a Prohibition Church, Established By a Critical and Complete Examination of Methodist History from 1743 to 1894.* Nashville, 1894.

Leftwich, W. M. *Martyrdom in Missouri, A History of Religious Prescription of Ministers of the Gospel, in the State of Missouri During the Late Civil War, And Under the 'Test Oath' of the New Constitution.* Two volumes. St. Louis, 1870.

McTyeire, Holland N. *A History of Methodism: Comprising a View of the Rise of This Revival of Spiritual Religion in the First Half of the Eighteenth Century, and of the Principal Agents By Whom It Was Promoted in Europe and America: with Some Account of The Doctrine and Polity of Episcopal Methodism in the United States, and the Means and Manner of Its Extension Down to A.D. 1884.* Nashville, 1885.

Newton, J. C. C. *The New South and the Methodist Episcopal Church, South.* Baltimore, 1887.

Norwood, C. W., compiler. *Georgia State Gazetteer and Business Directory. 1879-80.* Atlanta, 1879.

Poor, Henry V. *Manuals of the Railroads of the United States.* New York and London, 1877, 1881-1882, 1885.

Reilly and Thomas. *Atlanta. Past, Present & Future, Embracing Historical Sketches of Its Growth and Progress from Its Establishment to the Present Time, Together With Outline of Georgia History.* Atlanta, 1883.

Robertson, James I., ed. *The Diary of Dolly Lunt Burge.* Athens, 1962.

Rubin, Larry D., editor. *Teach the Freeman.* Two volumes. Baton Rouge. 1959. This splendid edition of letters concerning the Slater Fund's Activities—a majority of them to or from Rutherford B.

Hayes or Haygood—is a selection of the riches of the Hayes Memorial Library, in Fremont, Ohio.

Scott, W. J. *Biographic Etchings of Ministers and Laymen of the Georgia Conferences.* Atlanta, 1895.

Smith, George G. *The Life and Letters of James Osgood Andrew with Glances at His Contemporaries and at Events in Church History.* Nashville, Macon, and Galveston, 1882.

———. *The Life and Times of George Foster Pierce, D. D., LL. D. Bishop of the Methodist Episcopal Church, South, With His Sketch of Lovick Pierce, D. D., His Father, with Introduction by Atticus Haygood, D. D.* Sparta, 1888. This is an extremely valuable source since there are no Pierce papers extant. Haygood originally intended to write the volume.

Strahan, Charles M. *Clarke County, Georgia, and the City of Athens.* Athens, 1893.

Straker, D. Augustus. *The New South Investigated.* Detroit, 1885.

Vanderbilt University. *The Theologians of Methodism. Theses by Members of the Senior Class in the Biblical Department of Vanderbilt University. Printed Not Published.* Nashville, 1895.

Vincent, John H. *Chautauqua Movement.* Boston, 1886.

White, George. *Historical Collections of Georgia.* New York, 1854.

———. *Statistics of the State of Georgia: Including an Account of Its Natural, Civil, and Ecclesiastical History; Together With a Particular Description of Each County, Notices of the Manners and Customs of Its Aboriginal Tribes, and a Correct Map of the State.* Savannah, 1849.

Williams, Charles R., editor. *Diary and Letters of Rutherford Birchard Hayes, Nineteenth President of the United States.* Five vols. Columbus, 1922-1926.

Yarbrough, George W. Edited by Horace M. DuBose. *Boyhood and Other Days in Georgia.* Nashville, 1917.

PERIODICALS

The (Atlanta) *Methodist Advocate.* I, 1869. Erasmus Q. Fuller, editor.

The Educational Repository and Family Monthly (Atlanta). I-II, 1860-May, 1861. J. Knowles, W. H. C. Price, and Greene B. Haygood, editors.

The Gospel in All Lands (New York). 1891. Eugene R. Smith, editor. Missionary publication of the Methodist Episcopal Church.

Methodist Quarterly Review. LXII-LXXII, 1880-1890. Daniel D. Whedon, Daniel Curry, and J. W. Mendenhall, editors.

The Missionary Reporter. X-XII, 1890-1891. I. G. John, editor. Missionary publication of the Methodist Episcopal Church, South.

(Nashville) *Christian Advocate.* XXX-LVII, 1870-1896. Thomas O. Summers, Oscar P. Fitzgerald, and E. E. Hess, editors.

New Orleans Christian Advocate (also called *Louisiana Conference Edition Christian Advocate*). XXVII-XXXVII, 1880-1890, *passim*, Linus Parker, Charles B. Galloway and C. W. Carter, editors.

The Quarterly Review of the Methodist Episcopal Church, South (also called *Southern Methodist Review, Methodist Review,* and *Methodist Quarterly Review*). I-XX (XLIII), 1879-1896. J. W. Hinton, William P. Harrison, and John J. Tigert, editors.

Southern Christian Advocate (Charleston, Augusta, Macon). XXI-XLV, 1858-1882. E. H. Myers, F. M. Kennedy, and S. A. Weber, editors. John W. Burke, assistant editor until 1878.

The Sunday-School Magazine. I and V, 1871 and 1875. Atticus G. Haygood, editor.

Sunday-School Visitor. I, VI, New Series IX, 1855, 1860, 1875. Thomas O. Summers and Atticus G. Haygood, editors.

Wesleyan Christian Advocate. XLI-LV, 1878-1896. (Volumes from January, 1881, to end of 1890 bound as New Series III-XIII). Atticus G. Haygood, Weyman H. Potter, W. C. Lovett, T. T. Christian, and W. F. Glenn, editors.

NEWSPAPERS

Army and Navy Herald (Atlanta). II, 1865.

The (Athens) *Southern Banner,* 1844-1852; *Weekly,* 1861-1865.

The (Athens) *Southern Herald,* 1850. Until November, 1850, called *The Southern Whig.*

The (Atlanta) *Constitution.* (At first *The Constitution,* then *The Daily Constitution,* by the mid-1880's *The Atlanta Constitution*). 1868-1884, especially 1868-1870, and 1878-1884. W. A. Hemphill, publisher. J. J. Barrick, I. W. Avery, and Henry W. Grady, editors.

The Atlanta Intelligencer. (Also, *Daily Intelligencer and Examiner*), 1858, 1861. C. R. Hanleiter, publisher. *Weekly Examiner,* 1864-1866. Jared I. Whitaker, publisher. John H. Steele, editor. *Atlanta Daily Examiner,* 1857.

The (Atlanta) *Southern Confederacy,* 1863.

The (Covington) *Georgia Enterprise,* 1868-1872, 1883-1884. William L. Beebe, S. H. Hawkins, editors.

The Covington Star, 1889-1896. J. W. Anderson, editor and publisher.

Daily (Columbus) *Enquirer,* 1863.

The Macon Daily Telegraph, 1865. G. Clayland and J. B. Dumble, editors and publishers.

(Nashville) *Republican Banner,* May-July, 1870.

Nashville Union and American, July-August, 1870.

New York Tribune Extra, No. 36, September 23, 1876.

Rome Weekly Courier, 1868.

OFFICIAL PUBLICATIONS

Central University Charter. Proceedings of the Board of Trust and Address of the Board. Nashville, 1873.

De Puy, W. H., editor. *The Methodist Centennial Year-Book for 1884. The One Hundredth Year of the Separate Organization of American Methodism.* Cincinnati and New York, 1883.

Doherty, Robert R. *Representative Methodists. Biographical Sketches and Portraits of the Members of the Twentieth Delegated General Conference of the Methodist Episcopal Church, Held in the City of New York, May, 1888.* New York and Cincinnati, 1888.

Gaines, Wesley J. Edited by I. Garland Penn. *The United Negro: His Problems and His Progress, Containing the Addresses and Proceedings the Negro Young People's Christian and Educational Congress, Held August 6-11, 1902.* Atlanta, 1902.

Heriges, R. M. compiler. "Complete List of Members of the Book Committee, 1846-1926. Duties of the Book Committee. Official and Connectional Organs, 1846-1926, With Names of Editors." Typewritten, Nashville, ca. 1926.

———. "Appropriations Made from the Publishing House Funds By Order of the Methodist Episcopal Church, South, from 1854 to 1926, Also Recommendations." Typewritten. Nashville, ca. 1926.

———. "Connectional Officers Elected With Names of All Voted For, Commissions, Board, Committees." Typewritten. Nashville, ca. 1926.

———. "General Conferences of the Methodist Episcopal Church, South, 1846-1926. Publishing House, Agents, Editors, Book Committee, Report Made By Committee on Book Concern, Committee on Books and Periodicals, Committee on Publishing Interests." Typewritten, Nashville, ca. 1926.

———. "Publishing House M. E. Church, South. Legislation By the General Conferences, 1846-1922. Vol. I." Typewritten. Nashville, ca. 1926. These five bound volumes are the property of the Library of the Methodist Publishing House, Nashville.

John, I. G. *Hand Book of Methodist Missions.* Nashville, 1893.

Lafferty, John L. *Sketches and Portraits of the General Conference of the Methodist Episcopal Church, South. Held in Richmond, Va., May, 1886.* Richmond, 1886.

Methodist Episcopal Church. Freedmen's Aid and Southern Education Society. *Twenty-first Annual Report . . . for Year Ending July 1, 1888.* N. p., 1888.

———. *The Doctrines and Disciplines of . . . .* Edited by Thomas O. Summers and William P. Harrison. Nashville, 1859, 1866, 1890, 1891, 1894.

———. *Journal[s] of the General Conference. . . .* Edited by Thomas O. Summers. Nashville, 1866, 1870, 1874. (Held, respectively, in New Orleans, Memphis, and Louisville.)

———. *Minutes of the Annual Conferences* . . . 1858-1865, and 1866-1873. Two bound volumes containing eight yearly reports each. Nashville, 1859-1874.

Methodist Episcopal Church, South. Board of Missions. *Annual Report[s]*. . . . Nashville, 1877, 1883-1887, 1889-1893.

———. Georgia Conference. Edited by J. Blakely Smith. *Minutes*. . . . Macon, Atlanta, and Charleston, 1854, 1856-1860.

Methodist Episcopal Church, South. North Georgia Conference. Edited by Warren A. Candler, and H. L. Crumley. *Minutes*. . . . Atlanta and Nashville, 1880-1890.

———. Edited by Ellison R. Cook, Joel T. Daves, and John W. Heidt. *Year Book and Minutes*. . . . Macon and Atlanta, 1891-1896.

Methodist Episcopal Church, South. South Georgia Conference. Edited by Kosciuszko Read. *Minutes*. . . . Macon, 1890.

Peterson, P. A., compiler. *Hand-Book of Southern Methodism. A Digest of the History and Statistics of the Methodist Episcopal Church, South*. Nashville, 1884, 1891.

Redford, A. H. *Exhibit of the Publishing House of the Methodist Episcopal Church, South, for the Four Years ending April 30th, 1870*. Nashville, 1870.

The Trustees of the John F. Slater Fund. *Documents Relating to the Origin and Work . . . 1882 to 1884*. Baltimore, 1894. (Occasional Papers, No. 1).

———. *Organization of the John F. Slater Fund for the Education of Freedmen*. Baltimore, 1882.

———. *Proceedings*. . . . 1884, 1885, 1887, 1888, 1889, and 1890. Baltimore and Hampton, Virginia, 1885-1890.

PAMPHLETS AND SERMONS

Brown, Joseph E. *Letter . . . to His Excellency John B. Gordon, Upon the Subject of Betterments, Placed By the Lessees Upon the Western and Atlantic Railroad*. Atlanta, 1890.

Brown, Joseph M. *A Commercial Revolution Which the Opening of Muscle Shoals Will Bring About for the People of Georgia and the Southeast. The Western & Atlantic Railroad One of the Chief Beneficiaries*. Atlanta, 1889.

Burrus, John H. *Educational Programs of the Colored People in the South*. Nashville, 1889.

Caldwell, John W. *Slavery and Southern Methodism: Two Sermons Preached in the Methodist Church in Newnan, Georgia*. N. p. 1865.

Callaway, Morgan. *Our 'Man of Macedonia;' His Needs and Our Duties. Preached before the students of Emory College and the Citizens of Oxford, Ga., January 22, 1883, on the occasion of Dr. Callaway's taking leave of them*. Nashville, 1883.

Candler, Warren A. *Georgia's Educational Work. What It Has Been—What It Should Be.* Oxford, 1889.

———. *Georgia's Educational Work; What It Has Been: What It Should Be.* "Hammond's History" Corrected, Etc. Atlanta, 1893.

———. *Not Less Education, But More of the Right Sort.* Nashville, 1897.

———. *Speech . . . in the Georgia House of Representatives, July 23d, '89.* Atlanta, 1889.

———. , compiler. *Theater-Going and Dancing Incompatible with Church Membership.* Nashville and Dallas, 1904. (First published in 1884).

Curry, Jabez L. M. *Difficulties, Complications, and Limitations Connected With the Education of the Negro.* Baltimore, 1895. (Occasional Papers, John F. Slater Fund, No. 5).

Hamill, H. M. *The Old South, A Monograph.* Nashville and Dallas, ca. 1904.

Jones, Charles E. *Education in Georgia.* Washington, 1889. (Bureau of Education Circular of Information, No. 4, 1888. Also, Herbert B. Adams, editor, Contributions to American Educational History.)

McIntosh, R. M. *The Case of the Missions Board and Ex-treasurer Stewart.* Atlanta?, 1894.

Mayo, A. D. *Southern Women in the Recent Educational Movement in the South.* Washington, 1892. (Bureau of Education, Circular of Information No. 1).

Tucker, J. L. *The Relation of the Church to the Colored Race. Speech . . . Before the Church Congress Held in Richmond, Va., on the 24-27 Oct., 1882.* Jackson, Mississippi, 1882.

I. ARTICLES

Boland, J. M. "A Psychological View of Sin and Holiness," *Quarterly Review of the M. E. Church, South,* XII (July, 1892), 342-54.

Cable, George W. "A Simpler Southern Question," *The Forum,* VI (December, 1888), 392-403.

Callaway, Morgan. "Every Seventh Soul," *Quarterly Review of the M. E. Church, South,* VI (July, 1884), 513-24.

Garrison, Curtis W., editor. "Slater Fund Beginnings: Letters from General Agent Atticus G. Haygood to Rutherford B. Hayes," *Journal of Southern History,* V (May, 1939), 223-45.

Leftwich, W. M. "The Law of Sanctification," *Quarterly Review of the M. E. Church, South,* XIV (July, 1893), 370-85.

Price, J. C. "The Negro in the Last Decade of the Century," *The Independent,* XLIII (January 1, 1891), 5.

Ralston, Thomas N. "Holiness and Sin—New Theory Noticed," *Quarterly Review of the M. E. Church, South,* III (July, 1881), 441-51.

Wilson, John S. "Atlanta As It Is," *The Atlanta Historical Bulletin*, VI (January-April, 1941), 7-161. Originally published in 1871.

Woodward, F. C. "The Freedmen's Case in Reality," *Quarterly Review of the M. E. Church, South*, VII (January, 1885), 1-12.

OTHER SOURCES

Books

Alexander, Gross, "History of the Methodist Episcopal Church, South," pp. 1-142 of Philip Scheff and others, editors, *The American Church History Series*, Volume XI. New York, 1894.

Brown, Oswald E., and Anna M. Brown. *Life and Letters of Laura Askew Haygood*. Nashville and Dallas, 1904.

Bryan, T. Conn. *Confederate Georgia*. Athens, 1953.

Candler, Warren A. *Bishop Charles Betts Galloway, A Prince of Preachers and a Christian Statesman*. Nashville, 1927.

———. *Young J. Allen, "The Man Who Seeded China."* Nashville, 1931.

Cannon, James, III. *History of Southern Methodist Missions*. Nashville, 1926.

Cannon, William R. *The Theology of John Wesley With Special Reference to the Doctrine of Justification*. New York and Nashville, 1946.

Crum, Mason. *The Negro in the Methodist Church*. New York, 1951.

Curry, Jabez L. M. *A Brief Sketch of George Peabody, and a History of the Peabody Education Fund Through Thirty Years*. Cambridge, Massachusetts, 1898.

Daggett, Stuart. *Railroad Reorganization*. Cambridge, Massachusetts, 1924. (Volume IV of Harvard Economic Studies).

Dempsey, Elam F. *Life of Bishop Dickey, Bishop of the Methodist Episcopal Church, South*. Nashville, 1937.

Du Bose, Horace M. *A History of Methodism Being a Volume Supplemental to "A History of Methodism" By Holland N. McTyeire ... Bringing The Story of Methodism With Special Reference To the History of the Methodist Episcopal Church, South, Down To the Year, 1916*. Nashville, Dallas, and Richmond, 1916.

Duren, William L. *Charles Betts Galloway, Orator, Preacher, and "Prince of Christian Chivalry."* Emory University, Georgia, 1932.

Faris, Hunter D. *The Circuit Rider Dismounts, A Social History of Southern Methodism, 1865-1900*. Richmond, 1938.

Flood, Theodore L., and John W. Hamilton, editors. *Lives of Methodist Bishops*. New York and Cincinnati, 1882.

Garrett, Franklin M. *Atlanta and Environs, A Chronicle of Its People and Events*. Three volumes. New York, 1954.

Hammond, Edmund J. *The Methodist Episcopal Church in Georgia, Being A Brief History of the Two Georgia Conferences of the*

Selected Bibliography

    Methodist Episcopal Church Together With a Summary of the Causes of Major, Methodist Divisions in the United States and of the Problems Confronting Methodist Union. N.p., 1935.
Harris, Corra. *As a Woman Thinks.* Boston and New York, 1925.
———. *A Circuit Rider's Wife.* Boston and New York, 1933.
Hesseltine, William B. *Confederate Leaders in the New South.* Baton Rouge, 1950.
Hollander, J. H. *The Cincinnati Southern Railway, A Study in Municipal Activity.* Baltimore, 1894. (Johns Hopkins University Studies in Historical and Political Science).
Hull, Augustus L. *A Historical Sketch of the University of Georgia.* Athens and Atlanta, 1894.
Jarrell, Charles C., editor. *Methodism on the March, A Study of Methodism As Mobilized.* Nashville, Dallas, Richmond, and San Francisco, 1924.
Jones, Charles E. *Georgia in the War, 1861-1865.* Augusta, 1909.
Leavell, Ullin W. *Philanthropy in Negro Education.* Nashville, 1930. (George Peabody College for Teachers, Contribution to Education No. 100).
Lee, Gordon C. L. *The Struggle for Federal Aid, First Phase, A History of the Attempts to Obtain Federal Aid for the Common Schools, 1870-1890.* New York, 1949. (Teachers College, Columbia University, Contributions to Education No. 957).
Logan, Rayford W. *The Negro in American Life and Thought, The Nadir, 1877-1901.* New York, 1954.
Memoirs of Georgia Containing Historical Accounts of the State's Civil, Military, Industrial and Professional Interests, and Personal Sketches of Many of Its People. Two volumes. Atlanta, 1895.
Morrow, Ralph E. *Northern Methodism and Reconstruction.* Chicago and Crawfordville, Indiana, 1956.
Nixon, Raymond B. *Henry W. Grady, Spokesman of the New South.* New York, 1943.
Northen, William J., editor. *Men of Mark in Georgia. A Complete and Elaborate History of the State from its settlement to the present time, chiefly told in biographies and autobiographies of the most eminent men of each period of Georgia's progress and development.* Six volumes. Atlanta, 1910.
Peabody, Francis G. *Education for Life, The Story of Hampton Institute Told in Connection With the Fiftieth Anniversary of the Foundation of the School.* Garden City, New York, 1919.
Pierce, Alfred M. *Giant Against the Sky, The Life of Bishop Warren Akin Candler.* New York and Nashville, 1948.
———. *A History of Methodism in Georgia, February 5, 1736-June 24, 1955.* Atlanta, 1956.
Posey, Walter B. *The Development of Methodism in the Old Southwest, 1783-1924.* Tuscaloosa, Alabama, 1933.

Range, Willard. *The Rise and Progress of Negro Colleges in Georgia, 1865-1949*. Athens, 1951. (Phelps-Stokes Fellowship Studies No. 15).

Redford, A. H. *Life and Times of H. H. Kavanaugh, D.D., One of the Bishops of the Methodist Episcopal Church, South*. Nashville, 1884.

Rice, Edwin W. *The Sunday School Movement, 1780, 1917, and the American Sunday-school Union, 1817, 1917*. Philadelphia, 1917.

Shaw, Beverly F. *The Negro in the History of Methodism*. Nashville, 1954.

Smith, George G. *The History of Georgia Methodism from 1786 to 1866*. Atlanta, 1913.

Smith, H. Shelton. *Changing Conceptions of Original Sin. A Study in American Theology since 1750*. New York, 1955.

Stevenson, Arthur L. *The Story of Southern Hymnology*. Roanoke, Virginia, 1931.

Stowell, Jay S. *Methodist Adventures in Negro Education*. New York and Cincinnati, 1922.

Talmadge, John E. *Rebecca Latimer Felton, Nine Stormy Decades*. Athens, 1960.

Tigert, John J., IV. *Bishop Holland Nimmons McTyeire, Ecclesiastical and Educational Architect*. Nashville, 1955.

Woodson, Carter G. *The History of the Negro Church*. Washington, 1921.

———. *The Negro in Our History*. Fifth edition; Washington, 1929. (First edition in 1922).

Woodward, C. Vann. *Origins of the New South, 1877-1913*. Baton Rouge, 1951. (Volume IX of a History of the South, W. H. Stephenson and E. Merton Coulter, editors).

———. *Tom Watson, Agrarian Rebel*. New York, 1938.

Pamphlets and Miscellany

Alexander, Will W. *The Slater and Jeane's Fund, An Educator's Approach to a Difficult Social Problem*. Washington, 1934. (Occasional Papers, John F. Slater Fund, No. 28).

De Butts, Harry A. *Men of Vision "Who Served the South!"* New York, San Francisco, and Montreal, 1955. (The Newcomen Society).

Trinity Methodist Church. *Centennial Program, 1854-1954 . . . . 100 Years of Service to a Great City*. Atlanta, 1954.

Winton, George B. *Sketch of Bishop Atticus G. Haygood*. Lynchburg, Virginia, 1915. (Occasional Papers, John F. Slater Fund, No. 16).

Periodical Articles

Bryan, T. Conn. "The Churches in Georgia During the Civil War," *The Georgia Historical Quarterly*, XXXIII (December, 1949), 283-313.

Selected Bibliography

Cuttino, George P. "Methodism in History," *The Emory University Quarterly*, XIII (December, 1957), 218-28.

Edwards, John E. "Petersburg, Virginia, and Its Negro Population," *Methodist Quarterly Review*, LXIV (April, 1882), 320-37.

Harwell, Richard B. "Atlanta Publications of the Civil War," *The Atlanta Historical Bulletin*, VI (July, 1941), 165-200.

Humphries, John D. "A Sketch of the Atlanta Bench and Bar Prior to 1890," *The Atlanta Historical Bulletin*, IX (November, 1936), 30-39.

McCallie, Elizabeth H. "Atlanta in the 1850's," *The Atlanta Historical Bulletin*, VIII (N. rd., no. 32), 92-106.

Melton, Wightman F. "When Bishop Haygood 'Toted' Bricks," *The Atlanta Journal* magazine section, June 13, 1926, pp. 11 ff.

———. "H. I. Kimball; His Career and Defense," *The Atlanta Historical Bulletin*, III (October, 1938), 249-83.

Pearne, Thomas H., "The Race Problem—The Situation," *Methodist Quarterly Review*, LXXI (September-October, 1890), 690-705.

Southall, Eugene P. "The Attitude of the Methodist Episcopal Church, South, Toward the Negro From 1844 to 1870," *The Journal of Negro History*, XVI (October 1931), 359-70.

Tankersley, Allen P. "Basil Hallam Overby: Champion of Prohibition in Ante Bellum Georgia," *The Georgia Historical Quarterly*, XXXI (March, 1947), 7-25.

Tillett, Wilbur F. "Albert Taylor Bledsoe," *Quarterly Review of the M. E. Church, South*, XIV (July, 1893), 219-42.

Index

African Methodist Episcopal Church, 54, 56, 83, 183, 195
Allen, Young J., 21-22, 24, 28, 34, 66, 107, 108, 199, 205
American Missionary Association, 184
Annual conference, 12, 28, 30, 77, 90, 93, 123, 153, 171, 207, 210, (See also *Georgia Conference, North Georgia Conference, South Georgia Conference*)
Arminianism, 14, 43, 46, 85, 99, 118, 120, 131, 134, 152, 164, 175, 198, 203
Askews (Martha Haygood's parents), 1, 6, 7, 27, 69
Athens, Ga., 1, 2, 4, 30, 63, 95, 105, 162, 174, 177, 178, 188
Atlanta, *ante-bellum*: 8, 9-10, 12; *wartime*: 39, 41, 44, 45, 48-50; *Reconstruction*: 51-53, 55, 56, 61, 62, 63, 65, 66, 67, 69, 70, 71-72, 75; *Bourbon period*: 84, 112, 114, 116, 118, 122-23, 124, 127, 129, 131-33, 139-40, 146, 148, 158, 163, 166, 172, 179, 183-84, 186, 188; *Populist era*: 192-93, 195-96, 202, 210
Atlanta Constitution, 70, 106, 109, 126-32, 135, 139, 142, 188
Atlanta University, 71, 147, 185, 187, 197
Augusta, *ante bellum*: 1, 2, 8, 19, 33; *wartime*: 44; *Reconstruction*: 56, 63, 66, 71; *Bourbon period*: 77, 103, 115, 158-59, 163, 166; *Populist era*: 196

Bacon, Leonard W., 144, 145-46, 185-86
Baptists, 3, 17, 43, 44, 45, 47, 54, 70, 75, 91, 92, 146, 157-58, 165, 175, 183, 187
Barber's Creek, 2, 5
Beecher, Henry Ward, 113, 133
Bell, H. P., 106, 132, 165
Bigham, R. W., 42, 84, 131

Bishops, 14, 29, 31, 35, 44, 57-58, 60, 72, 91, 109, 115-16, 150-52, 163, 174, 191, 196, 203, 210
Blair bill (Federal aid to education), 172-73
Bledsoe, Albert T., 164
Boland, J. M., 121, 164
Bonnell, John F., 98
Brown, Joseph E., 12, 37, 53, 91-92, 126, 128-29, 141, 171-72, 182
Brunswick, 123, 139, 148
Burke, John W., 30, 99, 114

Caldwell, John W., 55-56, 60-61
Callaway, Morgan, 94, 96-97, 125, 190
Calvinism, 14, 31-32, 43, 46, 87, 120, 152, 164, 175, 198
Campmeetings, 3-4, 13, 69-70, 118-19, 124
Candler, Warren A., *1870's:* 88, 92, 110, 124-25; *1880's:* 142, 154-55, 158-60, 163, 165-66, 168, 190, 202-03; *1890's:* 170, 175, 176, 179, 195, 205, 208, 210-11
Carlisle, James H. 74, 133, 135, 189
Cartersville, 63
Charleston, S. C., 2, 4, 56, 75
Chattanooga, Tenn., 61, 75, 133, 139, 141, 185
Church membership, 3-4, 53, 72, 167, 203, 207-08
Church music, 23, 32-33, 53, 59, 73, 80-83, 98-99, 119, 163-65
Civil War, 37-50
Claflin College, 185, 194, 204
Clark University, 184-85, 186
Clark(e), J. O. A., 91-92, 114
Clarke County, 1-2, 3, 8, 41, 43, 48
Cole, E. W., 75, 95, 139-41, 148
Colored Methodist Episcopal Church in America, 57, 59-60, 153, 190

250

Index

Colquitt, Alfred H., 74, 95, 101, 106, 115, 126-29, 131-33, 139, 141-42, 146, 158, 178, 182, 190, 200
Columbus, 30, 46-47, 56, 59, 70, 83
Conference, (See *Quarterly, District, Annual, General Conferences*)
Convict (labor), 127, 128, 173, 201
Covington, 18, 19, 21, 67, 71-73, 101, 103, 105, 170, 177, 194, 202
Curry, J. L. M., 145, 146, 189

Dalton, 45, 56, 61, 63, 98, 162-63
Darwinism, 24, 89, 100, 144, 175, 198
Deacon, 22, 26, 28
Decatur, 48, 49, 67, 201-04
Democratic Party in Georgia, 4, 11, 25, 35, 126, 128-30
District conference, 59, 62, 64-65, 160, 162, 164
Dodge, Asbury, 41-43, 72, 162, 166
Dodge, William E., 146
Dodge, William E., Jr., 160
Doggett, David W., bishop, 58
Dowman, Charles E., 105
Drinking, 3, 19, 22, 70, 121-22, 123-24, 132, 144, 155-60, 173-74, 209-10
Duncan, James A., 118
Duncan, W. W., bishop, 151
Dunlap, W. C., 162, 190

Education, public, 11-12, 25-26, 36, 64, 68, 71, 90, 101-02, 169-74
Educational Repository and Family Monthly, 36-37, 113
Elberton, 63, 166
Elders, 26, 28-29, 41, 158
Emory College, *ante-bellum*: 17-27, 30; *1860's and '70's*: 64, 68, 74, 88-110, 121, 133, 134; *1880's and '90's*: 136, 140-42, 146-48, 150, 154-55, 159, 161, 164-66, 170, 172, 174-81, 186, 189-90, 195, 201-04, 210-11
Evans, Clement A., 63, 105, 162
Evans, J. E., 57, 161-62, 178, 190, 202
Evans, W. W., 112, 159

Felton, W. H., 64
Feminism, 86, 116, 127-28, 155, 160, 168, 204
Few literary society, 18-19, 24, 88, 103, 176, 189
Fisk University, 75, 147, 185-87
Fitzgerald, O. P., bishop, 151
Franklin College, (See *University of Georgia*)

Fraternities, at Emory College, 19, 25, 102-03
Fulton County, 9

Gaines, Wesley, bishop, 188, 195
Gaines, William, 56
Gainesville, 63, 106, 161-64
Gaither, Henry, 105, 195
Galloway, Charles B., bishop, 151, 157, 160, 195
Garland, Landon C., 74, 118
General Conferences, 14, 41, 56-60, 66, 74, 76, 86, 90, 114, 116, 121, 131, 143-44, 153-54, 157, 167, 190, 201
Georgia Conference, M. E. Church, South, 28, 33, 40-41, 44, 49, 55-56, 199, (Also see *North Georgia Conference, South Georgia Conference*)
Georgia Railroad, 2, 18
Georgia Teachers Association, 71, 101, 172
Gilman, Daniel C., 146, 186-87, 201
Gordon, John B., 71, 91, 126, 128-29, 140, 182
Grace, 26, 28, 30-32, 119, 158, 160-61, 166-67
Grady, Henry W., 106-07, 109, 126-31, 132, 135, 137, 203-04
Granbery, John, bishop, 151
Greene County, 1

Hancock County, 34-35, 37-38, 53, 101, 109, 196
Hardeman, R. U., 19, 22, 208
Hargrove, R. K., bishop, 151
Harris, Lundy H., 98, 110, 159, 175, 195, 205
Harrison, W. P., 53-54, 55, 57, 60, 76, 176
Hayes, Rutherford B., 117, 145-47, 173, 185-87, 201-03
Haygood, Atticus G., *birth*: 1; *boyhood*: 7, 9, 12-13, 15-16; *children*: 30, 34, 39, 42, 44, 47, 65, 68-69, 74, 93, 111-12, 202, 205; *college career*: 17-27; *editorial career*: 112-34, 140-42, 147-49, 170, 175-79, 180-81, 199, 201, 208; *educational philosophy*: 12, 20-21, 25-26, 37, 71, 89-90, 120-21, 169-70, 173-74, 175-79, 201; *episcopacy*: 150, 154-55, 166-68, 196-97, 201, 205-10; *health*: 5, 7-8, 14, 20, 201-02, 205, 206, 208-11; *lecturing*: 133-34, 145, 150, 172-73, 194, 201; *married life*: 27, 37, 39, 40, 42, 46-47, 68-69, 111-12, 202-06; *naming*: 5; *negrophilia*: 6, 30, 42, 64, 85, 108, 111, 123-24, 126, 130, 135-36, 142-44, 182-94; *personality de-*

velopment as adult: 67-71, 96, 103-104, 107-11, 124, 131, 134, 159-60, 200, 204; *physical activities:* 7, 111, 206; *presidency of Emory College:* 94-111, 134, 140-42, 147-49, 170, 175-79, 180-81, 199, 201, 208; *presiding elder:* 61-67, 71-73; *professional career as preacher:* 27-29, 30-32, 42-43, 47, 51, 109, 113, 150-54, 160-66, 199, 200, 203; *prohibition writing and lecturing:* 131-32, 158-68; *reading:* 7, 23-24, 31-32, 125-26, 203; *religious life:* 12-13, 15-16, 26, 69-70, 89-90, 99, 100, 124, 134, 136, 162, 198-211; *secularism:* 7, 13, 26, 29, 42, 86, 89-90, 99, 100, 124, 134, 136, 162, 198-211; *Sheffield residence:* 179, 204-05; *Slater Fund Agency:* 145-48, 181-94, 201-02; *Sunday school secretaryship:* 73-94, 114, 121, 199; *war chaplaincy:* 37-40, 44-50; *West Coast residence:* 154, 205-08; *writing:* 36-37, 65-66, 73, 78-79, 84-86, 112-15, 120-21, 131-32, 134, 153-54, 167, 173, 203, 208-09, 211

Haygood, Atticus G., Jr., 74, 111-12, 202, 205
Haygood, Greene B., 1, 5, 6, 8, 10-11, 18, 24, 30, 36, 41, 44
Haygood, Laura, 5, 7, 48, 68, 111, 112, 172, 205, 210
Haygood, Lollie (A. G.'s daughter), 93
Haygood, Mamie, 68, 99, 160, 202, 205
Haygood, Marsha Askew, 1, 5, 6, 30, 48, 68, 112, 201
Haygood, Mollie Yarbrough, 30, 34, 47, 65, 68, 74, 84, 93, 97, 111, 112, 159, 202, 205-06, 210
Haygood, Paul (grandson of Atticus), 202, 205, 206
Haygood, Wilbur F., 47, 68-69, 99, 111-12, 121, 160, 201-02, 204-05
Haygood, William (Willie), 5, 12, 41, 44, 48, 68, 111-12, 172, 180
Heidt, John W., 19, 21, 22, 83, 166
Hemphill, W. A., 70, 72, 126
Hendrix, E. R., bishop, 151
Holiness movement, 43, 109, 121, 124, 154-55, 159, 161-67, 174, 190, 198, 201, 209
Holsey, Lucius H., bishop, 57, 192
Hopkins, Isaac, 19, 22, 97, 176, 178, 179
Hoss, E. E., 177

Jack-Knife and Brambles, 208
Jackson, James, 74, 106
Jarrell, Anderson J., 41-43, 162, 165-66, 174

Jesup, Morris K., 146, 186, 201, 204
Johnson, John Calvin, 43
Jones, John J., 106
Jones, Sam, 158, 160
Justification, 14, 109, 199

Kavanaugh, H. H., bishop, 28, 58, 151
Keener, John C., bishop, 151, 154, 191
Kelley, D. C., 85, 151-52, 153, 165
Key, Joseph S., bishop, 152, 180, 201, 202
Kimball, H. I., 60, 131, 158

Lamar, L. Q. C., 19, 103, 172
Languages, study of, 20-21, 26, 94, 96-98, 101, 176, 185-86, 196-97, 209
Law profession, 1, 3, 5, 10, 26, 68, 101, 177-79
Lee, James W., 163, 166
Liquor, (See *Drinking, Prohibition movement*)

McFerrin, John B., 44-45, 76, 93, 119, 122
McGhee, C. M., 139, 148
McIntosh, R. M., 81-83, 99, 107, 177, 179, 203, 208
McTyeire, Holland N., 55, 57-58, 62, 64, 75, 77, 89-91, 111, 113, 151-52, 166
Macon, 19, 44, 59, 70, 93, 95, 96, 114-15, 124, 139, 140, 148, 166, 171, 188, 192, 196
Man of Galilee, The, 153, 154, 203
Marvin, Enoch, bishop, 58
Means, Alexander, 25, 54, 98
Mercer University, 17, 91, 95
Methodism, Southern, 6, 12-15, 19, 22, 24, 54, 59, 69, 72, 74, 78, 81, 85, 87, 90-91, 99, 117, 119-21, 154-55, 157, 161, 200, 203, 208, 209
Methodist Episcopal Church, (also *Northern Methodism*), 54, 57, 58, 60-61, 63, 73, 115, 117, 124, 133, 138, 142-43, 152, 157, 185, 187, 192
Methodist Episcopal Church, South, *missions:* 21, 28, 63, 66, 71-72, 85-86, 94, 148, 205-08; *organization:* 13-14, 32, 56-60, 133, 151-53, 207-08; *problems in reconstruction:* 54-70, 191; *prohibition positions:* 120-21, 131-32, 157-60; *Sunday school literature:* 75-80
Methodist theology and discipline, 14-15, 30-31, 34, 46, 96, 115-16, 119-23, 125, 151, 157-59, 160-67, 198, 207
Methodists in Georgia, 3-4, 31, 80-92, 118-25, 157-68, 174, 181, 190-91
Milledgeville, 17, 33, 35, 48, 55, 162, 173

Index

Miller, C. W., 164
Miller, H. V. M., 64
Miller, Hugh, 23-24
Missions, 13, 21, 28, 63, 66, 71-72, 85-86, 107-08, 205-08, 210
Monk and the Prince, The, 167, 208-09
Myers, E. H., 46, 55, 57-58, 65, 72, 105

Nashville, 30, 73-76, 77, 81, 83, 93-95, 104, 107, 111, 122, 141, 155, 165, 177, 192-94, 210
Nashville Christian Advocate, 75-77, 86, 90, 115, 142, 151-52, 209
National Education Association, 172, 177-78
Negroes, *as voters:* 129-31, 137, 144, 156, 182, 189, 191-93, 196-97; *in churches to 1865:* 3, 28, 30, 42; *in churches after 1865:* 51-52, 54, 56, 61, 63, 72, 83, 115, 117-18, 128, 144, 191, 197; *reconstruction status, and after:* 51, 64, 87, 111, 126, 143, 194, 196; *schools and colleges:* 4, 75; 128, 130-31, 135, 143, 145-47, 153, 169, 178, 182-88, 189-96; *slavery:* 2-4, 25, 33, 42-43, 49, 55-56, 108, 143
Negrophilia, 55-56, 85, 123-24, 126, 128-30, 144, 189-92
Negrophobia, 11, 129, 154, 156, 188-89, 191-92, 194-96
New Orleans Christian Advocate, 75, 115, 151, 190
"New Puritanism," 155, 156, 163, 167
"New South," 75, 108-09, 126-28, 131, 135-37, 142, 145, 194, 200, 203
Newton County, 21, 23, 160
Norris, John, 63
North Georgia (Conference), 132, 150, 155, 159, 162, 165-67, 169, 173-74, 190

Oconee County (See *Clarke County*)
Oglethorpe University, 17, 91
Orr, Gustavus J., 26, 71, 128, 130, 135, 169, 172-73, 200
Our Brother in Black (as title and phrase with variations), 137, 140, 142, 144, 153, 166, 183, 188, 191, 194-95, 200, 203
Our Children, 120, 122
Oxford, *1850's-'60's:* 19, 21, 27, 31, 48, 67-68, 72-73; *1870's:* 93, 96, 99, 102-07, 110-12, 118; *1880's-1890's:* 135-36, 143, 145, 155, 159-61, 164, 172, 175, 177-79, 190-91, 194, 196, 201-02, 206, 208, 210

Paine, Robert, bishop, 58
Paine College, 190, 197, 201

Parker, Linus, bishop, 151, 191
Patillo, William, 23
Patriarchal social elements in the South, 3, 14, 35, 57-58, 102, 110-11, 168
Phi Gamma literary society, 18-19, 21, 23-24, 27, 88, 103, 176, 189
Pierce, George Foster, bishop, *1854-1870:* 17, 22, 27, 31, 33-35, 38, 44, 48, 54-59, 64-65, 74; *1871-1884:* 79-80, 87-95, 99, 101, 105, 109-10, 113, 116-18, 124, 134, 147, 151, 153, 160-63, 176, 180, 190, 192, 196, 199-201, 205
Pierce, Lovick, 27-28, 30-33, 43, 65, 103, 109, 121, 124, 152, 164, 199, 205
Pleas for Progress, 203
Potter, Weyman H., 115, 178
Preachers, *attitudes toward education:* 169-71; *descriptions:* 19, 22, 41, 45, 49, 65, 90-91, 98, 197, 207; *professional and social status:* 4, 7, 11, 14, 17-18, 26, 28-29, 33, 52, 66, 99, 105, 117, 122, 128, 133, 162-63, 167, 189, 197, 206
Preaching, 26-27, 30-31, 37, 53, 69, 152, 158-59, 167
Presbyterians, 17, 26, 44, 46-47, 49, 54, 70-71, 75, 91, 118, 152, 175
Presiding elders, 14, 29, 30, 42, 55, 61-67, 70, 72-73, 88, 104-05, 151, 164, 207
Probationers; probationary system of Methodism, 13, 28, 31, 33, 53, 58-59, 157
Prohibition movement, 131-32, 156-60, 201
Publishing House, Southern Methodist, 30, 31, 74-77, 80, 83-84, 86, 93-94, 118, 153, 196

Quarterly Conference, 13, 68

Railroads, 2, 10-11, 75, 87, 95, 102, 123, 127, 132, 138-41, 146-48, 178, 180
Ralston, Thomas, 164
Redford, Alfred H., 74, 76-77, 80, 82-84, 89, 93, 153
Revivals, 22, 26-27, 103
Richardson, F. M., 12, 49, 51-52, 84, 126
Richmond, Va., 37, 39
Rome, 28-29, 45-46- 61-64, 70, 114, 139-40, 143

Salem Camp Ground, 21, 26, 116, 160
Salvation, 14-15, 22, 31-32, 58-59, 69, 90, 108, 120, 134, 158, 161-67, 200
Sanctification, 22, 27, 31, 43, 121, 161-67

Sassnett, William J., 25, 34
Savannah, 53, 56, 69, 71, 122-23, 178, 192
Scomp, Henry A., 97-98, 158-59, 192
Second Blessing, (See *Salvation, Sanctification, Holiness movement*)
Sectarianism, 32, 34, 45, 58, 79, 81, 116, 152, 167
Secularism, (See *Haygood, Atticus G.; Secularism*)
Seney, George I., 136, 138-42, 147-48, 176, 180-81, 200-01, 204-05
Sheffield, Ala., 179, 204-05
Simpson, Matthew, bishop, 35
Slater, John F., 144-46, 180, 184-86, 200, 204
Slater Fund, 145-48, 153, 160, 178, 182-88, 190-94, 196, 201, 203
Slavery, (See *Negroes, Slavery*)
Smith, O. L., 88, 93-94, 96, 102, 103, 105
South Georgia Conference, 152, 162, 166
Southern Christian Advocate, 75, 92, 110, 112, 114-15, 200
Southern Masonic Female College, 71, 176
Sparta, 33-34, 36, 55, 191
Speer, Eustace W., 123, 171
Spelman College, 184
Spencer, Herbert, 24, 120
Stewart, J. S., 106
Stone, George W. W., 25, 94, 96, 180
Stone, Harry H., 96
Stradley, W. B., 166, 205, 207
Summers, Thomas O., 31, 72, 75, 77, 78, 82-83, 123
Sunday-School Visitor, 73, 76-78
Sunday schools (s), 13, 28, 52, 59, 60, 64-65, 70, 72-75, 78-80, 85, 124, 128, 152, 172

"Sunshine" (Bishop Pierce's home), 35, 55

Theological training for ministers, 59, 89-91, 99-100, 118, 165-66, 177, 189
Thigpen, Alexander, 51-52, 56, 63
Tillett, Wilbur F., 161, 167
Tougaloo College, 184

Uncle Jim, Haygood's friend, 5-6, 111, 194
University of Georgia, 4, 17, 89-92, 95, 105, 106, 123, 124, 155, 171-72, 174-75, 177-78, 196

Vanderbilt University, 89-91, 98, 167, 175, 177, 189, 196, 205
Vincent, John H., 73, 78-79, 172

Watkinsville, 1-4, 41-43, 48-49, 68, 114, 162
Watson, Richard, 31-32, 78, 125, 199
W. C. T. U., 155-56, 160
Wesleyan Christian Advocate, 95, 109-10, 112, 115-16, 123, 128, 130, 135, 139, 141-142, 147, 151, 157, 159, 164-65, 171-72, 177, 197-98, 200, 210
Whig Party in Georgia, 4, 8, 10-11, 32
Wightman, William, bishop, 58
Wilson, Alpheus W., bishop, 107, 166
Wright, J. I., 63, 106

Yarbrough, George W., 23, 38, 39, 47, 163
Yarbrough, John W., 23, 30, 54-55, 60-61, 72, 110, 112, 205
Yarbrough, Mary (Mollie), 23, 26-27, (Also see *Haygood, Mollie*)